Industrial Policies in
Western Europe

edited by
Steven J. Warnecke
Ezra N. Suleiman

The Praeger Special Studies program—utilizing the most modern and efficient book production techniques and a selective worldwide distribution network—makes available to the academic, government, and business communities significant, timely research in U.S. and international economic, social, and political development.

Industrial Policies in Western Europe

PRAEGER SPECIAL STUDIES IN INTERNATIONAL POLITICS AND GOVERNMENT

Praeger Publishers　　New York　Washington　London

Library of Congress Cataloging in Publication Data
Main entry under title:

Industrial policies in Western Europe.

    (Praeger special studies in international politics
and government)
    Includes index.
    1. Industry and state—European Economic Community
countries—Addresses, essays, lectures. 2. European
Economic Community countries—Economic policy—Addresses,
essays, lectures. 3. Trade and professional associations—
European Economic Community countries—Addresses, essays,
lectures. I. Warnecke, Steven Joshua. II. Suleiman, Ezra N.,
1941-
HD3616. E83I53   338. 94   75-23998
ISBN 0-275-01670-6

PRAEGER PUBLISHERS
111 Fourth Avenue, New York, N.Y. 10003, U.S.A.

Published in the United States of America in 1975
by Praeger Publishers, Inc.

PREFACE

During the last two decades intrasectoral and intersectoral pressures on industries in both the national and global context have become more complex and intense. In order to insure continued domestic economic growth national governments and firms have had to undertake a variety of policies in response to changing patterns of domestic and international competition. This has not only led to a new balance of power between the public and private sectors, particularly as many governments have developed "industrial policies," but business-state relations have been modified as additional claimants who wish to influence industry have begun to exercise power through political parties and interest groups. Thus classes and regions which have been affected adversely by prior stages of industrialization now seek to participate in determining the direction and rate of future industrial development as well as the distribution of benefits to be derived from the expansion of this sector of the economy.

Moreover, these are not entirely domestic issues, since national industrial policies have an impact on each other. In the case of the European Community, the member states have recognized that politically and economically they are too small to deal with the problems of their industries within the confines of their limited national markets. Thus, the EC, in part, is an effort to establish a larger geographic base for national industrial policies and private sector activities. In addition, supporters of European political and economic union have considered the evolution of a "European" industrial network essential for the consolidation of the Common Market.

The essays in this volume are an effort to address some of these problems. They include contributions on national industrial policies and the problems of specific sectors as well as on the implications of public and private policies toward industries for workers and trade unions and for government efforts to develop active manpower policies. The research on which they are based was made possible by a generous grant from the Ford Foundation to Dankwart A. Rustow, Ezra N. Suleiman, and Steven J. Warnecke who would like to express their appreciation to the Foundation for its support of this project. The project was conducted under the auspices of the Foundation's program to encourage studies on common problems of advanced industrialized societies. We would also like to thank the Center for European Studies of the Graduate School of the City University of New York under whose auspices research was pursued and where the initial findings were presented at a conference held in

April, 1973. The editors would also like to thank David Rudnick of the Royal Institute of International Affairs in London for translating Chapter 8. One editorial note is necessary concerning references to the European Community. For consistency's sake it is referred to either as the EC, the Community, or the European Community, even though it would be more correct to refer to it as the European Economic Community or EEC for the period from the signing of the Rome Treaty in 1957 until the late 1960s. References to the Commission or the Council of Ministers mean EC institutions.

CONTENTS

LIST OF TABLES AND FIGURE

Industrial Policies in Western Europe

INTRODUCTION
Steven J. Warnecke

The establishment and evolution of industries and industrial structures have played a fundamental role in the development and governing of the growth-oriented economies of North America and Western Europe. However, this process has generated and continues to generate intense domestic and international conflicts. Nationally, conflicts have involved the struggle among different parties and groups to control not only the direction of industrial expansion and change but the distribution of the political, economic, and social rewards derived from growth. Internationally, since the continental countries began to emulate England in the nineteenth century, conflicts have arisen between states as the expansion of existing industries and the establishment of new ones has led to competition for markets. For liberal optimists free trade theory served to explain through the principles of comparative advantage and regional specialization why industrial expansion and competition would be complementary rather than a source of continuing domestic and international antagonism. This approach with its emphasis on the primacy of the private sector underestimated or took no account of the extent to which the state was involved in fostering industry and trade. For Lenin, however, there was little doubt about the relationship between the state and industry and about the implications of the capitalist system for the international economy. The expansionist pressures inherent in industrial capitalism increased the necessity to protect old markets and sharpened the conflicts for new ones. Inevitably these tensions led to imperialism—the highest stage of capitalism, in which the global struggle for raw materials and markets terminated in world war.

In recent years the increased interest in providing a more coherent understanding of national policies that affect industry is a result of the even more systematic and conscious efforts (since 1945) by governments of developing countries as well as of advanced industrialized nations to influence the evolution of their domestic industrial structures.[1] For the former this entails the classic process of industrialization to transform rural into advanced economies, whereas for the latter it involves the protection and upgrading of existing industries and the introduction of new ones in the face of domestic and international pressures released by prior stages of industrial development. Thus the interdependent industrial networks that have replaced the local economies of traditional societies have increased the sensitivity of national political economies to disturbances in the patterns of production and

1

the rhythms of growth. In addition as domestic groups have become politically aware, better organized and more active, and have insisted upon a better standard of living, continued industrial expansion has been necessary to increase aggregate wealth. Moreover, these groups have intensified their pressure on governments to deal with class and regional disparities that have been exacerbated by the evolution of modern industry and by the patterns of ownership and control of financial resources and firms.

However, the pursuit of strictly domestic goals through policies toward national industries is influenced and even limited by international competition. The traditional liberal model for trade assumed slow changes in comparative advantages that would reduce the pressure for rapid adjustments; international specialization leading to complementary rather than competitive industrial developments; and national control over domestic firms and banks. Increasingly, national trade, industrial, and adjustment assistance policies have been and remain necessary responses to the effects of international trade liberalization, for the model does not correspond to the reality of interstate economic relations. Thus rapid changes in comparative advantage have had destabilizing effects on industries as diverse as steel, textiles, electronics, and shoes. The political and economic dimensions of these difficulties have led to numerous exceptions to trade liberalization in order to stabilize existing market shares and the distribution of industry. Moreover, such liberalization without counterbalancing public and private policies would simply reinforce the competitive advantages of established industries in other countries. Therefore, in a broader sense, national interventions can be seen as one element in the struggle to influence the international distribution of industry. In fact as an increasing number of states aspire to be or are counted among those considered industrialized the dynamics of intrasectoral and intersectoral competition and change on a national and global basis become more complex. Since the fulfillment of domestic demands, in part, depends upon success in maintaining the domestic industrial base, nations, whether capitalist or socialist, must influence the evolution of this base.

Furthermore, these national policies are also a response to a fundamental change in the traditional structure of international trade resulting from the internationalization of production and capital. (Although the role of banks, particularly international consortia, is of great importance in determining global industrial development, they are not one of the subjects of this book.) Multinational banks and corporations as a result of their organization and strategies have weakened national efforts to influence industrial activity in key sectors. Increasingly, these banks and firms have played a major role in determining the distribution of important industries not only between the advanced nations and the developing states but also among the industrialized countries too. On the one hand, the multinational corporation has reduced the achievement of national goals through trade negotiations by its use of transfer prices, its control of technology, and its access to resources. This has allowed it to narrow the area in which the free market can function. On the other hand, it has limited the possibility for interstate agreements on the operation of businesses. Before 1950 the national organization of most international firms allowed cartels to be formed on a geographic basis. The development of the global corporation has impeded the conclusion of such agreements; moreover, global firms are provided with leverage against industries that are not organized on a worldwide basis like themselves. These structural changes raise the question of whether in those sectors where these firms operate the units of analysis and policy making should be the nation and its relative factor costs or the multinational corporation and its interests. This relationship is of particular importance since trade negotiations have been based on the assumption that the traditional components of the theory guiding these negotiations—national industries—and the components of foreign relations—states—were complementary.

Ironically, although governments' responsibilities for domestic welfare have increased, the growing interpentration of advanced socieites (of which the internationalization of production and finance are two dimensions) has posed a challenge to traditional notions of sovereignty over domestic economic and social policies. As liberal capitalism in the postwar international economy has resulted in the mobility of capital, industry, and technology across national frontiers government control over the private sector has been undermined. This has made it more difficult for policy makers to achieve domestic goals that require some capacity on their part to insure the competitiveness of domestic industries. Consequently, a shift in the balance of public and private power has been taking place as governments increasingly intervene to modify the impact of domestic and international market forces on their industrial structures. Depending on the case this may reflect the unwillingness or inability of the private sector to either respond effectively to changing patterns of competition or develop industries which the state considers essential to support its domestic and foreign policies. Therefore, since 1945 many European states have strengthened their existing national agencies or created new ones to correct the structural weaknesses of the private sector. Examples of this range from the introduction of indicative planning in France to the expansion of the Instituto per la Ricostruzione Industriale (IRI) and establishment of the Ente Nazionale Idrocarburi in Italy in 1953, to the creation in Britain of the National Economic Development Council and the Industrial Reorganization Corporation. These actions have been paralleled by an expansion of public-controlled financial institutions for granting long-term credits to support state interventions in the industrial sector.

Naturally, such national policies toward industry have had their impact on international economic and political relations; they have led to new patterns of conflict and competition for the global allocation of growth and power as well as to the necessity for developing new forums to manage and resolve these tensions. As a result of these trends the Organization for Economic Cooperation and Development (OECD) conducted studies of its members' domestic policies and subsequently published the findings in *United States Industrial Policies* (1970), *The Industrial Policies of 14 Countries* (1971), and *The Industrial Policies of Japan* (1972). In addition, in *Policy Perspectives for International Trade and Economic Relations* (the "Rey Report" of 1972), a high-level group of public officials surveyed the conflicts that arise from industrial policies, but did not offer any solution for resolving them. And as a result of a U.N. report titled *The Impact of Multinational Corporations on Development and on International Relations* (July 1974) the United Nations has established a commission to develop policies aimed at the internationalization of production and finance.

At present, however, both intrasectoral and intersectoral conflicts are dealt with on a bilateral basis or through the multilateral rules of the General Agreement on Tariffs and Trade (GATT) concerning subsidies, quotas, and dumping. But the continuing increase in petroleum prices has exerted new pressure on governments to foster their industries, and it is very questionable whether the existing forums for dealing with problems that arise as a result of international competition can be handled on the basis of the existing rules.

WHAT IS INDUSTRIAL POLICY?

The term "industrial policy" is rather amorphous. It has been used indiscriminately to include all policies that can aid industry, and has raised the expectation that there can be a policy which is universally applicable. Since there are, in fact, innumerable instruments available to governments to influence the diversity of the production structure, the geographic distribution of firms, and their organization, it would be more useful to discuss this term in regard to the goals industrial policies can serve. In part, many of the chapters in this book deal with one aspect of such policies: the increasing resort of governments to public policies to correct structural weaknesses in capitalism while efforts are made to preserve as large an area for the private sector as possible. Analyses of this relationship have been marked by the ideological premises of the debate between proponents of capitalism and those of socialism. However, the relevance of these premises for delineating policies toward industry has been called into question as much by the limitations of the ideologies as by the evolution of the specific systems based upon these philosophies. Thus national industrial policies involving state influence and intervention are an indication that private initiatives and market forces alone may be insufficient for meeting not only the broader needs of society and the interests of the state but also those of the individual firm. Even the planned economies of Eastern Europe and the Soviet Union have had to face the limits of attempting to deal with intrasectoral and intersectoral evolution through administrative methods, as indicated by efforts to introduce some features of market-governed relations. Moreover, as the experience of Russia and the Eastern European states shows, the political determination of the complementary distribution of industries can be used to subordinate smaller states to the interests of their larger neighbors. Finally, centralized planning also severely restricts or eliminates the freedom of individuals and groups such as trade unions.

Consequently, from the perspective of individual firms in advanced countries, government policies may be necessary to help them meet increased foreign competition in home markets as well as to assist them in expanding the size of their export markets. Broadly speaking these policies can be divided between those which are domestic and those that deal with the relationship between domestic industries and the international economy.[2] In the domestic context these can range from general measures such as company and tax law and fiscal policy to specific measures for intervening in particular sectors. In regard to the international economy domestic policies to protect or to improve the competitiveness of national industries may be dovetailed with foreign trade and exchange rate policies. These in turn may be tied to efforts to expand the gross national product in order to deal with structural problems in the operations of the private sector, such as unequal distribution of income, regional underdevelopment, and insufficient opportunities for employment.

However, these ends can be simultaneously linked with considerably larger goals that depend upon the level of national political, social, and economic development. Thus policies toward industry have been used to further national unification (Germany in the late nineteenth century),[3] the political consolidation of a new regime (the Soviet Union),[4] the modernization of outmoded structures that have contributed to a decline in national power and wealth (France since 1945),[5] the maintenance of a unitary system challenged by linguistic and political divisions (Belgium since 1945), and the democratization of societies that have already become industrialized through efforts to reorganize the management of businesses (codetermination in West Germany and the Yugoslav system of worker management). In addition, as Ota Sik has noted, changes in the overall management and structure of a command economy (Czechoslovakia) can contribute to the democratization of a Communist state.[6] Finally, as in the case of the European Community, the evolution of a "European" industrial network as the result of the establishment of a customs union is seen as one of the foundations for political and economic union. The customs union also has been viewed as the only vehicle through which the member states of the Community can have access to an economic base upon which they can establish internationally competitive European multinational corporations with which to challenge American and Japanese firms.

INTERNATIONAL DIMENSIONS OF
INDUSTRIAL DEVELOPMENT

Even before the Second World War the states of Western Europe were economically and politically too small to deal adequately on a national basis with the domestic impact of changing patterns of international competition. In spite of these limitations former great powers such as the United Kingdom and France still sought to maintain a semblance of the industrial base that they thought would continue to provide them with some degree of independence and autonomy in the postwar world while insuring their economic growth. Industrial policies were required which fostered sectors that both reflected the illusory status that these states sought and contributed to national economic well-being. In the contemporary world the image of the structure of production that embodied these states' images of themselves led inevitably to the continued support of existing advanced industries such as avionics and petrochemicals and to efforts to introduce and develop new industries such as computers, nuclear reactors, uranium enrichment facilities, and aerospace.

However, the choice of industries was fraught with difficulties. On the one hand, since the domestic economies were too small economically to support such industries these sectors could be internationally competitive and profitable only through access to the markets of other countries. On the other hand, if these states sought only to encourage industries that were competitive and profitable within the economic limits imposed by the domestic political economy this might have required them to forego capacities popularly identified with being a great power. This conflict as it emerged in France has been analyzed by Lionel Stoleru, who cites as examples of it the support of such uneconomical projects as the Concorde for reasons of national prestige and the slighting of investment for the unglamorous machine tools industry.[7] Moreover, the pursuit of international prestige through industrial policy had a profound domestic consequence in France. President de Gaulle's determination in the 1960s to develop a nuclear capability was a policy so costly for the nation's resources that it was not without impact on regional, transportation, and other policies. Nor for that matter was it without its impact on the nation's political structure contributing as it did eventually to de Gaulle's downfall.

However, as J. J. Boddewyn indicates in his study on Belgium in this book, a country that also no longer constitutes an optimum economic area to support certain types of industries necessary for national autonomy can still achieve a high level of growth. But this requires foregoing the ambition to imitate the industrial structure of nations such as the United States. This includes allowing and even encouraging a greater degree of foreign investment and ownership as well as even more reliance on export markets. Such small states are in a position of trying to manage both the speed at which they become intertwined with the international economy and the impact of the dependencies which result. The interventions of the American government and the Commission of the European Community during the legislative history of the Belgian Economic Expansion Bill illustrate both of these points. The establishment (in 1957) of the European Community provides another example.

CUSTOMS UNIONS AND NATIONAL INDUSTRIES

For both France and Belgium, as well as the other members of the Common Market, the formation of the EC was a recognition that domestic markets were too small for effective and efficient firms in certain sectors and also too limited for national policies toward industries. These countries hoped that market integration would lead to greater economic growth for the member states, make their industries more competitive internationally, and assist them in dealing more effectively with the problems of structural change and dislocation caused by the changing patterns of international competition and trade. In addition, as a result of access to a larger market industrial developments that would have been uneconomical in a national context now became possible. Moreover, the proponents of a supranational Community posited a direct link among the establishment of the customs union, industrial restructuring on a cross-frontier basis, and the establishment of an independent political and economic base for the EC.

As expected, regional trade liberalization has increased the size of the markets available for national industries, but the member states and their firms have been able to take advantage of these opportunities for increased trade while still pursuing public and private policies toward industry on a national basis. This has led to conflicts both among the states and between them and the proponents of a supranational Common Market. Thus as Ezra N. Suleiman notes in this book, the existence of the EC has allowed French policy makers to follow through more effectively in inducing economic concentration to increase the competitiveness of French enterprises on the international market and thereby contribute to national prestige and domestic economic growth. In fact, so relentlessly have they pursued this goal that no country in Europe has had a higher rate of mergers in the past twenty years than France. However, this has been a policy of encouraging mergers among French enterprises, not between French and foreign ones, even though the consequences of this policy have been to reduce economic competition in France and to restrict the integration of French industry in the "European" industrial network sought by the supranationalists. This is clearly a political choice directed against cross-frontier concentrations that could potentially support more authority for the EC institutions in Brussels. In addition, to the extent these policies were intended to lead to French international corporations designed to meet the "American challenge," they have not always had the desired results. American predominance in sectors like computers and avionics has severely restricted French firms in these areas. And not unexpectedly, French firms that have become global in scope like Pechiney have tended like other multinational corporations to be selective in their responsiveness to government pressures.

As I indicate in Chapter 6, the French case is not unique, since a variety of economic and political factors have led the other Community governments and their industries to seek solutions on a national rather than a Common Market basis. Consequently, the integrative effects expected from industry have not taken place. Instead each country has pursued a national policy. Moreover, not only has industrial reorganization and concentration occurred almost entirely within states, but specialization on the basis of new patterns of comparative advantage have, by and large, not taken place. This is contrary to the developments expected from the formation of the customs union and is particularly disappointing for those who support some form of supranationalism because it would have contributed to the process of regional integration. Nowhere has this been more evident than in key sectors. Supporters of the EC hoped that the member states and their firms would cooperate in a wide range of sectors, such as aircraft, telecommunications, computers, and nuclear reactors, where individually they were too small. But instead of these high-technology industries being developed on a cooperative basis, they have been developed on a national basis and have thus neutralized each other's efforts. The result has been a failure to establish significant national or Community capacities that are economical and can challenge American corporations. The outcome of the French policy toward computers is examined by John Zysman in Chapter 9.

However, as the Shah of Iran's billion dollar investment in the French uranium enrichment program demonstrates, uneconomical national industries undertaken for foreign policy reasons can pay off both in being economical and serving the foreign policy goals for which they were designed. But such national policies of maintaining domestic industrial bases both for domestic and foreign economic policy reasons make the Community an unstable bloc, because the policies are predicated on competition with the other Common Market countries as well as with industries in non-Community states. The impact of the petrodollar problem on its member states and their industries demonstrates one facet of the Community's instability. It has intensified the necessity among the states for expanding exports on the existing industrial base and requires adjustments of this pattern of production in respect to future export opportunities. This has resulted in a "strategic" sense of the economy and its industries that further impedes intra-Community cooperation. Thus the policy of negotiating bilateral arrangements with the

Third World, and particularly with the Organization of Petroleum Exporting Countries (OPEC), is one that will have a significant effect on the industries the Common Market nations will choose to encourage. However, such efforts will simply follow upon prior national strategies that have been directed toward maintaining some industrial autonomy as a hedge against changes in the distribution of economic and political power in the international system.

Moreover, if conflicting national policies have reduced the capacity of Community firms to take advantage of the more optimum economic area provided by the Common Market, the internationalization of capital and production has impeded the efforts of the member states and the Community as a whole to use certain sectors for geographically limited political and economic purposes. As explained above, the establishment of the Common Market unintentionally contributed to this process by expanding the scope for the private sector without transferring sufficient power from the national governments to the Community to regulate private activity. In the crucial area of energy, as noted by Dankwart A. Rustow in Chapter 7, autonomous national policies, much less a Community policy, presupposed adequate control over the corporations that organize the upstream and downstream components of this sector. Before OPEC began to change the balance of control between the petroleum producing countries and the international oil firms the Common Market and its member states were confronted by corporations whose horizons were global and whose seats are often located outside the Community while the responsibilities of the states were limited to their own territories. As a result of the continued existence of truncated international firms and assertive oil producing states the member states of the Community have intensified their efforts to expand or establish national oil companies to explore for new sources of petroleum as well as to buy, refine, and distribute petroleum. This has been paralleled by bilateral political and economic diplomacy particularly with the Middle Eastern members of OPEC. Not only have these factors undermined the mild and unsuccessful efforts of the EC Commission to formulate and implement an EC energy policy, but the different geographic sources of energy of the member states have also blocked intra-Community solutions.

NATIONAL DIMENSIONS OF INDUSTRIAL POLICY

In advanced societies the organization and operation of industries are simultaneously a major source of conflict and key elements through which the continuous processes of political, social, and economic integration are achieved. Thus if the supporters of industrial capitalism like to see it as the basis for stability because of its contribution to increased aggregate wealth, its detractors point to its structural weaknesses that have led to regional disparities and class antagonisms. Interestingly, even the Marxist envisions industry as a source of integration, although this depends upon a reorganization of factory management and an adaptation of liberal principles such as complementary regional specialization to a planned economy.

As Boddewyn's analysis of Belgian industrial legislation illustrates (see Chapter 2), public policies toward industry may be a decisive element in turning a static private sector into a dynamic one. In the Belgian case such a transformation has also been a necessary response to the linguistic, cultural, and political cleavages that have divided that country. In pursuing industrial policies the government has had to pay particular attention to the geographic distribution of industrial development to lessen these antagonisms; consequently, as is often the case, national policies toward industry cannot be separated from policies to foster regional development. Moreover, in achieving these goals national officials have had to mediate among a variety of conflicting subnational, national, and international pressures that impinge in one way or another on the domestic industrial structure.

Significantly, in regard to the subnational element the demand of economically deprived regions to be brought into the mainstream of national industrial life is a major development since 1945. In fact, these claims pose a challenge to long-established views on the causes of and remedies for unequal industrial development within a nation. Previously the location of industry in a particular region has usually been viewed as depending on a series of objective conditions—availability of manpower, transportation, and access to markets and raw materials. Underdeveloped regions have lacked these resources, and in those cases involving regions with declining industries like textiles the presumption has been that there would be a move by labor to where employment was available rather than a move by investments to where there was abundant surplus manpower. Increasingly, the alleviation of a region's relative backwardness has been given priority by the state in an effort to complete national unification (Italian policies toward the Mezzogiorno), to prevent overconcentration of industries in congested and overindustrialized regions by establishing new "poles of growth" particularly in underdeveloped areas (France), and to deal with the abovementioned cultural and political cleavages that coincide with geographic divisions (Belgium). In other words, many of the political, social, and regional conflicts with which public authorities must contend are a result of the unimpeded patterns of industrial growth and location followed by the private sector in the past.[8] This does not imply that governments must necessarily make a trade-off between policies that are economically rational and policies that meet these noneconomic needs. The changing determinants of what constitutes comparative advantages for many industrial sectors often reinforce public policies to influence the location of industry in those regions which have been peripheral to the national economy.

Finally, hand in hand with Europe's relentless drive toward industrialization in the 1950s and thereafter has gone the necessity of paying particular attention to certain groups that industrialization tends to render more or less obsolete. Of particular importance in this respect are farmers and shop-keepers who continue to represent a sizable minority, particularly in France and Italy. The organization of small shopkeepers in France has consistently been able to obtain concessions from the government, some of which are considered startling. For example the passage of the Royer Law in 1974 gave them a majority voice on commissions having the right to decide whether supermarkets or large discount stores could be opened in urban centers; this is in effect a corporatist law reminiscent of legislation under the Vichy government and gives legislative authority to a nonelected body. Yet while a large number of deputies abstained from voting for the law no deputy voted against it. The policy of placating and catering to the small shopkeeper at the same time that a policy designed to encourage mergers and bigness is being pursued may be illogical. But it shows the extent to which the dependence of mass production industries on mass marketing and distribution funda-mentally disrupts an older social economic structure based on small, privately owned shops. Thus the inherent conflict between industrialization and social stability continues so long as significant groups have not been incorporated into the forms of organization which modern industry seems to require. The problems caused by this conflict are all the more serious if these groups that are threatened or displaced vote for extreme parties of the Right or the Left.

THE BALANCE OF PUBLIC AND PRIVATE POWER

Whatever the reasons have been that have led Western European govern-ments to become increasingly involved in managing their domestic economies, the result has been a gradual but significant modification in the re-lationship of the state to the private sector.[9] For leftist critics of capitalism this change has only been a cosmetic one since government still remains the representative and defender of the owners of the means of production.[10] Such an ideological position, however, is too undifferentiated for analyzing the components of the new balance that has emerged; at the very least a rough distinction must be made between two elements to which it refers simul-taneously and which should be treated separately from one another. On the one hand, the structural soundness and competitiveness of industry and the processes through which intrasectoral and intersectoral competition are regulated are the concern of all groups in society. These are problems irrespective of the patterns of ownership and class organization, and at a minimum they involve the mechanisms that determine the international dis-tribution of industries. On the other hand, the wider impact of industrial decision making such as that regarding patterns of employment, income distribution, regional development, and conditions of work may be ignored or underemphasized by the managers of firms. Consequently, it is of great importance whether the state in asserting its powers to influence industry induces firms to relate production-oriented decisions to these broader issues. However, it is possible for public and private officials to cooperate to solve the former without addressing themselves to the latter.

Socialist governments have attempted to exclude the disruptive effects of market-determined structural changes by isolating their economies from dependence on foreign trade. This has been coupled with centralized planning—that is, a national industrial policy—and the implementation among the Comecon countries and the Soviet Union of what has euphemistically been called the complementary Socialist division of labor and production. However, as the political and economic limitations of these methods have become clear in Eastern Europe and in Russia some elements of price setting have been introduced in the market to improve the domestic and international allocation of resources and to cope more efficiently with intrasectoral and intersectoral changes.[11] In contrast many Western industrialists have attempted to preserve the illusion of an autonomous private sector and a functioning market while simultaneously seeking state support in private and publicly deriding government intervention as stifling economic initiative. If centralized planning restricts flexibility and mis-allocates resources, the increased necessity for Western governments to assist industry to adjust to changing patterns of competition as well as to take into account the domestic ramifications of industrial decision making is an indication of the limits of relying on the voluntarism and spontaneity of the private sector.

This development has led to a progressive erosion of the distinction tradi-tionally made between the public and private sectors—that is, government and business. But as Suleiman notes in Chapter 1, the weakening of this distinction in France as a result of indicative planning has not only depended on the state formally assuming more power over the economy. The gap between the public and private sectors has also been bridged by an elite with a common social background and training whose members circulate among the key posts in government, business, and banking.[12] Such a network is essential for providing a general consensus upon which efforts at national planning can be based. Jack Hayward examines in Chapter 5 the interrelationship of the public and private sectors in his discussion of the representative bodies through which governments and firms conduct their contacts with one another. As he points out, "The increased interpendence of business and government has meant that both in France and Britain a system of de facto power sharing has developed within an institutionalized system of reciprocal influence." However, employer associations such as the Confederation of British Industries are not as important as has been assumed. The real bargaining goes on among the actual holders of bureaucratic and managerial power. Moreover, the establishment of the European Community has introduced an additional dimension into this domestic balance. As previously noted, the EC has extended the geographic market for the private sectors of its nine member states without a concomitant expansion of the geographic scope and powers of national authorities. This situation has allowed business more leeway to evade national regulations without the risk of confronting insurmountable controls by the Commission of the Common Market.

Within these "mixed economies" it is not always clear just how powerful the state is in specific instances, although it is generally assumed that such relations almost always work to the advantage of the private sector. Thus contrary to some myths about French planning, Stoleru has suggested that despite all its powers the French state has ultimately to "convince" industrialists to follow the most "sensible" direction; in the final analysis the state is "condemned to seduce,"[13] particularly if its goals are to modify and not replace the market and the private sector. As the Zysman study (see Chapter 9) of the French electronics sector illustrates, an excessive use of government power too frequently ends up backfiring.

Many of these changes in the balance of public and private power are analyzed in the various chapters of this book that deal with particular sectors. In the case of a declining sector, textiles, Camille Blum indicates in Chapter 8 that the structure and organization of this industry as well as the capacity of individual firms are not adequate to meet either intrasectoral competition from firms located outside the Community or intersectoral competition from synthetic fibers produced by the EC chemical industry. In addition, because textile firms tend to be concentrated in depressed regions that are dependent on a single industry their failure to make necessary structural adjustments can have a disproportionate negative social and economic impact on their employees. As a result of the patterns of competition faced by textile firms, policies to assist them cannot be formulated and implemented on a strictly national basis. Such policies require coordination and cooperation among the national governments of the EC and the Commission as well as with the GATT. Since the Community is responsible for trade and tariffs domestic policies have been supplemented by Community participation in the Long-Term Arrangement to stabilize international competition in the textile industry. In contrast, the incentives available for EC firms to restructure and improve their productivity are granted almost exclusively by the public authorities of the member states. In regard to lead industries governments are frequently so concerned about the kinds of industries the nation supports that this has led to political intervention to establish firms in key areas even when such policies were overridden by economic considerations. The role of the Commission, however, in formulating sectoral policies has been minimal, since it does not have the authority, organization, or structure to influence individual national efforts.

LABOR AND TRADE UNIONS

In general the efficient management of industry and the evolution of industrial sectors are directly related to the flexibility of labor and trade unions in adjusting to changes in production. This requires mechanisms not only for reallocating labor within firms but also for matching the labor supply with the domestic labor market.

However, workers and their unions in trying to respond simultaneously to the needs of industry and the interests of labor are confronted by contradictory forces inherent in a society in which growth depends on technological innovation and on the adaptation of individuals to new processes of production. On the one hand, it is in the aggregate economic interest of labor to respond positively to these changes to ensure the competitive efficiency and the structural flexibility of firms. To a large extent, however, the management of firms and the operation of national labor markets have emphasized the convenience of industry; this means the existence of a geographically mobile, trained reservoir of workers who will fit the needs of industry. Although unions have frequently been the initiators of improvements in conditions of work and the administration of the labor markets, the demands of contemporary labor are qualitatively different from those of previous generations. They have expanded beyond insuring better wages and shorter hours to include job security and greater participation in the management of firms. In other words, workers increasingly reject a role of passively adjusting to changes in factory organization or to regional variations in employment opportunities. In part, the debate over regional policy involves these issues. In the past it was considered self-evident and more reasonable that labor should migrate to industrial centers where employment was available. As Italian efforts to develop the Mezzogiorno have indicated, among the many reasons for the state to attempt to reverse this process by inducing industry to move to chronically depressed regions is the higher priority of preserving existing social structures that are healthy and viable. The failure to achieve this end is reflected in the problems of Turin and Milan resulting from migrations of workers from the south of Italy to the north.

Both Roland Tavitian and Hans Günter, in Chapters 3 and 4 respectively, describe how Western European governments in the postwar era have preferred to rely on macroeconomic policies to attain full employment and on general measures to establish the optimum conditions for encouraging labor mobility. These have included the removal of some of the more formidable barriers to the free circulation of labor within the Common Market, but not the adequate development of corresponding policies to deal with the social and economic problems of such workers. However, as Tavitian mentions, even in the midst of high levels of employment the changes in the demands of the capitals and goods markets for workers have only rarely been matched by the changes in the labor market, which has caught up slowly if at all. Furthermore, since growth alone is no longer a panacea for achieving full employment both the expansion of existing government responsibilities for the labor market and the acceptance of new ones are necessary. These include retraining programs, greater job security, more generous compensatory schemes in cases of shutdowns or outright dismissals, and retirement benefits.

In addition to the traditional goals that labor and trade unions have pressed with national governments and during contract negotiations with employers a new issue has emerged—participation in the formulation and implementation of policies that have a significant effect on the operations and structure of industry. This is, in part, a result of the increased influence—even direct involvement—of the state in the policies of firms and in the development of particular sectors, and, in part, a derivative of older demands for workers' control of firms.

However, unions have faced a number of difficulties in participating in this process. In part, this is a result of their domestic organization according to industrial sectors, which has led to vested interests in the health of the industries where their members are employed. Thus the goals of those unions which represent textile and chemical workers, for example, may sharply conflict when questions of intrasectoral and intersectoral restructuring are involved. In addition, the internationalization of production has not been matched by cooperation among trade unions either within or outside the Common Market. In fact, the appeal to the solidarity of labor in the face of the management of multinational corporations breaks down as a result of competition among firms located in different nations. In spite of these problems demands for direct participation in the management of firms have become more important.

In this regard the Lip affair is indicative. Whether the workers who occupied the Lip factory wanted to keep their jobs or wanted to run their own factory is not clear. But the political support that this generated for "autogestion" in France suggests that the question of industrial democracy is not merely a theoretical issue.[14] This is perhaps best illustrated by the fact that President Giscard d'Estaing formed a commission headed by Pierre Sudreau to study the question of the reform of industrial enterprises. Workers' participation, however, is fraught with difficulties: What issues should they try to regulate through firms and what goals should they pursue through trade unions and national political institutions?

At one extreme have been the solutions of the Communist parties and unions for insuring workers' rights through the overthrow of the existing order and its replacement by institutions based on economic democracy. As the examples of workers' control under wartime communism and in Yugoslavia have demonstrated, such devices combined with strictly formal changes in the locus of ownership do not do away with the basic managerial problems of industrialized societies. In fact, they may even make them worse. Once the political and moral victory of shifting authority from managers to workers has been achieved the same problems of industrial management, of maintaining internal discipline and relying on expertise limit the extent to which workers can democratically run a firm. Moreover, one of the greatest dangers of workers' control is its parochialism. As the successive modifications of the Yugoslav system have revealed, the interests of the individual factory must be related to those of the entire economy, and this can only occur if there are institutions at higher levels to coordinate decisions made at the level of the firm.

Socialist unions and parties have supported more practical forms of worker participation that include issues of immediate concern to workers such as conditions of work and personnel policies. In the case of the West German codetermination law this also extends to major changes in the structure of a firm, particularly if a reduction in the size of the work force is involved. Although the unions of West Germany have become actively involved in the implementation of the law since its passage in the mid-1950s its legislative history is relevant for the light it sheds on the background of the proposal. The Christian Democratic party under then Chancellor Konrad Adenauer, representing the interests of industry, included provisions in the bill to prevent workers' councils from becoming the extended arm of the trade unions as well as being the lowest component of a series of economic parliaments parallel to the political parliaments at the state and federal levels. These provisions were in response to a draft submitted by the Social Democratic party in collaboration with the Federation of German Trade Unions during the first session of the new Bundestag the purpose of which was to establish the institutional framework for economic democracy in the fledgling West German republic.[15]

These practical forms of participation, when combined with some form of nationalization of industry through which the state becomes the owner and potential manager of key sectors, contain certain dangers. All intermediaries are removed between the government and the worker, and a new and more volatile pattern of confrontation can result. Moreover, the spontaneous effort at workers' control by the employees at the Scottish Upper Clyde Shipyards illustrates another dimension of the parochial horizons of workers—the self-defeating unwillingness or inability of workers and trade unions to formulate and administer policies for dealing with redundancies and improving productivity. The anxiety about job security may outweigh all other considerations, and this is partly understandable if there are insufficient opportunities for new employment as well as inadequate national institutions for matching workers to jobs; however, the anxiety may also rest upon an inability to distinguish between different forces that impinge upon a firm. On the one hand, worker reaction against the closing of an enterprise may be a manifestation of a conflict between the financial mentality of investors, bankers, and managers who see the firm only as a negotiable asset and workers whose lives are tied to a particular skill, geographic location, and social milieu. On the other hand, codetermination has provided the representatives of German labor on managing boards with direct knowledge of the external competitive factors to which management must respond to keep a firm viable. To some extent awareness of these factors has modified the tendency of workers to respond negatively to decisions that adversely affect them, so long as it can be demonstrated that there is a collective interest on the part of labor and management in sharing the burden of adjustment.

In fact, both managers and workers may have a collective interest in the survival of their unit of production against other domestic plants, because the complex patterns of production that characterize advanced economies also lead to involved patterns of competition. In other words, the notion of class interest is bisected by concern about the future of the firm where one works and the sector to which it belongs. Moreover, the appeal to class solidarity that transcends national boundaries intersects with the more tangible interest in the success of national firms—a factor which is not negligible in the struggle for the global allocation of growth.

NATIONAL INDUSTRIAL POLICIES
IN THE NEXT DECADE

The rapid change in the price of petroleum and the incipient efforts of other raw material producers to improve their terms of trade will have a significant impact on the industries and national policies of the advanced countries. Currently the United States and the members of the European Community have focused their attention on the immediate difficulties caused by the financial aspects of recycling petrodollars. This has diverted attention from the long-run problem that is of equal importance: the effect that recycling, resource nationalism, and the more intense industrialization efforts of the developing countries will have on the evolution of patterns of production and trade in the advanced nations.

If, at present, the OECD countries are concerned about domestic industries, their concern is limited to expanding exports on the basis of existing sectors to finance oil deficits. However, as a result of the basic structural changes in the world economy—of which the OPEC demands are one element—these nations will also have to consider whether their current range of industries will be adequate for the new conditions that are determining international competition. And if not, what impact will this have on the balance of public and private decision making in planning how national industries will respond? What policies will be necessary to stabilize or change existing patterns of production and trade, and to what extent will private financial institutions be subject to government influence in allocating their credits? And, finally, how will these developments affect relations among the OECD members who now compete in similar product lines?

These are not hypothetical questions, since the Common Market states have been more prepared than the United States to intervene to assist and improve their industries through a combination of foreign political and economic policies and domestic industrial policies. In the case of the Community such policies have been necessary not only to insure national growth rates, but the continued economic expansion of the nine member states, a sine qua non for the maintenance of the Common Market and its ability to defend its commercial interests in foreign markets. In the course of the 1960s the American government viewed these policies as contributing to the establishment of a large economic bloc whose existence was considered contrary to U.S. interests. The contradictory reactions within the EC to new pressures on its industries and trade have not stilled the anxiety of policy makers in Washington.[16] The EC's liberal mandate for the GATT negotiations is counterbalanced by a number of bilateral agreements between countries like Iran and individual member states of the Community. In addition, the Europeans as well as the Americans have become even more concerned about what constitutes unacceptable foreign ownership of domestic industry. In the case of Britain the effort to reassert greater national control over domestic industries is reflected in the Industry Bill submitted to the House of Commons in January 1975.

Even the American government will have to fundamentally reverse its response to intrasectoral and intersectoral changes in domestic production. Until now the dynamics of this process have been determined primarily by the private sector. The specter of a national energy policy implicitly contains such a new direction for the federal government. This development would require greater willingness on the parts of management and labor to adapt to the exigencies of structural evolution. However, it is questionable whether union leaders are prepared to accept an active manpower policy which would inevitably threaten the power bases of many trade unions, and, in addition, it is unclear how a national system of "planning" would blend with the existing practices of the private sector. In fact, what appears to be the onset of a flirtation with planning[17] occurs at a time when countries such as France are experiencing the limitations inherent in the approaches which were followed in the 1950s and 1960s, but which apparently still exert an influence on American thinking.

NOTES

1. Jacques R. Houssiaux, "American Influence on Industrial Policy in Western Europe since the Second World War" in Charles P. Kindleberger and Andrew Shonfield, eds., *North American and Western European Economic Policies* (London: St. Martins Press, 1971), pp. 351-363.

2. For contrasting French and German approaches see Jean Saint-Geours, *La politique économique des principaux pays industriels de l'occident* (Paris: Editions Sirey, 1969), chap. 6, and Egon Tuchtfeldt, "Die volkswirtschaftliche Rahmenplannung im Widerstreit der Meinungen," *Weltwirtschaftliches Archiv,* vol. 94, 1965, pp. 10-39; for a general discussion of government policy and changes in post-1945 West European industrial structures see Heinz-Dietrich Ortlieb and Friedrich-Wilhelm Dorge, ed.,

Wirtschaftsordnung und Strukturpolitik, 2d ed. (Opladen: Leske Verlag, 1970), chap. 3.

3. A basic nineteenth century work on the relationship between tariff barriers, industrial development, and national unification is Friedrich List, *The National System of Political Economy* (1885; reprint ed., New York: Augustus M. Kelley, 1966).

4. I. S. Koropeckyj, *Location Problems in Soviet Industry Before World War II: The Case of the Ukraine* (Chapel Hill: University. of North Carolina Press, 1965), see particularly chap. 4.

5. Robert Gilpin, *France in the Age of the Scientific State* (Princeton, N.J.: Princeton University Press, 1968).

6. Ota Sik, *Der dritte Weg: Die marxistisch-leninistische Theorie und die moderne Industriegesellschaft* (Hamburg: Hoffmann und Campe, 1972).

7. Lionel Stoleru, *L'impératif industriel* (Paris: Editions du Seuil, 1969).

8. See "The No-Growth Society," *Daedalus,* Fall 1973.

9. Andrew Shonfield, *Modern Capitalism: The Changing Balance of Public and Private Power* (London: Oxford University Press, 1965), particularly the chapters on France, Britain, Italy, and Germany.

10. Ralph Miliband, *The State in Capitalist Society* (New York: Basic Books, 1969).

11. Ota Sik, *Der Stürkturwandel der Wirtschaftssysteme in den osteuropäischen Ländern* (Zrich: Verlags AG die Arche, 1971).

12. Ezra N. Suleiman, *Politics, Power and Bureaucracy in France* (Princeton, N.J.: Princeton University Press, 1974).

13. Lionel Stoleru, "L'Etat condamné à séduire," *L'Expansion,* April 1972, pp. 125-133.

14. See Francois Bloch-Lainé, *Réforme de l'entreprise* (Paris: Editions du Seuil, 1963); the traditional worker-employer relationship since 1963 has been increasingly contested in France, as elsewhere.

15. For a book that had a great influence on the development of a socialist model for economic democracy during the early years of the Federal Republic of Germany see Fritz Naphtali, *Wirtschaftsdemokratie* (1928; reprint ed., Frankfurt: Europäische Verlagsanstalt, 1966).

16. See Steven J. Warnecke, "The Political Implications of Trade for European-American Relations," in a forthcoming book edited by Ernst-Otto Czempiel and Dankwart A. Rustow.

17. For a report on the Javits-Humphrey bill proposing a national system of planning see the New York *Times,* May 13, 1975, p. 47.

PART

I

NATIONAL POLICIES
TOWARD INDUSTRY

1

INDUSTRIAL POLICY
FORMULATION
IN FRANCE
Ezra N. Suleiman

THE NEW FRENCH ECONOMY

In traveling through France today one is bound to be struck by the general wealth and industrial activity of the country—so much so that many surely ask themselves whether this is the same country that they knew in the 1950s or even the 1960s. And if they did not know the country first-hand during those years they probably wonder whether this can be the same country that they had been used to reading about in the most pessimistic terms. For most analyses of the French economy written during and before the 1950s not only sought to explain the reasons for the static nature of the French economy, but indicated generally that the future could not be radically different from the past. In a 1951 essay, "French Business and the Businessman," David Landes concluded: "Thus the urgent, the critical dilemma hangs over France today: to change and, in changing, die; or not to change, and risk a swifter death."[1] This analysis was essentially Schumpeterian, for just as Schumpeter had argued that the disappearance of the entrepreneurial function would spell the doom of capitalism,[2] so Landes mantained that the bourgeois ethos prevented the rise of the entrepreneurial type in France. The distinctive precapitalist mentality of the French businessman hindered the development of a competitive, production-and-

I wish to acknowledge the financial assistance I received from the American Council of Learned Societies and from the American Philosophical Society for an ongoing study of the relationship between public and private elites in France.

23

profit-oriented economy. France in this view was destined to remain a nation of shopkeepers. As Landes noted:

> The concept of free enterprise as developed in England in the nineteenth century and transplanted to the United States with its postulate of a competitive struggle for markets and drastic penalties for failure, and with its emphasis on earning more and more through producing more and more for less and less, has never really been accepted in France. Instead, France . . . has continued to cherish the precapitalist ideology that underlay the guild organization of the pre-Revolutionary period. This ideology may be summed up briefly as follows: every man has his place in society, should produce enough goods and services of quality to maintain his place, and has a right to the living earned in this manner. In other words, the justification of survival lies not in the ability to make a profit, but in the correct performance of a social function.[3]

Whereas Landes stressed the connection between cultural values and entrepreneurship, other observers, following Max Weber's thesis expounded in *The Protestant Ethic and the Spirit of Capitalism* (1920), placed the emphasis on the religious factor to explain the abhorrence of profits and hence the static nature of the French economy.[4] In other words, as a Catholic country France lacked the Protestant "profit ethic."

A third popular explanation for France's economic backwardness has centered on the effects of the centralized state. The high degree of administrative centralization in France which, according to de Tocqueville, antedated the Revolution of 1789 has brought under the state's net all aspects of the economic and social life of the country. Centralization has in other words sapped much of the energy of a potentially dynamic private sector. If the state took on greater and greater responsibilities during the course of the nineteenth century it could be expected to fill still more vacuums. In this way it discouraged the development of private initiative.

Bourgeois values, religion, and the Jacobin tradition have been seen as the key factors impeding the development of a modern economy in France. Most analysts of France's economic backwardness expected little change to occur in any of these factors and thus could not foresee the day when France would take its place as a leading industrial nation. Yet no one any longer denies that a profound transformation has taken place in France's economy. It is even common to speak of France's "economic miracle." In fact, attempts to explain France's historical economic stagnation have now given way to attempts to explain its rapid industrialization. One such explanation noted in looking back: "It could be said, in summary, that the image of *'la bonne vieille France'* represents a cast of mind acquired over the past 150 years—a cast of mind that gradually became a tradition as the France of the pre-revolutionary, revolutionary and Napoleonic eras receded into oblivion."[5]

The Hudson Institute study conducted by Edmund Stillman completely reverses the picture of the static French economy, arguing in effect that few modern economies are or will be as dynamic. This study notes that since the late 1950s France has experienced the highest rate of economic growth in Western Europe; has known the highest rate of growth (5.8 percent per year) in the world except for Japan and the Soviet Union; has a labor force that can be considered as the most hard-working, best educated, and most productive in Europe; and finally, has a higher rate of investment than even Germany. Projecting from these trends into the 1980s Stillman and his associates maintain that by 1985 France will become, with Sweden, the richest country in Europe. The Hudson Institute projections are certainly open to challenge and their euphoric nature is of little relevance to us here. Whether France will or will not be the richest country in Europe within a decade is a question that should not detain us. Let it simply be noted that the old analyses of the French economy have in fact been shattered and that within a period of less than twenty years France has moved from being an agricultural country to one of the world's most industrialized countries. My purpose is not to attempt to explain the reasons for this transformation, though I will obviously touch on some of them. Rather it would be of greater interest to attempt to see the ways in which the relationship in France between the state and the private sector has had a bearing on industrial development. The traditional gulf separating the public and private sectors has to a very considerable extent been narrowed. It is the narrowing of this gap, which itself (as will be noted below) is the consequence of a number of complex factors, that has facilitated France's industrial development.

THE STATE AND THE GROWTH
OF INDUSTRIAL ENTERPRISES

Just as formerly the state was generally recognized to have played an important role in hindering industrial development, so now it is credited with having played a major role in the transformation of the French economy. Whether through the Plan or through selective policies designed to encourage particular industries the state has without a doubt played an active role since the 1950s. One writer has noted that "one answer to the question of how and why 'dynamic France' overcame 'static France' is that there was a change in elite behavior and popular attitudes."[6] By this the writer simply means that it was the agents of the state, "the technocrats," as he refers to them, who initiated and took responsibility for the changes that led France into its industrial and postindustrial era. This thesis is well documented but it represents, as we will see, only a part of the answer to the general question of how and why France has overcome its industrial backwardness.

That there have been changes in "elite behavior"—that is, in the behavior of those who are chiefly responsible for conducting the state's activities—can hardly be questioned. Nowhere has the change in the state's attitude been more radical and nowhere has it represented a sharper break with the past than in its desire to encourage the development of large industrial enterprises. To this end the state has followed a determined policy of encouraging mergers. This has had both political and economic consequences. Politically it has strengthened the ties between big business and the state and weakened those between small business and the state. This is of considerable importance particularly when one considers the many generations during which economic policy consisted largely in catering to the small independent businessman. Economically the push toward mergers has had the effect of encouraging a certain degree of competition and efficiency. This is because the concentration of industrial enterprises presupposes an important element of competition if only because at its early stages it involves the big swallowing up the small. Hence it is the clearest manifestation of the abandonment of the "live-and-let-live" attitude that has been often described as characterizing the French business mentality.

To be sure, it is important not to exaggerate the degree of competition that the process of industrial concentration entails. At the outset competition may be very fierce, but beyond a certain point, a point which is reached when an industry becomes monopolistic or oligopolistic, the degree of competition that actually prevails may be minimal. It is at this point that a state's antitrust divisions become more active. But in France, as V. G. Venturini has noted, there is no antitrust tradition. He is right in noting with regard to France: "The economico-legal structure of a country is determined not only by the technical processes particular to each type of production but also by the heritage of a long past. The continuum from such past is 'protectionism.' "[7]

France has known the highest rate of mergers in Europe in the postwar years.[8] The logic of the "industrial imperative" has required, it is generally believed, that the state should take it upon itself to encourage the concentration of industrial enterprises. Stoleru, one of the chief spokesmen for the "industrial imperative," may be regarded as having expressed the official view when he noted: "In fact, the problem at this point is no longer just to stop opposing this trend but rather to encourage it openly and actively, for the existing lag is already disquieting."[9]

Table 1.1 shows the extent to which the largest French enterprises have undertaken to merge; and Table 1.2 shows that the industries that have known the highest rate of concentration have been chemicals, electronics, and steel. John H. McArthur and Bruce R. Scott found in their study of the French state's intervention in the key sectors of the economy that the industries concerned could be divided into three categories: where the degree of state influence was high; where it was moderate; and where it was low. It is interesting to observe that the state was found to have little or no influence

TABLE 1.1

**Number and Remuneration of Concentrations Effected
by the 500 Largest French Enterprises**

Year	Number of Operations of Concentration	Total Remuneration (millions of francs)	Average Remuneration of each Operation (millions of francs)
1950	21	58.61	2.79
1951	9	2.98	0.33
1952	22	42.02	1.91
1953	41	147.96	3.60
1954	16	17.91	1.11
1955	41	45.83	1.11
1956	52	25.32	0.48
1957	36	67.31	1.86
1958	45	40.52	0.90
1959	68	101.61	1.49
1960	75	165.47	2.20
1961	70	230.29	3.28
1962	93	201.77	2.16
1963	131	298.04	2.27
1964	113	164.31	1.45
1965	96	279.16	2.90
1966	79	817.08	10.34
1967	57	759.49	13.21
1968	56	720.12	12.85
1969	72	1,287.10	17.87
Total	1,193	5,466.90	4.58

Source: *Direction*, February 1970.

with regard to two types of industries or firms. The first of these is the group of small firms: "In general, these firms knew relatively little about the shape and direction of national policy, and they expressed considerable frustration concerning their contacts with the State."[10] The reported attitude of the state officials toward these companies is extremely revealing:

For their part, the Government officials we met viewed small businesses and businessmen in stereotyped and unsympathetic

TABLE 1.2

Number of Operations of Concentration Effected by French Firms, by Sector

Year	Foodstuffs	Banks, Insurance	Construction	Mechanical and Electrical Industries	Chemicals	Steel and Metallurgy	Textiles	Transport	Other	Total
1950-60	85	183	54	181	149	98	58	41	0	849
1961	12	16	3	9	17	18	10	20	15	120
1962	17	24	3	29	30	7	4	3	10	127
1963	22	17	23	27	25	4	8	9	15	150
1964	44	49	21	46	39	20	12	7	27	265
1965	29	30	19	25	29	8	7	5	12	164
1966	33	52	11	32	28	22	13	25	33	249
1967	13	43	12	10	17	22	8	9	10	144
Total	255	414	146	359	334	199	120	119	122	2,068

Source: A. P. Weber, "Fusions et Concentration d'Entreprises en France," p. 14.

terms. Indeed, the role, competence, motives, and contribution of small businessmen was often regarded with considerable contempt and suspicion. Even the contributions made by the professional managers of some of the largest companies were sometimes called in question by Government and administration people. It was not uncommon for us to encounter strong value judgments in official circles about the relative social roles. Even so, there was an important difference in attitudes toward large and small businessmen.[11]

The second group of companies that the state appeared to have little interest in "comprised companies in certain industries that seemed to be regarded as falling outside the pale of twentieth-century respectability."[12] The two most important examples cited in this group were textiles and food, both of which are not characterized by large-scale firms, do not have strong organizations, are internally divided, and do not attract the type of skilled management that would gain them entry into the official network.[13]

In following a policy that aims at encouraging the development of large industrial conglomerates the state believes it encourages competition. Since mergers that lead to oligopoly often have a negative effect on competition French policy has an inherent contradiction. However, looked at from the perspective of the goals set for French industry, competition and oligopoly may appear to be reconcilable. Stephen Cohen has observed that the concentration of industrial enterprises is seen very differently in France from the way it is seen in the United States:

> The French attitude towards concentration and *ententes* differs from that of American economists. The American generally studies industrial concentration with the assumption that high concentration prevents competition, permits monopoly and profits and reduces competition. The French economist generally looks at industrial structures to see whether concentration is high enough to allow for big, efficient firms.[14]

A brief look at the oligopolistic industries where the degree of state intervention has been high shows that these industries all attempt to compete internationally. Thus although it is often argued that economic competition is still not widely accepted in France by the business community, it should be noted that French industrial policy has tended to distinguish between international and national competition and has chosen to place the greatest emphasis on the former. In other words, the trend toward oligopolistic industries is encouraged because while it reduces the degree of domestic competition it also increases the competitiveness of French firms internationally. A French economist has effectively expressed the apparent contradiction in French policies toward mergers:

Schematically, it is possible to distinguish two clearly different attitudes. On the one hand, the public authorities examine the market conditions, define the criteria of abuse and incriminate all those whose intention it is to interfere with competition. On the other hand, these same authorities encourage and favor the formation of large sectoral oligopolies and monopolies that can effectively meet international competition.[15]

It should also be noted that industrial concentration, which leads to large conglomerates with international markets, accords well with Gaullist foreign policy. McArthur and Scott in fact observe that the political leaders of the Fifth Republic have been aware that "a strong economy depends in large measure on strong competitive enterprises. Even here, however, the idea was not so much to compete with one another as with outsiders."[16] And A. P. Weber notes that this policy antedates the Fifth Republic: "From a historic point of view, it seems that since the Second World War the concern for industrial policy has little by little taken precedence over the concerns relative to the advantages of a policy of competition."[17]

What accounts for the turnabout in French industrial policy, a policy that has shifted its preoccupation from the small businessman to the large industrial enterprise? First, international prestige certainly figures as an important factor. To pull some weight and figure prominently in the diplomatic arena, de Gaulle judged it necessary to have a nuclear striking force, however small and insignificant such a force might be. Similarly, to figure prominently in the economic field it has also been judged essential to promote enterprises with an international character. If one examines the history of the Concorde project one finds beneath all the proclamations of "scientific progress" a fervent desire to be in the forefront of the aircraft industry. That this industry is one that has accounted for a heavily subsidized national megalomania in innumerable countries only confirms the French desire to be one step ahead. In other words, it is important not to under-estimate the impact of foreign policy goals on industrial policy.

The Common Market has been a second key factor in influencing French industrial policy.[18] The Treaty of Rome facilitated for the other European countries their access to French markets. This made it all the more necessary for the French government to consider means to acquire markets in the countries of its European rivals. But if France, as a result of being in competition with its European neighbors, has found it necessary to promote large competitive enterprises this policy has received an added stimulus from the fact that French enterprises have looked at American firms as constituting the greatest threat. This was made clear in the Fifth Plan:

The benefits of the establishment of a European Common Market will not be fully realized unless French firms participate in the construction of larger conglomerates. Such European consolidation must be all the more encouraged and aided since, in a number of cases, only they will permit resistance to the financial and technical power of the large American firms.[19]

The policy of establishing "national champions" was, if not instigated, at least supported by the need to resist the *défi américain*; in other words French industrial policy has aimed to develop firms that are large enough and efficient enough to resist the American challenge and that are able to compete with American firms beyond French borders. To be sure, the problems posed by the multinational corporations are at once political and economic. That is, these corporations come to have an influence, sometimes more imperceptibly than directly, on the industrial and economic policy of the host country.

The third important factor accounting for the industrial policy that seeks large, internationally competitive enterprises is that this policy facilitates the whole process of French economic planning. By "planning" I refer to more than the guidelines laid down by the Plan, for the cooperation between the public and private sectors that takes place outside the Plan is perhaps of greater significance. Andrew Shonfield described the earlier period of French planning as a "conspiracy in the public interest." It was, he noted, "a very elitist conspiracy, involving a fairly small number of people. . . . It relied essentially on the close contacts established between a number of like-minded men in the civil service and in big business. Organized labor, small business, and, most of the time, the ministers of the government of the day were largely passed by."[20] Whether this has radically changed since that time is perhaps not of crucial importance, for as McArthur and Scott note, the "important force shaping corporate strategies and strategic planning was a close relationship between business and the State." It became evident to McArthur and Scott from the outset of their investigations that "the *state-company relationship*, and not the planning process, was the most important determinant of corporate strategic planning and strategies in France."[21] Cohen reached much the same conclusion in his study: "The *économie concertée*, is a partnership of big business, the state, and, in theory though not in practice, the trade unions. The managers of big business and the managers of the state run the modern core of the nation's economy—mostly the oligopoly sectors."[22]

If French industrial policy does hinge to a large extent on the close cooperation between "the managers of big business and the managers of the state," it becomes important to understand the bases for this cooperation.

COOPERATION BETWEEN PUBLIC
AND PRIVATE SECTORS

The development of oligopolistic enterprises in postwar France is, as noted above, the result of policies that the public sector has pursued and that have been embraced by the private sector—a form of cooperation between the two sectors that represents a sharp departure from previous patterns. The traditional businessman described by Landes and others has not disappeared in France but has given way nevertheless to the manager of the large enterprise which, as in the United States, has come to fulfill the modern entrepreneurial function. Thus the economic policies of the Third Republic that sought above all to protect the small businessman and the farmer have been largely replaced by policies that seek to develop large, competitive enterprises. No longer can France be characterized as *"La République des petits."* Nowhere is this more evident than in the Fifth Republic's treatment of the small shopkeeper who, finding himself squeezed by the conglomerates, appeals more and more desperately to the government. Being still a part of a rather sizeable group he is still able—mostly at election times—to obtain some concessions from the government. (Sometimes the concessions accorded to small businessmen are astounding, as in the case of the Royer Law that grants shopkeepers a veto power in departmental councils when the establishment of supermarkets or department stores are at issue.) Otherwise he can no longer be said to figure prominently in the state's economic policies, which have been aimed at overcoming old habits and making France an industrial nation. Giscard d'Estaing could declare to Roger Priouret in 1969:

> I consider that my mandate at the Ministry of Economy and Finance runs until 1976. My objective is, by that date, to bring France to an industrial level about equal to that of Germany and England. I would prefer to attain this objective without inflation. But if I have to choose, I would opt for industrial development and regard the fight against inflation as secondary.[23]

Priouret notes that Giscard d'Estaing was equally of the opinion that the industrialization he sought should be the responsibility of the large enterprises, whose power should remain in the hands of their directors. The extent to which the Fifth Republic has favored big business, either by passing new laws or refusing to apply old ones, is the theme of Priouret's book.

Perhaps most important, however, is the fact that the relationship between the public and private sectors is no longer characterized by a mutual hostility. The traditional mutually hostile perception of the two sectors, which for a long time seriously affected their relationship, has been well described by Henry Ehrmann:

> The feelings of the bureaucracy towards organized business are not free from ambivalence. The civil servants admittedly need the practicality and the experiences of the business world, especially as long as in their own training an almost exclusive emphasis was placed on rhetoric, mathematics, law, and economic theory of the nineteenth century. But they will criticize quite openly those

practices of the trade associations and the cartels that lead to
"economic Malthusianism." As long as such practices continue to
protect the marginal firms, irrespective of costs, the civil servants
hold that big business is hypocritical if is complains about the
political demagoguery favoring the "little man." They regret and
sometimes ridicule the overcautious attitude of industry towards
problems of investment and modernization. They castigate what
they consider the employers' slovenliness towards housing and other
social problems, and are aware of the need for protecting
unorganized interests, especially those of the consumer. They blame
many of the difficulties that stand in the way of European economic
integration on the reluctance of French business to face the
competition of a wider market. Especially the younger
administrators who have already reached high positions show an
increasing amount of impatience with the ingrained habits of the
business community.[24]

If the perception of the managers of the private sectors and those of the
public diverged in the past this was to a large extent because the two sectors
were indeed different. Today both the civil servants and the heads of the large
industrial enterprises see themselves as managers. The distinction between the
art of managing in the private sector and managing in the public sector is no
longer made in France. In fact, whereas the higher civil servants make
categorical distinctions between politics and administration,[25] they make no
distinction whatever between "managing" in the public and private sectors.
The reason for this is that the private sector in France is no longer composed
of small businessmen. The managers of the state now feel they have an
"interlocuteur valable." They feel they can deal on an equal footing with their
counterparts in the private sector whose functions are not very different from
their own and whose goals they come to share. As noted by Ehrmann:
"Characteristically enough, the views of the high bureaucracy and those of
business leaders on the proper organization and the functions of a modern
employers' movement are almost identical. Both groups wish to see that
solidly organized trade associations in the major branches of economic
activity assure the flow of information and control in either direction."[26] Both
groups want to see highly centralized and representative professional
associations. That is the only way in which each side can actually know who
its *"interlocuteur"* is. For the state this can be seen from the distinctions its
agents establish among various interest groups, distinctions that are of crucial
importance because actions are based on them. It is perhaps worth
elaborating on this because of the importance it has in determining the pattern
of relationships established between the private and public sectors.[27]

The term "interest group" or "pressure group"—*groupe d'intérêt* or
groupe de pression—has very specific connotations for the higher civil
servants. Such a group is not representative, seeks limited and selfish ends for

its members, and by implication is of highly questionable legitimacy. This type of group is known, with extremely pejorative connotations, as a "lobby," and it is distinguished from professional organizations. Thus an associational group or a professional organization represents something totally different to the civil servants, who do not consider such organizations as interest groups or lobbies. Such a distinction between interest groups and professional organizations certainly appears illogical but it nonetheless has important implications in France. One official noted: "We have no contact with interest groups here. We only have contact with professional organizations." One of the most influential directors in the Ministry of Finance stated: "One has to make a distinction between interest groups and professional organizations. An interest group—that is, a lobby—is one that defends its specific interests. A professional organization is one that defends not a private interest but a group interest." And a director in the Ministry of Equipment and Housing stated in similar fashion that "an interest group or a pressure group has very limited interests, whereas professional organizations represent the interests of a whole profession." One ministry director who also made this distinction provided some examples: The Chamber of Commerce and the Union of Textile Industries are professional organizations whereas the PME (the organization of small and medium-sized enterprises) is a lobby. It was pointed out to this director that the PME also represents a "profession" or a collective group and seeks ends for the entire group, much like the unions of mechanical industries and textile industries or magistrates or notaries. Nevertheless the director maintained there is in fact a distinction between the two types of groups.

The distinction between interest groups and professional organizations makes perhaps little concession to logic but it reveals what is an undeniable bias in favor of strong, representative organizations. This bias is premised on the administration's choice of groups that it considers representative, which in turn affects the type of relationship established between the administration and the favored groups as well as the latter's method or style of intervention. It was the same director who made the abovementioned distinction between the Union of Textile Industries and the PME who noted in another context: "We've decided to have close contact with dynamic groups. The others try to oblige us to take Malthusian decisions. It's obvious for example that certain unions defend the large numbers of unproductive shopkeepers and not the few productive and dynamic ones. We must not therefore be forced to become intoxicated by the nondynamic groups. This is what the administration has to guard against." Every administration decides for itself which groups it will have close contact with and which groups will receive less than equal treatment. But what distinguishes "dynamic" from "Malthusian" groups? In the instance in which these terms are used above they clearly have an economic connotation. The dynamic groups are those whose economic strength is such that they cannot be ignored. More importantly they are the groups who are considered legitimate because their own demands accord with government policy. The Malthusian groups, on the other hand, as the director in the Ministry of Finance noted, are those whose demands run counter to government policy. Not surprisingly, this director repeated several times the example of PME as a group that constantly attempted to put pressure on the government to take wrong decisions—that is, to support them in their fight against the large-scale business enterprises.

PUBLIC AND PRIVATE MANAGERS

"The key fact in French planning," wrote David Granick some years ago, "is that the same type of men are sitting in the management and civil service posts in this cartel: men of the *grandes écoles,* present and former civil servants who consider themselves technocrats."[28] Another writer has argued that these are the men who "penetrated the centers of public decision-making and turned the state into an instrument for rapid industrialization."[29] Whether these are in fact the true technicians on whom modernization has depended is perhaps debatable. What is less debatable, however, is the fact that the large industrial enterprises in France, the nationalized industries, and the public sector are all to a very large extent run by the members of the Grands Corps.

A 1972 study of industrial managers in France concluded that "the most characteristic trait in the careers of the sample studied is the frequency of the PDG (President Director-General) coming from the public sector."[30] The study noted that this type of career does not simply involve the seduction by the private sector of an elite whose sense of public service has been diluted. Rather it ought to be seen, the study noted, as "an essential element in the training (acquisition of competence and of relations) of the industrial managers in France."[31] Another study, done by *L'Expansion*, has shown how different France is from other countries in this respect (see Table 1.3). Equally important, as the study indicates, is the fact that those leaving the public sector for the private almost always enter large enterprises:

> We have seen that a considerable proportion of French PDG's—a proportion that is higher in the bigger than in the smaller firms— come from the public sector. This interpenetration of business and government, resulting from the mobility of high-level directors from the public to the private sector, is one of the particularities of French society.[32]

The homogeneity in the educational and professional backgrounds of the directors of French industrial enterprises implies three things: they have

TABLE 1.3

The European Company President: Professional Background
(percentages)

Background	France	Britain	Italy	Belgium	Holland
General administration	75.3	56.6	69.2	64.2	65.2
Marketing	3.9	16.4	16.5	7.5	13.0
Finance	2.6	9.0	2.2	0	2.2
Manufacturing	13.6	7.4	8.8	22.6	13.1
Other (law, etc.)	4.4	10.6	3.3	5.7	6.5

Source: "Portrait-Robot du PDG european," *L'Expansion,* November 1969, p. 137.

usually been trained in state academic institutions (specialized schools—the *grandes écoles*—as opposed to the universities); at least a part of their career has been spent in the public sector; and they graduated in the top 15-20 percent of their class. It is this last factor that enables them to choose entry into one of the elite corps. Those who graduate at the top of their class at the Ecole Polytechnique enter the corps of mines and the corps of civil engineers; those who graduate at the top of their class at the Ecole Nationale d'Administration enter the Inspection des Finances, the Conseil d'Etat, and the Cour des Comptes. Entry into these technical and administrative corps is regarded as of the utmost importance not only for a successful administrative career but for a successful career in the private sector. What indicates above all that the hostility between the public and private sectors is a relic of the past is that the *grandes écoles* no longer see themselves as training only agents of the state. They have come to have closer relations with the private sector and they have willingly accepted as a fact of life that a considerable proportion of each graduating class will enter the private sector forthwith. Table 1.4 shows that the Ecole Polytechnique, whose original function was to train military officers, now trains fewer and fewer officers; indeed the percentage of those who resign from the public service immediately upon graduation and choose employment in the private sector is continually on the increase. Furthermore, the particular type of training that the heads of French enterprises receive distinguishes them from their European counterparts. As noted in the *L'Expansion* study:

> It is immediately apparent that the directors of French industries are the ones who are the most educated, whereas the English directors

TABLE 1.4

Distribution of Ecole Polytechnique Graduates, by Sector

Sector	Class of 1935-36		Class of 1956-57		Class of 1964-65	
	No.	%	No.	%	·No.	%
Military						
Army	279	60.5	16	3.0	5	0.8
Military engineers	82	18.0	139	24.0	125	21.4
Total	361	78.5	155	27.0	130	22.2
Civil						
Civil corps	84	18.0	181	32.0	194	32.6
Research	0	0	19	3.0	81	13.6
Resigned	16	21.5	213	38.0	190	31.9
Total	100	21.5	413	72.5	465	77.8

are the least educated. A detailed examination shows that more than half of the French PDG's included in this study were trained in *grandes écoles*, and of these, half were trained at the Ecole Polytechnique. In France, the educational level is the measure of one's worth and a *polytechnicien* is considered to be of superior and universal intelligence.[33]

In his study of the Inspection des Finances, Pierre Lalumière has shown that the phenomenon of *pantouflage* (the move from the public to the private sector) has been a normal career move for the members of this corps.[34] In fact, since the early 1900s the percentage of Inspecteurs des Finances moving into the private sector has varied between 25 and 50 percent but has generally averaged about 30 percent; the figure is about the same for the corps of mines. Table 1.5 shows that the percentage of members of the corps of mines who are at any given time civil servants has been declining, whereas those departing from the corps in order to serve in the semipublic and private sectors have been increasing.

The Grands Corps were originally established for the purpose of training high-quality recruits for specific activities all of which fall within the state's purview. These corps continue to fulfill the functions for which they were

TABLE 1.5

Distribution of Members of Corps des Mines, by Sector

Section	1949		1961		1970	
	No.	%	No.	%	No.	%
Civil servants	109	43.4	115	37.1	120	35.9
Public and semipublic	69	27.5	98	31.6	109	32.6
Private	73	29.1	97	31.3	105	31.5
Total	251	100.0	310	100.0	334	100.0

Source: Erhard Friedberg and Dominique Desjeux, "Fonctions de l'Etat et Rôle des Grands Corps," p. 569.

originally created and such functions constitute their *raison d'être*.[35] But whereas these functions have continued to decline in importance (for example mines no longer occupy an important position in the economy) the corps themselves have not. In fact the corps are now utilized as springboards to illustrious careers in the administration and in the private sector. Three principal reasons account for this: recruitment into these corps necessitates the highest intellectual attainments; the number of members admitted into these corps has remained severely restricted; and, perhaps most important, these corps have been sufficiently flexible and adaptable to meeting changing economic and social conditions. Thus academic success in the *grandes écoles* leads forthwith to the attainment of high posts in the public sector, which in turn leads to high managerial posts in the private sector.

Given that the members of the Grands Corps move to the private sector it becomes important to know what areas of the private sector they gravitate toward. Although it is difficult to obtain precise data on this a clear indication can nevertheless be obtained.

There is no doubt that members of the different corps prefer different sectors. This is in part due to the fact that their training and professional background predispose them for particular activities. It is also due to a large extent to the access they have to particular sectors as a result of the imprint already made in those areas by their *camarades*. Thus the banking and credit sector is the one most favored by the *inspecteurs des finances*. This is of profound importance insofar as the concentration of industry is concerned. As Michel Drancourt has noted: "The role of the banks here is crucial. It appears that they favor the development of the large enterprises rather than the accession of the medium enterprises to the level of the big ones.[36] That the *inspecteurs des finances* favor the banking and credit sector is by no means a novel situation:

> The sectors in which private firms needing credit dominated [before 1914] had their preferences. In particular, the institutions of finance capitalism, the financing source for the entire economy, were colonized by those who resigned [from the Inspection des Finances].[37]

The other sectors that attract the *inspecteurs des finances* (besides banking) are the mechanical, chemical, metallurgical, and steel industries, though they do not dominate in any of these; this is because it is the corps of mines that strongly colonizes these industries. As Dominique Desjeux and Erhard Friedberg observe: "The mining engineers in the private sector always concentrate in the heavy industry sector; such as chemicals, mechanical, metallurgy and steel, the industries which have been the ones that have traditionally welcomed the *pantouflards* of the corps and in which [the] corps has been reinforcing its presence. Moreover, the corps has considerably increased its presence in the sectors that are peripheral to the industrial sector proper, namely, in [the] banking sector and in the consulting firms."[38] Lalumière's conclusion regarding the Inspection des Finances can be said to apply to all the Grands Corps:

> The *Inspecteurs des Finances* who leave [the Inspection des Finances] gravitate toward the most active sectors of the economy. They maintain a very strong position in the area of finance capitalism whose principal institutions they direct. At present, they are infiltrating the chemical and automobile industries which are experiencing expansion. They tie their fortunes to the most dynamic aspects of capitalism.[39]

The question may legitimately be raised as to how the restricted number of members of the Grands Corps can allow these corps to continue occupying most of the directorial posts in both the private and public sectors particularly in an expanding economy when the number of these posts must be increasing. Is there not a contradiction between the desire of these corps to continue restricting their membership and their desire to occupy the key posts in the public and private sectors? In effect not only is there no contradiction between these two aims but they are perfectly compatible. This is because French industrial policy has aimed at the concentration of economic power in much the same way as political and administrative power is concentrated. Consequently the rapidly expanding French economy has not entailed a corresponding expansion of key posts. It may in fact have entailed the contrary. This also helps to explain the newly established cooperation, previously mentioned, between the public and private sectors.

CONCLUSION

It can be concluded that not only do the members of the Grands Corps occupy, as indicated, key positions in the private sector but they occupy these positions almost exclusively in the most dynamic sectors of the economy. In a separate study I am currently undertaking, on the relation between public and private elites in France it has been found that the members of the Grands Corps in the public sector believe there is little basis for conflict between the public and private sectors. Indeed it is generally affirmed that it is undesirable that there should be much separation between the two sectors. This is a remarkable assertion particularly when one considers the extent to which the agents of the state have traditionally seen themselves as the sole guardians of the general interest.

The preliminary results of this study also reveal that the managers of industrial enterprises, as well as the state's officials, believe if any conflict exists it is now confined to the area of price controls. When asked what areas displayed the greatest cooperation they most often mentioned industrial, investment, and export policies. It was generally maintained that the expansion of the French economy had led to a concordance of views between public and private sectors. (This raises the question of whether the cooperation between the two sectors is due simply to the fact that both have embraced the goals of economic growth, implying that were the state to set different goals for the economy and for the society hostility might resurface between the two sectors; this question is treated in my larger study.) Now it happens that the industries which have experienced the greatest expansion are also the industries in which the state has shown the greatest interest. These are also the industries in which the members of the Grands Corps are to be found in the directorial posts.

It is important to note that French industrial development and the newly established cooperation (or collusion) between the public and private sectors are not simply due to the fact that France is the country where the technocrat is "supreme"[40] and where the dynamic technocrats have been able to diffuse and implement their ideas. This is only partly correct. Credit should not be totally taken away from the politicians who were in large part responsible for shaping French industrial policy, the consequences of which have led to a more dynamic private sector and in turn allowed for the closer cooperation between public authorities and the private sector. The fact that members of the Grands Corps, the "arch technocrats" as they are often referred to, occupy directional posts in both the public and private sectors has perhaps insured the continuation of the closer cooperation. But for this cooperation to have been initiated it was first necessary for structural changes to occur in the private sector.

NOTES

1. David S. Landes, "French Business and the Businessman: A Social and Cultural Analysis," in Edward Meade Earle, ed., *Modern France: Problems of the Third and Fourth Republics* (Princeton, N.J.: Princeton University Press, 1951), p. 353.

2. Joseph A. Schumpeter, *Capitalism, Socialism and Democracy* (New York: Basic Books), pp. 121-124.

3. Landes, op. cit., p. 348.

4. Octave Gelinier, *Morale de l'entreprise et destin de la nation* (Paris: Plon, 1965).

5. Edmund Stillman et al., *L'Envol de la France dans les années 80* (Paris: Hachette, 1973), p. 35.

6. Richard F. Kuisel, "Technocrats and Public Economic Policy: From the Third to the Fourth Republic," *Journal of European Economic History* 2, no. 1 (1973): 53.

7. V. G. Venturini, *Monopolies and Restrictive Trade Practices in France* (Leyden: A. W. Sijthoff, 1971), p. 9.

8. Ibid., p. 350.

9. Lionel Stoleru, *L'impérative industriel* (Paris: Editions du Seuil, 1969), p. 49.

10. John H. McArthur and Bruce R. Scott, *Industrial Planning in France* (Boston: Harvard Graduate School of Business Administration, 1969), p. 391.

11. Ibid.

12. Ibid., p. 392.

13. See ibid., pp. 392-401.

14. Stephen Cohen, *Modern Capitalist Planning: The French Model* (Cambridge, Mass.: Harvard University Press, 1969), p. 75.

15. A. P. Weber, "L'Economie industrielle de 1950 à 1970: Concentration des entreprises et politique économique," *Revue d'Economie Politique* 80, no. 5 (September-October 1970): 770.

16. McArthur and Scott, op. cit., p. 229.

17. A. P. Weber, "Fusions et concentration d'entreprises en France," *La Documentation Française*, January 1969, p. 35.

18. See Raymond Vernon, ed., *Big Business and the State* (Cambridge, Mass.: Harvard University Press, 1974), p. 116.

19. Weber, "Fusions et concentration d'enterprises en France," op. cit., p. 36.

20. Andrew Shonfield, *Modern Capitalism* (New York: Oxford University Press, 1969), pp. 130-131.

21. McArthur and Scott, op. cit., p. 8.

22. Cohen, op. cit., p. 51.

23. Roger Priouret, *Les Française Mystifiés* (Paris: Grasset, 1973), p. 121.

24. Henry Ehrmann, *Organized Business in France* (Princeton, N.J.: Princeton University Press, 1957), p. 266.

25. See Ezra N. Suleiman, *Politics, Power and Bureaucracy in France* (Princeton, N.J.: Princeton University Press, 1974), chap. 9, 10, 12.

26. Ehrmann, op. cit., p. 271.

27. The following two paragraphs are derived from Suleiman, op. cit.

28. David Granick, *The European Executive* (New York: Doubleday, 1964), p. 147.

29. Kuisel, op. cit., p. 54.

30. Dominique Monjardet, "Carrière des dirigeants et contrôle de l'entreprise," *Sociologie du Travail*, no. 2 (1972): 1411.

31. Ibid.

32. "Portrait-Robot du PDG Européen, *L'Expansion*, November 1969, p. 137.

33. Ibid., pp. 139-140.

34. Pierre Lalumière, *L'Inspection des Finances* (Paris: Presses Universitaires de France, 1959), p. 72.

35. See Suleiman, op. cit., chap. 9.

36. Michel Drancourt, *Les clés du Pouvoir* (Paris: Fayard, 1964), p. 30.

37. Lalumière, op. cit., p. 86.

38. Erhard Friedberg and Dominique Desjeux, "Fonctions de l'Etat et Rôle des Grands Corps: Le cas du corps des mines," *Annuaire International de la Fonction Publique*, Autumn 1972, p. 579.

39. Lalumière, op. cit., pp. 87-88.

40. Granick, op. cit., p. 72.

2

THE BELGIAN
ECONOMIC EXPANSION
LAW OF 1970
J. J. BODDEWYN

THE LEVELS AND IDEOLOGICAL CONTENT
OF INDUSTRIAL POLICY

The Internationalization of
Industrial Policy

The concept of "industrial policy" has a strong national connotation in Western Europe because it has long been associated with various plans and programs for industrialization, reconstruction, reconversion, or "restructuration" within a single country. In fact, however, Western European countries have not been able to carry out such programs independently, as significant autarky in these countries has been impossible particularly since the loss of their colonies. The post-World War II period also has witnessed an impressive recognition of the international economic interdependence among Western and other developed countries. This is exemplified by various European, Atlantic, and global initiatives such as the Marshall Plan, the European Community (EC), the General Agreement on Tariffs and Trade (GATT), and the Organization for Economic Cooperation and Development (OECD). This interdependence, occasionally resisted or resented, has undoubtedly reduced the freedom of national economic planners, policy makers, and administrators.

In a less visible fashion bilateral treaties of "Friendship, Navigation, and Commerce" have limited national maneuverability in the field of industrial policy. This is particularly true when a partner in such treaties has been the United States, which has been able to use its widespread influence to raise questions about the impact of industrial policy on U.S. firms and other American interests. Foreign influences are thus significant in industrial policy.

Furthermore, the European economic integration movement which culminated in the EC and precipitated the formation of the European Free Trade Association (EFTA), has marked the further decline of the purely national concept of industrial policy. This resulted when the Treaty of Rome (1957) and the Stockholm Convention (1959) imposed various limitations on national sovereignty so far as the formulation and implementation of economic and social policies are concerned. The EC Commission has itself made various proposals for a European industrial policy, and has drafted several partial programs in this area.[1] Supranational dimensions of industrial policy are therefore increasingly evident.

Such economic and political developments have simultaneously broadened and narrowed the scope of national industrial policy. On the one hand, they have forced European governments to extend their vision to the outside world by developing their own multinational firms. On the other hand, these governments have lost some room for maneuver as a result of obligations restricting their sovereignty. These limitations, however, have been circumvented—through simple violations of international obligations or through new measures violating their spirit—by governments that have wanted to retain or regain maximum autonomy in the face of new economic and social problems affecting their stability and future (for example the problems associated with monetary and energy policies in the 1970s).

The Subnationalization of Industrial Policy

The explicit consideration of subnational regions in national industrial policy is a relatively new addition to the earlier focus on sectoral targets in particular industries, such as cement, steel, computers, and energy. Motives for developing subnational regions or for restructuring declining ones have been broadly social. That is to say, they have been concerned with eradicating or at least reducing inequalities in standards of living among the different geographical parts of a country. Among the regions of member nations of the EC and EFTA this is true also for humanitarian and moral reasons. Yet it is obvious that political motives have been as significant as—and perfectly compatible with—such economic motives as creating larger national markets as well as with social aims. This is due to the fact that individual politicians as well as entire political parties have had a stake in furthering the cause of the stepchildren of economic development.

Intense subnationalism has emerged or reemerged in various parts of Western Europe. This has usually found a strong base in charges of neglect or exploitation by the "core" area; Wales, Scotland, and Northern Ireland have made such charges against England. The "outlying" new members of the EC—Britain, Ireland, and Denmark—similarly have voiced fears that they would become "deserts" for the benefit of the central EC regions. As a result, they have obtained commitments for a stronger regional development assistance policy.

Within this context of supranational, foreign, and subnational factors increasingly affecting the formulation and implementation of national industrial policy an analysis will be given below of the enactment and application of the Belgian Economic Expansion Law of 1970, since Belgium is particularly exposed to these three sets of influences.

The Ideologizing of
Industrial Policy

Another reason for studying the Belgian legislation is that it provides an opportunity to verify whether industrial policy is as free of political ideology as its image usually implies. There are, of course, underlying values associated with industrial policy, such as growth, efficiency, (workable) competition, and innovation. But these values have become largely apolitical to the extent that they are widely shared by ruling parties and elites in Western Europe. The choice of particular objectives and instruments associated with industrial policy as well as the attitudes and behavior of those who implement them usually reveal a political vision and will. Here again the 1970 Belgian Economic Expansion Law makes it possible to check whether any difference resulted because the law's major sponsors and executors were members of the Belgian Socialist party, which has been part of recent coalition governments.

Consequently, this study tests two hypotheses: that industrial policy can no longer be conceived and implemented in a strictly national context; and that industrial policy is not a purely technocratic exercise but has also a significant ideological content.

The subject is obviously vast. It can only be partially handled here in the process of analyzing the genesis of the 1970 Belgian bill and the application of the resulting law during the 1970-73 period. The analysis rests on parliamentary and executive documents, personal interviews with key actors, and various general and special studies.

BACKGROUND OF THE 1970 LAW

Industrial Evolution

The 1970 Economic Expansion Law—sometimes referred to as the Leburton Law for Edmond Leburton, then Belgian Minister of Economic Affairs and its chief sponsor—succeeded related pieces of legislation going back to 1953. All of these reflected the fundamental problems facing Belgian industry in the postwar period.

Following the example set by England, Belgium had been the first country on the continent to industrialize in the nineteenth century. Coal mining, iron-and-steel works (soon relying almost entirely on imported ore), processing of copper and other nonferrous metals (mainly from the former Belgian Congo), glass and cement making, and textile manufacturing (including carpets) were the major industries in which Belgium obtained its early lead in the 1800s. And they were still the mainstay of Belgian industry in the 1950s. Since the country had experienced little destruction during World War II and enjoyed excellent demand for basic materials and semimanufactured products in the immediate postwar period, there was no need for massive reconstruction and modernization. As a result, Belgium received relatively little in Marshall Plan funds.

By the 1950s Belgian industry, overwhelmingly owned by private interests (there have been no nationalizations outside transportation and little public ownership outside utilities), had lost much of its entrepreneurship and inventiveness. In part this was a result of the lethargic control over industrial development exercised by giant conglomerate "holdings."[2] The government's fundamentally noninterventionist stance in regard to industrial restructuring failed to reverse the inertia of the private sector.

Meanwhile, of course, the competing neighboring nations rebuilt (Germany and France), industrialized (the Netherlands), expanded, and modernized their economies. This left both Belgium and Britain progressively behind in the race for economic development. Furthermore, developing nations—a traditional market for Belgian exports—began their own industrialization precisely in those relatively unsophisticated sectors where Belgium was strong.

Consequently, a number of Belgian industries declined for lack of competition. This process was accelerated by the problems of the basic coal and steel industries. Belgian coal, which had to be mined deep underground, became too expensive in the face of cheaper sources from abroad and the shift to oil-based energy. This led the government in the 1960s to assume de facto responsibility for the closing down of some mines and the survival of the remaining ones. Throughout Europe the steel industry began its move to the seaside, away from proximity to the coal mines. Belgium found it hard to follow this trend although a new complex was developed near Ghent and the estuary of the Scheld River. The loss of the Belgian Congo in 1960 upset the copper-processing industry and further weakened the finances of the controlling holding companies that were largely based on such older industries.

Social, Cultural, and
Political Factors

This unfortunate economic evolution resulted in serious social dislocations. Employment suffered, especially in the face of a growing population—up from 8 to 10 million between 1940 and 1970. However, the upheaval took place mainly in Wallonia, the French-speaking part of Belgium. It is there that the nineteenth century Industrial Revolution had started, as Wallonia was the original coal and iron ore site. Flanders suffered also because of its dependence on textiles.[3] But new industries such as petrochemicals could more readily locate in Flanders since it borders on the sea and is close to the estuaries of major rivers. This applied particularly to Antwerp and Ghent on the Scheld. In addition, the work force of Flanders has until recently been considered more docile than that in Wallonia, where Socialist influences were much stronger than the Social Christian (Catholic) and Liberal (conservative) ones that have predominated in Brussels and Flanders. This made Flanders more attractive to new investors including Americans.

The economic decline of Wallonia and the ascendancy of Flanders have been accompanied and exacerbated by the cultural-political-social quarrels between the two major linguistic groups. French-speaking Belgians have historically dominated the country's economic, social, cultural, and political life since the advent of independence in 1830, although the Flemish were definitely more numerous. At the present time 55 percent of the population resides in the Flemish part of the country, 35 percent in Wallonia, and 10 percent in bilingual but predominantly (80 percent) French-speaking "Greater" Brussels.

Francophone predominance came to an end after World War II; and the Flemish are now clearly equal—if not predominant—on account of their number, strong political ambitions, and the greater economic development of their region. This political configuration definitely affects the creation and implementation of major legislation. One such example is the 1970 Economic Expansion Law which provides incentives for areas and sectors in need of new jobs, financing, and technological development.

THE 1970 ECONOMIC EXPANSION LAW

Precedents

Government Bill (Senate) no. 354 of April 1970, which resulted in Belgium's Economic Expansion Law of December 30, 1970 must be understood in the context of at least three related laws:[4] The first of these was the law of July 17, 1959 (still in force), which was intended to remedy such general problems as high unemployment, low profit margins and the concomitant low level of investment, the lack of a modern industrial base producing high demand products, and uneven regional development. It applies to all of Belgium, but has a strong sectoral focus. The second related law, that of July 18, 1959 (no longer in force), was uniquely concerned with the development of certain regions troubled by economic and social problems. While the maintenance of an adequate level of employment, the importation of new technologies, and the modernization of industrial structures were largely achieved through granting various incentives under the two 1959 laws, regional development kept lagging. Thus a supplementary but temporary law of "exceptional assistance" enacted on July 14, 1966, was intended to promote and accelerate the reconversion and economic development of the declining coal mining regions (mainly in Wallonia and in the eastern part of Flanders) and of certain other areas confronted with critical or urgent problems. Improvement would be achieved by diversifying their economic activity, installing rapid growth or high-value-added industries, providing work, or promoting scientific research. This 1966 law (now eliminated) increased both the amounts of subsidies available for development areas and the extent of these areas—particularly in Flanders.

Under these three laws incentives were provided for investment in (1) fixed assets; (2) intangible assets (organizational studies, research and development, and new product development); and (3) other basic costs related to the marketing of new products thus developed. Financial assistance was available through (1) interest-rate subsidies (the main form); (2) direct capital grants; (3) state guarantees; (4) tax advantages; and (5) interest-free advances for research and development. Each type of incentive was linked to a certain category of aid.*

Priorities thus evolved from 1959 to 1966 as the problems of depressed

---

*It is interesting to observe that an ad hoc measure was taken in January 1968 immediately after the U.S. Office of Foreign Direct Investment (OFDI) restricted the export of U.S. capital to developed countries; the Belgian government offered the assistance of the National Investment Society (SNI), which was willing to take up to 90 percent of the equity of a foreign firm while leaving control with the U.S. partner, because investments in companies owned less than 10 percent by the American investor were exempted from OFDI controls.

areas became progressively paramount—a phenomenon also observable elsewhere in Western Europe. While the Belgian government increasingly placed greater though still limited emphasis on project analysis as a condition for state aid all firms locating in the development areas officially delimited by the 1966 law were generally assisted in some manner. They also benefitted from larger incentives than those given to firms located elsewhere; firms with sites in or near Brussels and Antwerp, which were considered fully developed, received even less or nothing.

The 1966 law succeeded in creating employment in depressed areas, particularly through foreign investment. On the other hand, it did not result in either significantly greater diversification, the establishment of new rapid growth or high-value-added industries, or the promotion of scientific research—its other major goals. These were somewhat incompatible with the creation of more employment through traditional labor-intensive but low-growth and research-poor ventures.[5] Moreover, the less affluent provinces obtained fewer new investments because competition among areas (and with foreign countries) meant that investors were offered much the same assistance in all eligible localities. As a result they tended to gravitate to places better endowed in terms of infrastructure and proximity to suppliers and customers, thereby perpetuating the problems of outlying and less developed parts of the country. "Need" had thus not proved to be the commanding criterion.

As a result of this situation the Belgian government, which had reached similar conclusions, proposed a restatement of objectives and the revamping of instruments. This led to the 1970 expansion bill designed to replace the temporary 1966 regional law whose duration had already been prolonged past its original two-year limit.

Objectives of the Bill

As the title of the bill indicates, "economic expansion" remained the paramount objective;[6] the creation of new jobs and the modernization of Belgian industry in the context of balanced and properly distributed regional development were sought. These now traditional goals, however, were cast in a new light and supported by new means. Particularly evident in the bill were the steps taken by the state vis à vis private enterprise; the use of contractual devices to influence business responses in the desirable direction; and the granting of a larger role and greater resources to the National Investment Society (SNI).

The Role of the Private Sector

The government expressed the desire not to reduce the scope and initiative of private enterprise, provided the latter responded voluntarily to achieve official goals. However, a rather strong "or else" was implied, with state-backed institutions such as the SNI acting as reserve instruments to "prompt initiatives," whether private, public, or mixed. In addition, the bill revealed the government's interest in making its intervention in the economy much more permanent. Thus the new legislation was to provide a more flexible instrument linked to the achievement of recurrent official plans rather than to the solution of transitory or "special-case" problems, as with the 1966 law.*

In particular, the bill and its commentaries stressed that firms seeking participation in the economic expansion plan would be more carefully scrutinized; they would have to commit themselves more explicitly to achieve public purposes encompassed in the plan, particularly when contracts were used; and their fulfillment of such commitments would be more carefully scrutinized—and penalized if found deficient (Articles 3 and 37-40). For that matter, the disbursement of subsidies would increase to match a firm's pace in fulfilling its promises. This would avoid the recurrence of a few situations where companies that had received various incentives at the outset had failed to live up to their commitments within a reasonable period of time.†

In the case of the relatively more important projects the state could place its own observer inside a firm in order to supervise the fulfillment of the contract and advise the management (Article 23). Firms in need of reconversion or "restructuring" would have to submit first to a thorough investigation by an agent of the government. The resulting contract could be undertaken by a third party which would acquire control of such firms for that purpose. In the latter two situations the SNI could have a role. Additionally, the bill's provisions envisioned that selectivity could be used in assisting firms—for example, to favor large firms of a multinational character because they were considered better able to remain competitive or to assume a leading role.

In another vein, the bill professed to avoid the kind of "futureless protectionism" connected with defending the hopeless cause of declining industries or firms, although social measures outside the scope of this proposed law might also be necessary in these cases. One way of avoiding such circumstances would be to have recipient firms invest some of their own funds

---

*The Planning Bureau, which in 1970 succeeded the Bureau of Economic Programmation created in 1959, is charged with preparing the draft plan and with following up the application of the laws approving the plan (usually of a five-year duration) and its annual adaptations. The plan is imperative as far as public firms and administrations are concerned; contractually binding on private firms accepting government assistance in return for committing themselves to achieving some part of the plan; and indicative for other firms.

†For example, Article 14 provides that employment premiums will be paid at the end of each year on the basis of the jobs actually created, with reimbursement due if employment is not maintained for at least two years.

in any rescuing project. At the same time government assistance of the type covered by this bill would never exceed 75 percent of the total investment.

While acknowledging the contributions made by foreign (mainly American) investors the bill's proposals stressed the importance of not being too dependent on foreign goodwill. Yet the bill itself singled out only take-overs: It proposed that the approval of the Ministries of Economic Affairs and of Finances be obtained when at least one-third of the capital of a firm with a net worth in excess of BF100 million (about $2 million) was to be acquired by persons or companies (1) having their habitual domicile or seat, central administration, or main establishment outside of the member states of the European Community; and (2) being directly or indirectly under the control of such persons or companies (Article 36).*

The Role of Incentives

The traditional incentives—interest subsidies, capital grants, state guarantees, and tax advantages—were retained but were to be complemented by the alternative of employment premiums for each job created.

While incentives could be granted by simple ministerial decision in regional development zones the bill stressed the new "contracts" that could be entered into by benefitting firms in order to foster: (1) technological and industrial-commercial development (progress contracts and technological promotion contracts); (2) overall managerial improvement (promotion contracts); and (3) the reconversion of declining firms (reconversion contracts). Contracting firms would benefit from regular incentives such as cheap loans and subsidies, government purchase orders for goods, contracts for research and development work, and export assistance; but government assistance would be better aimed and integrated. The firms could also have the government pay up to 25 percent of the cost of the services of management consultants; and they could receive interest-free advances (up to 80 percent) for technological research. Such contracts would in principle be linked to the achievement of some of the plan's objectives.

The dual character of this new legislation is observable here. On the one hand, it succeeds the 1966 law in assisting regional development. However, it also has a strong sectoral and technological bent along the lines of the

---

*The State Council, which has to comment on all government bills, was to raise many objections about this article because of its vagueness (for example, who was to ask for the permission?) and the lack of consideration of the seller's interests (p. 64 of the bill). The old exchange rate of BF50 to $1 is used throughout this study since it prevailed at the time of the law's enactment, and therefore reflects the magnitudes relevant then.

economic and scientific plans, thereby paralleling the goals of the more general law of July 17, 1959.* Thus Article 5 provides that incentives can be granted outside development zones for "sectoral and technological projects of particular interest," with the government specifying the relevant criteria and application rules (also Article 11). Additional incentives—namely, higher interest subsidies and employment premiums—would be available if "advanced technology" were involved and if a progress contract had been signed.†

Yet the new law was intended to be politically neutral in its definition of the zones entitled to assistance, and to avoid "partisan preoccupations, whether political or linguistic" in order to "normalize relations" among contending groups. The seriousness of economic-social problems was to be the leading criterion in order to achieve equality among zones with similar difficulties. It may be added that the bill encompassed not only industry but also crafts (*enterprises artisanales*) and services—a welcome addition in light of the traditional emphasis on narrowly defined "industry."[7]

The Role of the SNI

The National Investment Society (SNI) was created at the initiative of the Belgian government in 1962, but it is partly owned by private financial institutions. It is designed to assist in the creation, reorganization, or extension of industrial and commercial firms in the interest of the Belgian economy. Regional Investment Societies (SRIs) were also authorized in 1962.

The 1970 bill expanded the SNI's role as a "chosen instrument" to be used whenever the private sector is unable or unwilling to move toward the achievement of the plan's objectives (Article 20); but this role was conceived as being more complementary and cooperative than competitive. For its new purpose the SNI's authorized capital was to be increased by BF2 billion (about $40 million) to BF5 billion. (This figure must be compared with the BF130 billion of industrial investment provided by the Belgian government during the 1959-69 period out of a total investment of BF267 billion.) And the government's guarantee was to be available to protect the SNI's various interventions on behalf of the state. The SNI, which can acquire and hold the

---

*The law of July 17, 1959 was to remain effective, with its nationwide and sectoral emphasis, while the laws of July 18, 1959, and July 14, 1966 (and related legislation)—with their regional emphasis—were to be replaced by this new one whose regional character is not evident from its title.

†Article 14, paragraph 2, specifies that employment premiums can be doubled if the investment helps create a "pole for regional industrial development," if it is of an advanced-technology character, or if it brings in an industry that does not yet exist in the country.

shares of other companies, was also authorized to participate in European and multinational projects of benefit to the Belgian economy (Articles 34-35).

Moreover, the bill stressed that the government should have the right to audit (*droit de regard*) the recipient firm's management when state assistance was involved, and that the government should benefit from some of the profits resulting from its aid. Hence the bill provided that in the case of investments over \$2 million (BF100 million) the state could ask to have part of its loans covered by convertible debentures to be administered by the SNI; the beneficiary firm could, however, redeem them before maturity.

Other Provisions

According to other provisions of the bill the government could commission all necessary studies (Article 43); and companies would be penalized for failure to meet their commitments (Article 38). On the other hand, there were various tax benefits to facilitate mergers and spin-offs (Articles 44-45).

Belgian provinces, communes, and other public institutions would be further assisted in acquiring land (through interest subsidies, grants, and state guarantees), in purchasing equipment, and in providing other forms of "welcoming infrastructure" (*infrastructure d'accueil*), such as buildings suitable for manufacturing, warehousing, and research, which could be sold or rented to firms (Articles 30-31 and 42). Such assistance was to be linked to the expansion and modernization of the industrial and service parks provided for in the regional sections of the plan.

Finally, the bill acknowledged the need to coordinate the work of the various Belgian ministries. While the Ministry of Economic Affairs was charged with applying the new law it was to coordinate its work with the Finance Ministry, the subministries (*Sécrêtariats d'Etat*) connected with regional (Flanders and Wallonia) economic development, and other relevant public institutions.[8]

FACTORS AFFECTING THE CONTENTS OF THE BILL

Zeitgeist and Foreign Examples

The bill and the resulting law represent an interesting microcosm of the goals fashionable in the late 1960s—economic growth, regional development, and high technology; there is no mention of environmental problems and other "limits to growth" that become prominent shortly thereafter although the law deals briefly with water pollution and water resources (Article 33). In particular, the emphasis on "advanced technology" mirrors a period when discussion of "technological gaps" and of the "American challenge" was current. Even the very mild anti-Americanism—particularly in the matter of take-overs—was de rigueur.[9]

The new instruments must also be studied in the context of received ideas and foreign innovations. "Indicative planning" à la France had a very good press during the 1950s and 1960s; even West Germany finally adopted it. Government subsidies to reconstruct, reconvert, or restructure industry were common in practically every European country. And the second half of the 1960s saw great interest in "government reorganization corporations" following Italian (IRI, ENI) and British (IRC) models. These latter inspired the creation and expansion of the Belgian SNI. In addition, the system of incentives had quickly become fairly uniform as European governments copied each other even though the incentives mix was not always the same. The Belgian bill of 1970 borrowed in particular from the French system of contractual agreements (*contrats-programmes*) between the state and private firms. This formalized the commitment of companies to contribute to public objectives, such as price stabilization, in return for various benefits from the state.

Since such goals and instruments had thus become part of the Belgian political consensus the politics of economic expansion no longer dwelt on their merits. The main concerns were twofold: the beneficiaries of the government's intervention in the expansion process; and the means to be used to achieve the various purposes.

Competition for Benefits

The issue of dividing the benefits and spoils of the assistance programs revolved around a central question, Who would gain most from the incentives: Flanders or Wallonia? Included also was the more specific problem of what particular cities and political districts would figure among the colored or shaded zones that represented the assisted areas on Belgium's white map (but this topic is not treated here).

The stakes were sizable, since during the 1959-69 period about half (BF 130/267 billion, or $2.6/5.3 billion) of Belgian industrial and mining investments had benefited from low-cost loans or state guarantees. This proportion is higher when other benefits, such as capital grants, interest-free advances for research and development, and tax advantages, are included. A number of assisted areas had been added by the 1966 law particularly in

Flanders. Of the $2.6 billion of assisted credits during the ten-year period, about $1.5 billion went to the Flemish-speaking part of the country, $1.05 billion to the French-speaking region, and $.07 billion to the Brussels region.

Subnational Competition

Where the zones to be assisted under the 1970 law would be located was clearly very important, but the bill remained largely silent on this topic. It did provide, however, that the listing of cities (*communes*) under the 1959 and 1966 laws would be retained until a new list could be drawn up on criteria of underemployment, industrial decline, low living standards, or slow growth rate (Article 11).

This relative silence may be explained by the fact that the implementation of the proposed legislation was to be linked to another pending bill on economic planning and regional decentralization (Government Bill no. 125), the exact contents of which were not yet known. (This regional decentralization law was passed on July 15, 1970, before the economic expansion bill became law.) In addition, the intention was to build as much flexibility as possible into the Economic Expansion Law in order to provide a more permanent framework for the management of economic expansion and regional development. The list of qualifying development zones would obviously have to change during the life of the law.

Two more fundamental problems also justified this discretion, however. One was internal to Belgium. It mirrored the growing discussion about the overall allocation of resources among the Flemish and French regions. Brussels was virtually left out of this issue because it was considered fully developed and probably too economically powerful for the good of the other two regions. The seats of practically all major firms and major government offices are in fact located in the capital.

Three views competed here. The first stressed need, which when measured on the basis of such criteria as unemployment and industries in need of reconversion, tended to favor Wallonia in the distribution of benefits although the Flemish have questioned this conclusion. A second view stressed solidarity and equality; it grew out of the nascent federalism increasingly advanced to replace the country's unitary system. Its proponents would simply have divided benefits equally among the two regions, with intraregional distribution based on need. The third view was power based and stressed that Flanders should receive more than Wallonia simply because it had a larger population. Flanders had also to pursue its long-delayed industrial development, now well underway, irrespective of any narrowly defined need, if only because industrial power has been an important source of political power during Belgium's modern history, and would thus reinforce Flemish numerical strength.[10]

This was a sensitive issue and hard to resolve explicitly at this point, because it was linked to the continuing overall discussions on the future of Belgium's unitary regime. Questions were raised about whether the country would go federal and about the nature and extent of the powers to be granted to the new formal regions—Flanders, Wallonia, and Brussels—in the context of the regionalization underway. Would the new regions be largely "cultural," for example, or would they also obtain a fair amount of economic, including budgetary, autonomy?* Under such conditions it was thought better to leave any definition of what were to be the assisted cities and zones to governments (that is, the Councils of Ministers), since the latter are eminently suited—if not always willing—to resolve such problems of political "dosage" in the light of changing coalitions and pressures.

Even such a topic as the types of incentives available had subnational implications. For the Flemish were opposed to large employment premiums to the extent that they saw the need for more capital-intensive investments in Flanders.

EC Objections

The other reason for leaving the regions and criteria unspecified was the fact that the EC Commission had complained about the criteria used by Belgium to select assisted zones under the 1959 and 1966 laws—criteria alleged to be in violation of Article 92 of the Treaty of Rome.[11] These criteria had at times been blatantly political. This is particularly true under the 1966 law where certain cities had been added to satisfy politicians, with the result that forty-one out of forty-three of the nation's districts (*arrondissements*) were included in whole or in part.

The EC Commission considers that incentives frequently distort competition, and urges that their appropriateness be assessed in light of the situation in the regions to which they apply—the clearest cases being such extremes as southern Italy and West Germany's eastern border areas. Belgium, on the other hand, was relatively developed. Its smallness and compactness hardly warranted singling out miniareas. These could be tolerated only if they were very few in number, instead of incorporating, as they did after 1966-67, close to 40 percent of the country's surface and 42 percent of its population. Even then the 20 percent of the population finally

---

*This second issue, by the way, was linked to the content of 1971-75 plan since the regionalization of planning was under consideration; it must be remembered here that the 1970 Economic Expansion Law was to be strongly linked to achieving the plan's goals.

included in the 1970 law—and increased to 25 percent in 1973—would encompass a significant portion of the territory once the major and normally excluded industrialized centers were left out.

The Belgian government had officially communicated the bill to the EC Commission on November 25, 1969, before the bill was issued—in compliance with Article 93 (paragraph 3) of the Treaty of Rome. While not official consultation, subsequent contacts with the EC Commission revealed serious objections emanating from that quarter. Consequently, the government followed the way out suggested by the Belgian State Council—namely, to consider the proposed 1970 Economic Expansion Law as a general enabling act (loi-cadre, or "framework" law) to be checked with the EC authorities only when implementing decrees were enacted. Such a check could be postponed until the government had made up its mind about drawing up a list of eligible zones. Meanwhile, the areas currently assisted would continue to receive aid.

Another issue was the matter of government support through such measures as public orders and export assistance. These two practices met increasing objections from the EC Commission on the grounds that they distort competition, since they are used to favor "national" firms (in violation of the Treaty of Rome).[12] The EC Commission was bothered also by the law of July 17, 1959, which (as noted above) was to be retained with its general and sectoral (rather than regional) scope. The incentives it provides are fundamentally unacceptable to the EC because they are seen as distorting competition and lying outside the regional exceptions allowed by the Treaty of Rome.

The Belgian government, on the other hand, was anxious to keep the 1959 law to help troubled industries located outside assisted areas. More generally, officials wished to be able to intervene wherever they felt some sector or project needed assistance. The reconversion of Belgian industry—particularly its technological, structural, and managerial upgrading—was seen as a permanent and pervasive task in which any required state intervention or assistance should not be limited to a fraction of the territory. In particular, the Flemish wanted to be able to assist the development of areas near Antwerp (refining and petrochemicals) and Ghent (steel) while the Walloons were thinking of installing inland refineries near Liège among other projects. One technical problem is that some Belgian industrial areas have little or no population, so that assistance cannot be justified on the basis of the crucial criteria of unemployment and low standards of living.

Hence, the Belgian government thought it better not to incorporate the substance of the law of July 17, 1959 into the 1970 bill, as had been intended originally, but to retain that legislation on the ground that "a bird in the hand is better than two in the bush." Furthermore, the government thought, it would be harder for the EC Commission to have an existing law removed from the books than to oppose some of the features of pending legislation as the Commission must be consulted only about new regulations.*

In any case, Article 5 of the law allows aid to be granted for "sectoral or technological projects of particular interest." This clause is not operational, however, since a royal decree must still specify for a project the applicable criteria and implementing means—both of which the EC Commission would immediately oppose. Indeed in June 1970 the Commission initiated a procedure whereby the Belgian government was automatically refused permission to put the proposed aid systems into operation until such time as the Commission had taken a final decision on the proposal. Subsequently, in April 1972, the Belgian authorities agreed to submit large individual assistance cases to the Commission as well as to communicate to it the draft regulations needed for implementing forthcoming laws.

Ideologies and Interventionism

The economic expansion and regional development laws (1959 and 1966) and the 1970 bill were not rammed through by the Socialists, but received as well the support—at times lukewarm or grudging—of the Social Christian and Liberal parties in the Belgian coalition governments that have prevailed in the postwar period. The more interventionist flavor of the 1970 bill reveals, however, definite Socialist influences.

With the previous laws the Belgian government had been content to "bring water" (that is, incentives) to the "horses" of private industry, and to wait and see if they drank it. Meanwhile, various means were being devised to make them "thirsty" and to bring in nonprivate "horses" as alternative drinkers. Thus the government was no longer simply going to observe whether events conformed to the economic forecasts and limited planning engaged in since 1960—an essentially "reactive" approach. It would instead try to make things happen that way in an active, or rather "preactive," fashion.

The views of the Belgian Socialist party (PSB) can be readily recognized in the 1970 bill, whose main sponsor (as noted previously) was the then Socialist Minister of Economic Affairs, Leburton. A first draft was actually prepared by Leburton's main collaborators within his private cabinet, who were Socialists also.

Belgian Socialism is not terribly "leftist" in a country generally known for its economic and social conservatism, and the PSB has not pushed for large-

---

*In a decision of March 11, 1974, the EC Commission decided to open the procedure provided for in Article 93, paragraph 2, of the Rome Treaty in relation to the law of July 17, 1959; the Commission's opinion was that this law can only be applied within a sectoral or regional framework.

scale nationalization except in the electricity generating field and the declining coal mines, whose fate depends on government subsidies anyway. Energy is another matter now.* It is probably more accurate to view the Belgian Socialists as interventionist and technocratic in the French tradition; that is, they fundamentally believe things happen only if one makes them happen, instead of relying on laissez-faire and chance—particularly in Belgium where large domestic firms are viewed as timid entrepreneurs. The government must therefore take an active stance in terms of making an inventory of problems and opportunities, of mapping out priorities, of prodding private enterprise, and of developing alternative ways of achieving public goals when companies do not respond to the call. This is the essence of French indicative planning and technocratic interventionism. The link of the 1970 bill to Belgian planning was obvious throughout the bill in its references to the plan's sectoral, technological, and regional objectives.

The French preference for coherence and discretionary powers is shared by Belgian Socialists, since modern planning implies a system where things hang together and pull in the same direction. But this also requires flexible action in the light of special situations and changing circumstances, and the 1970 bill certainly stressed both. An excellent example of this preference for discretion may be found in Article 2, which specifies the types of enterprises that can benefit from the available incentives; the article's last paragraph adds that a royal decree can "extend these benefits to firms other than those mentioned here."

To the objectives typically raised by the Belgian State Council, as well as by various legislators and qualified observers, concerning the vagueness of many clauses in the bill and the broad discretion granted to the executive, the government's standard answers were: (1) that all vague provisions would be clarified through subsequent implementing decrees;[13] and (2) that all relevant parties would be consulted before decisions were made. These are two fairly empty promises, since there is no effective mechanism for forcing the Belgian government to adhere to them.

High-level Belgian bureaucrats appear to welcome the provision of more interventionist instruments. Some of them are Socialists and favor such instruments as a matter of principle. Others are keenly aware of how much pressure is put on these instruments by ministers when crises develop. At such times it is "nice" to have more power and alternative means to cope with problems. And, to return briefly to the previous discussion of political benefits, increased interventionism has suited the growing number of Belgian politicians eager to use economic development as a tool for reinforcing the

---

*The Socialist-led Leburton coalition government fell in January 1974 on the issue of a government-controlled mixed venture with the Iranian state petroleum trust; and the Socialists campaigned on the theme of "With the Socialists, fight the petroleum trusts."

political power of their own region since it promised to give them more control over where investments would go. It is well to remember here that previous economic expansion laws were sponsored by Liberal party (PLP) ministers concerned about the entrepreneurial shortcomings of Belgian firms.

Belgian Socialists have worked for many years to set up institutions and place their men in key positions, so that planning and interventionism may be used successfully without appearing to alter Belgium's political economy fundamentally or rapidly. Thus, increasingly a Socialist has served as Minister of Economic Affairs, a position traditionally staffed by Social-Christians and Liberals until after World War II. This has offered many opportunities to place Socialists at the head of key government departments and state-sponsored organizations.

Furthermore, the launching of the Belgian Planning Bureau (1959) and of the National Investment Society (1962), both of whose means of action have been slowly but definitely extended, has provided additional tools in the interventionist arsenal.[14] The Industrial Promotion Office (OPI) was created in the context of the law of July 15, 1970, providing for the organization of planning and economic decentralization. The OPI is authorized to investigate profitable production opportunities and industrial problems referred to it by the government; to study the feasibility of selected projects to be proposed to the private sector or to be realized by new companies that would be created by the SNI or a regional development society, either alone or in association with the private sector; and to facilitate the commercialization of patents, particularly those generated by public bodies or with the financial assistance of the state. Moreover, the regional development societies, according to the law of July 21, 1970, can put up buildings, borrow funds, and undertake industrial projects, such as those suggested by the OPI, with the technical and financial assistance of the SNI "whenever the private sector fails in this respect."

Opposition Views

There was some opposition to the 1970 bill even within the Socialist party. When an early version of the bill was accepted by the Belgian Council of Ministers in November 1969, the Walloon wing of the Socialist party objected to it for its failure to create a truly active and selective industrialization policy—something unacceptable to the EC Commission, of course. Instead, the Walloons anticipated correctly that the law would assist almost anybody anywhere, without much selectivity and on a "political" basis. In other words, Flanders would get at least half of the assistance, irrespective of its needs.

Subsequent conflicting studies of which zones needed assistance will be discussed below.*

The Social Christians partners in the governing coalition objected to the large area of discretion left to the government, and to the wide powers granted to the national authorities to meddle in the business of assisted firms—a position reflecting their occasional ambiguous support of free enterprise and their doubts about state intervention. Since the president of the Senatorial Commission on Economic Affairs was a Liberal, conservative forces were given a chance to tone down the bill's interventionism. Among other items the 20 percent population limitation emerged from this commission as a result of pressures from non-Socialist legislators.†

Business itself opposed the more interventionist aspects of the bill, mainly through its Federation of Belgian Enterprises (FEB, previously FIB), which is influential with the Social Christian and Liberal parties. For example, whereas a September 1969 version of the bill had provided that assistance be granted *exclusively* through contracts between the state and the recipient firm the 1970 bill and law only made such contracts *possible*.[15] In general, business opposed public entrepreneurship as well as subsidies that distort competition; but it was pleased with the intention of greater selectivity in lieu of previous indiscriminate sprinkling of state aids.

American Pressure

The take-over of local firms by foreign companies is not the most popular form of economic penetration by multinational firms either in Western Europe or elsewhere.[16] Jean-Jacques Servan-Schreiber crystallized this and other negative reactions in his 1967 book, *The American Challenge*— especially in the case of a take-over combined with local borrowing of the capital needed for the acquisition ("They buy us out with our own money!"). Hence the bill included Article 36 requiring prior authorization from the government in the case of major take-overs by non-EC firms. This included U.S.-controlled subsidiaries incorporated in an EC country and thus legally "EC firms."

---

*Walloon Socialists also objected to the fact that workers would not be involved in the application of the law; this ultimately led to a floor amendment which granted an assisted firm's Workers' Council the right to be informed of the conditions and use of the assistance—Article 37 of the bill and the royal decree of September 25, 1972.

†The 1959 and 1966 economic expansion laws were enacted under Social Christian and Liberal sponsorships; and these parties would have come up with new such laws around 1970 even without Socialist support.

This was already the second version of Article 36. An earlier draft had required all firms—even "true" EC ones—to obtain such an authorization for large acquisitions. The latter were subsequently excluded in the light of EC Commission objectives, since this regulation would have restricted the rights of establishment guaranteed to firms in member states. Nevertheless, this second version was attacked by the EC Commission and by the U.S. Embassy in Brussels.

In 1969 the Commission had fought the French screening of "inward" investors, including firms incorporated in other member states. This practice allegedly violated Articles 58 and 221 of the Treaty of Rome; and the Commission had argued before the EC Court of Justice that a host nation had no right to investigate the ownership or control of firms in terms of their nationality. The case was settled out of court in a way which saved faces by allowing the French to retain their screening on the basis of foreign-exchange controls rather than investment controls in return for letting in EC-controlled firms in a quasi-automatic way.* Nevertheless, the Commission did not like this kind of distinction among EC firms on the basis of their ultimate ownership or control. It expressed its objections to the system of authorization proposed in the Belgian legislation, even though "true" EC firms were going to be spared.

The U.S. Embassy in Brussels also made various representations against Article 36 of the bill for its negation of the "national treatment" guaranteed to American firms under the Treaty of Friendship, Establishment, and Navigation (1961) between Belgium and the United States. Such a practice could, the Embassy noted, spread to other countries and even become part of an EC industrial policy.

More generally, the Embassy was concerned about what this clause revealed about the future of the very favorable investment climate for U.S. firms in Belgium. There had been some unfavorable reactions among Belgian unionists against the take-over of the important but troubled ACEC electrical equipment company in Belgium by Westinghouse because of fears of layoffs by profit-conscious Americans. In addition, ITT's unsuccessful attempt to acquire General Biscuit had elicited vigorous protests and countermoves by the owners of that Belgian firm.

The Belgian government, prompted in part by pressures from some unionists and Socialist parliamentarians, wanted to be able to do something in the case of take-overs deemed undesirable in the light of public policy, even if acceptable to the sellers.† It also wished to avoid worsening the investment climate and further antagonizing the EC in such a fairly minor matter.

---

*A similar case developed in 1972-73 when the British Treasury relaxed its foreign-exchange control, to allow EC-controlled firms to borrow in the United Kingdom—thereby denying this privilege to U.S. subsidiaries located in EC countries. Protests by both the Commission and the U.S. embassy led to the removal of this distinction.

†It could already intervene in the case of public take-over bids, following a revision of Article 108 of the Commercial Code.

The combined pressures of the EC and the U.S. Embassy eventually succeeded. The final text of the law only required prior notification of the Belgian government in the case of take-overs by foreign-controlled firms— even those controlled by EC nationals. This compromise was acceptable to the U.S. Embassy; but further pressure by the EC, on the basis of the procedure provided for under Article 169 of the Treaty of Rome, led ultimately to the enactment of the law of August 17, 1973, which eliminated the discrimination against foreign firms. All those who acquire firms whatever their origin may be (even Belgians) now have to notify the Belgian government of sizable acquisitions.

APPLYING THE NEW LAW

The application of the 1970 law does not appear to have fundamentally differed from that of the 1966 legislation which it replaced, at least so far as all the brave "Socialist" ambitions and innovations are concerned. There have, however, been significant compensations to the latter's views elsewhere. On the other hand, both subnational (Flemish-Walloon rivalry) and supranational (EC) influences have significantly affected the implementation of the 1970 law.

Defining Assisted Areas

On January 6, 1971, a royal decree sustained the zones defined in 1967 for implementing the regional law of July 14, 1966. These zones were still being used in the summer of 1974 because of fundamental disagreements among Flemish and Walloon ministers and the political opinions they represent, notwithstanding constant pressures from the EC Commission to have the zones redrawn.

The EC Commission had strenuously objected to the inclusion of the Belgian population in the 1966-67 zones; and the law had ultimately provided that no more than 20 percent could be included. Two categories of zones (I and II) were established based on the seriousness of a zone's economic problems. Both the zones and their categorization were to be reviewed periodically, according to Article 11; this article further provides that zones are normally chosen "in the context of the plan and with the advice of the Regional Economic Councils created by the law of 15 July 1970." This was actually an unsuccessful attempt to depoliticize the law.

Belgian Studies

Three separate studies of the zoning issue have been made—by the

Planning Bureau, the Walloon Economic Council, and the Flemish Economic Council. The latter two are official consultative bodies in the context of Belgium's growing decentralization (according to the law of July 15, 1970). Their aim in each case was to help choose the new zones on the basis of the aforementioned four criteria posited by the 1970 Economic Expansion Law, that is, actual and foreseeable structural underemployment, the real or imminent decline of important economic activities, an abnormally low standard of living, and slow economic growth—and within the 20 percent population limit.

Reflecting the choice of different indices for the application of these four criteria the three studies came up with strikingly different, if predictable, results. In ranking Belgium's forty-three administrative districts out of which the zones would have to be carved the Walloons managed to introduce the first Flemish *arrondissement* in seventeenth position whereas the Flemish concluded that 70 percent of the zones should be in Flanders. The Planning Bureau used a very complex method to come up with a more balanced distribution which, however, slightly favored Wallonia (twelve out of the most deserving twenty districts).[17]

These differences are practically irreconcilable unless some feeling of national solidarity prevails over a more technical and subnational approach. Such an attitude is very unlikely, however, in view of the fact that "linguistic" parties gained ground at least until March 1974 over the "national" parties—Social Christian, Socialist, and Liberal—which themselves are now split into Flemish and Walloon units.

The overall distribution of the zones among the two linguistic-political regions of the country is already a moot question to the extent that the budgets voted for carrying out the 1959, 1966, and 1970 Economic Expansion Laws have progressively favored Flanders. These budgets reflect both need and power on the part of the latter region.*

Although actual expenditures do not tally faithfully with budgetary allocations a policy of dividing assistance credits on a 50-50 basis between Flanders and Wallonia prevailed until 1971 when Flanders began to be favored. Later the Leburton government (which resigned in January 1974) decided that the new division of economic expansion funds for 1974-75 would be on the basis of 52 percent for Flanders, 39 percent for Wallonia, and 9

---

*It is notable that three major sources of funds are involved here: the Fund for Economic Expansion and Regional Reconversion, which comes out of the ordinary budget, and finances (through various departments) the application of the 1959 and 1970 economic expansion laws; the 1972 National Solidarity Fund (BF10 billion over 4 years), which comes out of the extraordinary budget and is to assist the most depressed areas in Flanders and Wallonia (there have been only two interventions as of mid-1974); and "compensatory credits" (BF1 billion a year after 1972 and for 8 years) granted to Wallonia to compensate for the acceleration of the development of Zeebrugge harbor (in Flanders). About one-third of the economic-expansion budget is spent on "nonregionalized" projects, that is, on sectors such as textiles, steel, and shipbuilding.

TABLE 2.1

Belgian State Assistance

Region	1967-70		1971-72	
	BF millions	%	BF millions	%
Flanders				
Value of assisted investments	115,554	59	56,721	62
Cost to the state	8,421	46	4,370	51
Wallonia				
Value of assisted investments	77,627	40	32,790	36
Cost to the state	10,005	54	4,163	48
Brussels				
Value of assisted investments	2,364	1	1,510	2
Cost to the state	51	0	39	1

percent for Brussels. This is a rough reflection of the distribution of Belgium's population. (See Table 2.1).

Further EC Interventions

The Belgian government and the EC Commission's Competition Directorate kept in touch during 1971 in regard to the objectionable parts of the 1970 law; and in September-October of that year the government sent to the directorate a tentatively revised list of development zones along with their justification.

The Commission, however, remained dissatisfied with the extreme spread of these zones to forty-one out of forty-three districts—on the grounds that this negated the intended "regional" character of the 1970 legislation. In addition, no distinction was made in this proposal between Zones I and II in terms of intensity of assistance; and the Commission was not satisfied with the analysis which led to the selection of so many districts. On the other hand, the Commission was aware of the political and technical difficulties besetting the choice of new development zones.

Therefore, after further consultations with the Belgian government, on April 26, 1972, the Commission decided that some provisions of the 1970 law were incompatible with the Treaty of Rome. This decision restricted permissible assistance to twenty-eight districts, and added four with some eligibility. The assisted zones would have to be chosen from among this group and submitted to the Commission for approval without delay. Without prejudice, Belgium must communicate to the Commission a new list of suggested development zones on the basis of detailed studies. This would enable the Commission to issue a further decision on these areas within a period of two years. The delay could be used by the Belgian authorities to work out, in collaboration with the Commission's staff, the technical problems of the criteria and the methods to be used in the designation of the zones.[18]

The list of zones subsequently decided upon by the EC definitely favored Wallonia as it included eighteen districts there versus ten in Flanders. The Commission also requested that the distinction between Zones I and II be reestablished and that, subject to EC approval, differentiated maximum aids be provided to reflect the acuity of the problems found among the zones. (After January 1972 EC countries were supposed to limit their assistance to 20 percent of the value of the proposed investment in "central" [developed] areas; and aids must be "transparent" [readily measurable] and truly regional in nature [not nationwide, and varying according to local need].)

While the Belgian government agreed to comply with this EC decision it could not come up with a revised list. The dissolution of parliament in January 1974, and the elections that followed on March 11, 1974, provided the government with a new respite, since a postponement of the April 26, 1974 deadline for drawing up new zones was easily obtained.

In any case the law of August 17, 1973 extended the share of the Belgian population in development zones from 20 to 25 percent, so that more districts can be "rescued." The EC Commission approved this extension as a way of assisting the Belgian government with its problems. The 25 percent limit is of course far less than the previous 42 percent. Moreover, EC pressures remain very strong in the matter of drawing up and differentiating among the zones within the 25 percent population limit. Therefore a suit before the EC Court of Justice over the location of assisted zones (which would elevate a technical issue to the political arena) is not out of the question.[19]

Regarding the sectoral aid permitted by Article 5 of the 1970 law, the Commission asked that an application of this article be submitted to it in advance. It pointed out that a distinction must be made between assisting an entire sector and helping certain firms within a sector, with the latter particularly frowned upon because of its obvious "rescuing" character.*

---

*For example, if an entire sector is to be helped the government must provide information about the sector's characteristics, its specific problems, the assistance program's objectives, and the types of aids and their modes of application; if only a few firms are to be helped each assistance case must be justified to the Commission when it exceeds BF100 million ($2 million) or 15 percent of the value of the investment (whatever its value).

In this context it is well to observe that, while unhappy with the Leburaton law, the EC Commission has nevertheless used the law to make some points about the desirable content of regional assistance policies in member countries and about the powers granted to it by the Treaty of Rome in this area. Here, however, Belgium has complained about being singled out when other EC countries were apparently committing as many or more infractions in the matter of incentives. Moreover, Belgium expects very little from the EC Regional Development Fund, which was supposed to start on January 1, 1974, since Belgium will not be a contributor to it. Still, the timing was right from the EC's point of view; and Belgium was a weaker country to challenge than France, for example.

Interventionism

According to a number of politicians, and civil servants interviewed by this writer, no notable use has been made of the new instruments provided by the 1970 Economic Expansion Law The examination of applications for assistance, it is noted, has not been significantly altered, although environmental impact has been considered in some cases. In addition, follow-up of the fulfillment of an investor's obligations has not markedly changed apart from improvement in matching state assistance to the degree of completion of a project.

Selectivity has been no better, since competition has remained acute among Belgian regions and provinces (and among European countries). The tendency for each Belgian secretary (subminister) for regional economy* and for the Interministerial Committee for Economic and Social Coordination, which ultimately decides about the assistance granted to investments over BF100 million, has been to let one region match what the other one offers and to allow the investor to choose if he has more than one region in mind. As one respondent put it: "We do not want to assist firms that are going to invest anyway. Yet we give assistance to everybody, on grounds of 'equity.' Really, what we need is 'judicious inequity.' Besides, we still do little to send the investor where we think he should go. Instead, he chooses among the sites we show him. Hence we end up in fact subsidizing what he will pay in the form of higher salaries due to inflation. Why do we do it that way? Because of international competition about incentives." For that matter the distinction between zone categories I and II has not been operative although the EC Commission keeps insisting on more discrimination among the revised zones to be assisted.

---

*There is one Sécrétaire d'Etat à l'Economie Régionale for Flanders, and one for Wallonia, plus one Minister for Brussels Affairs, but the capital has not been assited much under this legislation.

It is noted further that no contract has been signed between the government and a beneficiary firm, although contractual agreements were hailed as a major innovation in the process of improving the country's technological development, managerial ability, and reconversion. Progress contracts were signed, however, with the Siemens and Philips firms. The contracts stipulated that these firms were to set up or expand computer facilities in Belgium in return for each company's obtaining up to 25 percent of government orders for computers during a five-year period.* But these contracts were signed in the fall of 1970, before the Economic Expansion Law was enacted, through reliance on the legislation bearing on public purchases. There were also four comparable contracts relating to transportation equipment. It is possible that such progress contracts will become more common once the plan develops more refined goals. These could cover major firms as well, possibly in the context of the 1976-80 plan.

Also as a result of the law more is now being done to assist service types of investment such as those related to tourism. And Article 32 of the law has introduced opposition to real estate speculation to the extent that the government must pay only the indexed price at which land was sold to a former investor when buying it back from him.

CONCLUSIONS

This analysis has revealed the inadequacy of considering industrial policy only in a national context, or as a purely technocratic exercise of matching means to ends. There are, of course, a number of factors that reveal the strong "Belgian" character of the 1970 legislation. The country's small size and relatively large degree of industrial homogeneity make it more difficult to differentiate among regions and zones without engaging in what appears to outsiders as an inordinate amount of "fine tuning." In addition, Belgium's particularly virulent linguistic quarrels give this case a subnational dimension not usually found elsewhere.[20] Belgium appears also to be one of the few countries to take its Treaty of Friendship, Establishment, and Navigation with the United States rather seriously, thus providing considerable room for foreign influences. This is true, too, when choosing France as the model for many governmental interventions in the economy.

---

*It appears that the Belgian government has refused to communicate details of the Siemens and Philips agreements to the EC Commission, which would oppose them if they amounted to a quota system for government purchases rather than being part of a regional incentive scheme. The U.S. embassy has also pointed out to the Belgian government that such arrangements restrict the access of U.S. firms to public-sector purchases.

Hence, whether the present case study provides only a unique illustration of these propositions about the nature and content of industrial policy can only be demonstrated or refuted in the light of analysis of other countries.

Can Industrial Policy Remain
National in Scope?

The answer to this question appears to be that industrial policy is now significantly constrained by subnational, supranational, and foreign factors. These constraints will remain in the foreseeable future although greater isolationism, protectionism, and autarky cannot be completely ruled out. This study, however, has not addressed itself to such an eventuality.

There are limits to the constraints because the influence process is typically a volatile affair. Even when the constraints are backed by legal commitments, such as treaties, the outcome is not necessarily clear-cut. This is well illustrated by Donald Puchala's preliminary conclusions about the processes of compliance and enforcement within the EC. His study applies quite well in the case of the Belgian Economic Expansion Law, which he cites briefly.[21]

The EC Commission fundamentally depends on government compliance with its directives and other decisions, because it lacks strong enforcement authority. Noncompliance on the part of member governments usually results more from national dilemmas than from malevolence or lack of interest in European integration: they cannot rather than will not. Here a strong national government is often of more help to the EC than a weak one because an "immobilized" government immobilizes the EC as well. Moreover, the EC Commission is often reluctant to push infracting governments into line when success is unlikely. This reluctance stems from its fear of intranational difficulties and of wasting precious "political capital" unnecessarily. In the Belgian case, according to Puchala, "The Commission authorities proved attentive to linguistic politics in Belgium, were warned against provoking a crisis in that country, and rather systematically overlooked infractions for a number of years, and then pressed ever so softly when they finally began enforcement procedures."[22]

Other EC member governments seldom press for action, because they share the same problems or commit the same or similar infractions. There seem to have been some French pressures on the EC in the Belgian case, however, since France resents the openness of Belgium to foreign investors, who are also attracted by the incentives. National governments typically bide for time, extensions, and respites until domestic dilemmas or pressures can be reduced, sorted out, or reconciled; and they seldom approach the Commission for clarifications or exemptions, but wait instead for it to complain either formally or informally. Then they take their own time in answering EC questions and requests for corrective action. Nevertheless the Treaty of Rome and the EC Commission could not be ignored by Belgium, and at the very least provided constraints or had a certain "nuisance value" as far as the Belgian government was concerned. The same may be said about the aforementioned bilateral treaty between Belgium and the United States. But subnational influences based on real political strength are more foreseeable and stable; it seems reasonable to predict that they will increase in importance and result in greater co-decision-making in industrial policy between national governments and these lower levels, such as those in the three emerging Belgian regions.

On the other hand, it is hard to imagine that the nation-state will not remain the major locus for the initiation, formulation, and implementation of industrial policies, even though there are significant attempts to shift part of this to the EC Commission, at least as far as particular industries are concerned. One can even detect attempts to map out some new "international division of labor" between developed and developing nations, as, for example, the efforts by the U.N. Conference on Trade and Development (UNCTAD) to gain preferential access to industrial markets, and among nations at similar levels of development through such complementary agreements as those among the Andean Pact countries.[23] But these broader issues related to the shape of the new international economic order cannot be analyzed here.

Was It a Socialist Law?

Compared to the above question the hypothesis that the 1970 Belgian Economic Expansion Law is "Socialist" is more ambiguously supported by the facts. For one thing the term "Socialist" has not been carefully defined. There is, of course, no such simple definition. As a result, any number of interpretations corroborating, qualifying, or negating this hypothesis can be provided. However, to the extent that "Socialism" is equated with what one respondent in this study calls "directed and discretionary interventionism by government in economic life in reaction to the randomness of private-enterprise action," a great deal of this may be detected in the new objectives and instruments introduced by the law. But then the 1970 law could have been labeled "technocratic" or "French" rather than "Socialist."

The application of this law has not been particularly "Socialist" in its results. These are very similar to those achieved by previous economic expansion and regional development laws applied since 1959 by ministers of various political stripes.

The Limits of Old-Fashioned Interventionism

An explanation of this failure to translate Socialist goals into action is superficially easy. There have been the obvious obstacles: the pervasive and intensive quarrels between the Flemish and Walloons; EC interventions against some of the law's key features; the recession of 1971, which slowed down investment; international competition; and the relatively short time since the law's enactment in December 1970. In addition, there have been two elections and several new Belgian Ministers of Economic Affairs. However, these were Socialists until March 1974.

The key problem has remained one of creating jobs. Socialist ministers have had to pay more attention to this immediate goal—as did their predecessors—than to achieving the more elusive and time-consuming objectives of upgrading technology and restructuring Belgian industry, processes that are going on with some success anyway.

The Belgian proclivity for compromise and *middelmaatism* (a preference for center-of-the-spectrum measures) may also be cited as well as the fact that much government intervention in the Belgian economy is of an ad hoc nature, such as rescuing a faltering firm. Thus the Val St. Lambert Crystal Works—a small but prestigious company eyed by Corning Glass—was made into a state enterprise in order to save jobs and to prevent the foreign take-over of a major symbol of Belgian craftsmanship. In such cases Belgian "Socialists" are simply "Belgians" in many ways; or as one respondent put it, "It is a Socialism of protesters who build, of opponents who administer."

Finally, some observers have pointed to a more personal factor, namely that Leburton, both as Minister of Economic Affairs and as Prime Minister later on, was not strong enough to impart much drive and direction to the implementation of this law.* There may, however, be more fundamental reasons linked to the evolving nature of modern government intervention and of Belgian Socialist elites.

The Emerging Interventionism

A great variety of instruments are available to the Belgian government. For example, it never relinquished most of the extraordinary powers

---

*The most common comparison is usually with the late Economic Minister Spinoy (also a Socialist), but one can also think of such strong ministers as Messrs. Simonet (Economics) and Vlerick (Finance).

progressively granted to the state after World War I. These were stimulated by reconstruction and inflationary problems in the late 1920s, by inflation again at various periods, and by other crises such as Korea and Suez. The lack of strong budgetary controls in a parliamentary democracy such as Belgium also gives the government some latitude in using its budgets. Hence it is usually possible to do something if there is a real desire to intervene in the economy unless the executive branch itself is divided on the issue, as in the designation of assisted zones.

In this context the 1970 Economic Expansion Law figures only as one instrument among many. It is an important one, to be sure, but it is hemmed in by various restrictions, including those imposed by the EC Commission, and plagued by political-linguistic problems for which there has been no "Socialist" answer. It is better then to use some other instrument if one really wants to intervene; thus the law on government purchases was invoked when Siemens and Philips were assisted in the fall of 1970.

The Socialist apparatus now includes some extremely capable and ambitious men who are eager to become public industrial leaders a la Enrico Mattei of ENI fame. But Belgium lacks the French capability of moving such public servants (*grands commis de l'état*) into top managerial positions in state enterprises or private firms (see Chapter 1). One reason is that there are very few major public enterprises bearing on Belgian industry except in the financial area, which includes the National Industrial Credit Society and the National Investment Society. Furthermore, Belgian Socialist elitists are unlikely to be invited to join large private corporations as directors or managers, since such positions are traditionally reserved for men of a more politically conservative hue.*

Consequently, the interest of key Socialist ministers and civil servants appears to be moving in the direction of creating real state enterprises or even holdings. Men of action anxious to intervene in the Belgian economy find the use of incentives to bend private enterprise to public purposes a cumbersome, slow, and at times frustrating process. They apparently feel it is better to have state enterprises directly responsive to state commands, in the face of the growing number of similar arrangements in France, Italy, and Britain.

---

*Someone like A. Vlerick, former Secretary of State for the Flemish economy, is a Social Christian and has strong links to commercial and investment banking to which he can return when out of the government. This is largely out of the question for such elite Socialists as H. Simonet (former Minister of Economic Affairs, and now EC Commissioner) and A. Baeyens (secretary general of the Ministry of Economic Affairs) who do not have similar options but must largely make their "industrial career" through politics—unless they choose to leave politics altogether, as was done by P.-H. Spaak, who later became associated with ITT in Europe. H. Neuman, president of the National Investment Society (SNI)—the mixed-ownership holding and management company—is a Socialist, however. So is R. Evalenko, who heads the Coal-Industry Reorganization Corporation; but these are largely appointive positions over which the government has control.

Moreover, some industrial sectors seem to be increasingly "natural" loci for state enterprises. This helps explain the interest of the Socialists within the Leburton coalition government in setting up a state refining company (IBRAMCO). This ultimately brought down that government in January 1974 because of various quarrels about its needs, financing, management, and anticipated contributions to the Belgian economy.[24] But this will certainly not be the last Socialist attempt to create "commanding heights" and levers through which needed changes can be made more directly and promptly.

In sum, then, the Leburton law has not proved significantly "Socialist" in its application. This is due in part to pragmatic difficulties in its implementation and in part to the fact that it has come to be seen as an already too traditional and cumbersome way of achieving public purposes in the Belgian economy. Hence the Socialists have turned to even more "Socialist" (interventionist) instruments for achieving their objectives.

The Dilemmas of Industrial Policy

Besides revealing the inadequacy of considering industrial policy in purely national or technocratic terms this analysis provides some insight into the contents, rationale, and processes of industrial policy.

First, industrial policy remains too amorphous, complex, and fluid a field for any government to claim that it now can master economic evolution. Instead there are only partial industrial policies, often of an ad hoc and opportunistic character.

Second, any incentives scheme, such as the one embodied in the 1970 Belgian Economic Expansion Law, can only be one among many instruments, including public enterprise, toward which Belgium seems to be moving—long after similar moves by other European governments.

Third, much of industrial policy is of a symbolic nature in that it is designed, at least in part, to prove to the electorate that government has "vision" and is ready and able to act on economic problems. The real effectiveness of plans and instruments and the ability of public administrations and structures to deliver results, as well as the real determination of politicians to make difficult decisions, often fall short of promises, though the promises have real political value nonetheless.

Fourth, and along the same line, much of what passes for an industrial policy is in fact of a social nature, since it amounts to various attempts to save or create jobs in order to alleviate or avoid serious dislocations and their political repercussions. The politics of industrial policy are thus fairly obvious because the creation or maintenance of jobs affects elections and because economic power continues to underlie the preservation and increase of political power.

Fifth, the distinction between "industrial" and "regional" policy is often blurred—as is evident in the dual "general" and "regional" character of the 1970 Belgian law. Smart politicians have come to realize that the continuing development of a region (district or zone) necessitates a corresponding restructuring of its economy through new industrial, commercial, financial, and managerial technologies. This requires helping areas that do not qualify as underdeveloped under certain criteria or that are declining and could well become so, either absolutely or relatively, if new industries are not brought in and if healthy "champion firms" are not further assisted.

"Regional" policy thus quickly assumes a "sectoral" dimension. And industrial policy itself soon focuses on particular industries and even on individual firms, instead of stressing the improvement of factor markets for labor, capital, technology, and entrepreneurship—the more classical approach to remedying structural problems in a country.[25] This double shift, however, clashes with the EC Commission's determination to oppose if not eliminate the distortions created by such "sectoral" policies when they are not conducted on an EC-wide (or at least plurinational) basis or under Community aegis.

Finally, one can observe how certain concerns materialize and then fade away. The 1970 Belgian law can be labeled as "preenvironmental" and "pre-Club of Rome," since it hardly reflects later concerns about the limits to growth. Yet even now it is doubtful whether in any new law of this sort the emphasis on expansion would be reduced; there will probably be more emphasis, however, on environmental protection in terms of screening applications and of state help to finance necessary investments. It is likely that land-use planning regulations will be used increasingly to bend industry to government plans since the state can readily use that instrument either to oppose industrial plans or to trade a building permit for some desirable contribution to public goals.

NOTES

1. See *Industrial Policy in the Community: Memorandum from the Commission to the Council* (Brussels: Commission of the European Communities, 1970); and J. J. Boddewyn, "EEC Policies Toward U.S. Investors," *Moorgate and Wall Street* (Britain), Autumn 1973, pp. 44-63.

2. For a good analysis of Belgian holdings see David Granick, *The European Executive* (New York: Doubleday, 1962). See also "L'Entreprise publique en Belgique," *Courrier Hebdomadaire du CRISP*, no. 630 (January 25, 1974) for an analysis of the growing public sector in Belgium.

3. For a good general analysis of Belgium see F. E. Huggett, *Modern Belgium* (New York: Praeger, 1969). Technically there are two "Flander"

provinces—East and West—bordering on the sea, with two more Flemish provinces inland (Antwerpen and Limburg); but the term "Flanders" is often used loosely to refer to the entire Flemish-speaking part of Belgium, including the Flemish part of the Province of Brabant where the bilingual capital, Brussels, is located. Similarly, "Wallonia" is not correctly applied to all French-speaking Belgians (*Francophones*), since the French-speaking inhabitants of Brussels do not consider themselves to be "Walloons," but it is often used that way.

4. Data in this section are largely drawn from G. R. Thoman, *Foreign Investment and Regional Development: The Theory and Practice of Investment Incentives, with a Case Study of Belgium* (New York: Praeger, 1973). In fact there were also the earlier laws of August 7, 1953 and July 10, 1957, aimed at industrial modernization. Additional data about the short-comings of the 1966 law can be found in three Belgian House bills—nos. 421 (May 23, 1967), 481 (November 22, 1967), and 502 (December 12, 1967).

5. Thoman, op. cit., p. 64. The 1970 government bill cites the creation of some 238,000 new jobs during the 1959-69 period.

6. This section rests on an analysis of Belgian government (Senate) bill no. 354, April 1970, and the official rationale (*exposé des motifs*) in its preamble; the bill was not enacted until December 30, 1970, and there were earlier drafts of the bill.

7. See J. J. Boddewyn, *Belgian Public Policy Toward Retailing Since 1789* (East Lansing, Mich.: Michigan State University, Graduate School of Business Administration, Bureau of Business Research, 1971), pp. 147-50 and *passim*.

8. An analysis of the Belgian laws and of comparable legislations in other EC countries can be found in Ph. de Castelbajac, "Les aides à l'expansion industrielle régionale dans les pays du Marché Commun," *Notes et Etudes Documentaires*, no. 3917 (Paris: La Documentation Française, September 11, 1972).

9. See J. J. Boddewyn, "Western European Public Policies Toward U.S. Investors," *Bulletin* (New York: New York University, Graduate School of Business Administration, Institute of Finance), no. 93-95 (March 1974).

10. *IRES, Service Mensuel de Conjoncture*, June 1973, and *Le Soir*, September 1, 1973. It appears that during the period from 1950 to 1972 defensive (or rationalization") investments have predominated in Wallonia, while they have been of the "expansion" and "new-sector" types in Flanders. The Walloons tend to stress the jobs lost because of industrial decline while the Flemish emphasize the need for new jobs in the face of a larger youth group which will soon reach the labor market.

11. For a discussion of this issue see Pierre Mathijsen, "State Aids, State Monopolies, and Public Enterprises in the Common Market," *Law and Contemporary Issues* (Spring 1972), pp. 376-91; and European Communities, *First Report on Competition Policy* (Brussels, April 1972), pt. 2, particularly pp. 127-129.

12. For a discussion of this topic see OECD, *Issues of Regional Policies* (Paris, 1973), pp. 154-159 and 235-245.

13. See particularly the State Council's objections—the bill, pp. 58-59, 63-64—for example to Article 36 on the proposed regulation of take-overs by foreign firms. The government answered in the bill's commentaries that ensuing regulations would clarify these matters once the broad principles had been agreed upon by the legislators (p. 27). The State Council was quite bothered by such discretion, wondering how the basic principle of "All Belgians are equal before the law" would fare in the face of so much vagueness about assistance goals, criteria, and instruments; and it was worried about the proposed legislation's possible conflict with other institutions whose autonomy was threatened (pp. 58-61).

14. For a recent analysis see Pierre Stiévenart, "De la SNI à la SBI," *Enterprise* (Belgian ed.), no. 855 (January 28, 1972). The SNI's capital was recently increased by BF2 billion to the new BF5 billion limit provided by the 1970 law. Technically the SNI is not a state enterprise but a mixed-ownership corporation endowed with a public purpose.

15. For a more recent statement of this position see *Mémorandum de la Fédération des Entreprises de Belgique au gouvernement* (Brussels, March 1974). It must be added that small business was given forms of assistance (Article 14) that better reflected their needs and means (for example their labor-intensiveness).

16. J. J. Boddewyn, "Western European Policies toward U.S. Investors," *Bulletin* (New York: New York University, Graduate School of Business Administration, Institute of Finance), no. 93-95 (March 1974), pp. 46-48.

17. For details see Christian Tacquenier, "Le point sur l'application de la loi d'expansion," *Enterprise* (Belgian ed.), no. 855 (January 28, 1972); and three articles in *La Libre Belgique* (June 16-18, 1971), "Remous autour de la loi d'expansion économique."

18. EC Commission, "Décision de la Commission du 26 avril 1972 concernant les aides accordées au titre de la loi belge du 30 décembre 1970 sur l'expansion economique" (Brussels, COM/72/435). In application of this ruling, the Commission vetoed in September 1973 Belgian aid to refining investment in the Antwerp region by Shell and Esso—France being the main objector to this proposed assistance to a well-developed area, which was expected to result in overcapacity and downward pressure on oil prices and company profits in the EC.

19. For a discussion of this distinction see Helen Wallace, *National Governments and the European Communities* (London: Political and Economic Planning, European series no. 21, April 1973), pp. 13-15.

20. Werner J. Feld, "Subnational Regionalism and the European Community: Ambitions and Fears of Subnational Legislators and Officials" (Paper presented at the March 1974 meeting of the International Studies Association in St. Louis).

21. Donald Puchala, "A Report to the Ford Foundation Concerning Research Supported by a Ford Faculty Fellowship for the Academic Year 1972-73," mimeographed (New York, 1973).

22. Ibid.

23. J. N. Behrman, *Decision Criteria for Foreign Direct Investment in Latin America* (New York: Council of the Americas, 1974), pp. 25ff.

24. See *International Herald Tribune*, January 21, 1974. It should be added that the IBRAMCO affair as well as the general election campaign of March 1974 have revealed that all major Belgian parties are now in support of state enterprises, albeit with varying degrees of enthusiasm and reservations.

25. For a summary of this see "European Regional Participation," *Kredietbank Weekly Bulletin*, June 28, 1974, pp. 229-234.

LABOR, TRADE UNIONS, AND EMPLOYER ASSOCIATIONS

3

PROBLEMS OF
EMPLOYMENT POLICY
IN THE EC COUNTRIES
Roland Tavitian

During the 1960s the original members of the European Community seemed to be on the way toward solving their employment problems. Although the existence of some regional unemployment problems was recognized especially in the south of Italy it was generally felt that the successful rates of growth which had been achieved would tend progressively to absorb such pockets. Consequently, the emphasis in policy formulation was placed on shortages rather than on surpluses of labor and this was reflected in the first EC program for medium-term economic policy (1966), which emphasized potential sources of additional labor such as immigrants and women.

This optimistic mood began to recede about 1968-69 when it appeared that the maintenance of high rates of growth no longer resulted in the reduction of unemployment rates. In fact the latter even increased in France and Italy. Moreover, the enlargement of the Community to include Britain and Ireland introduced two countries where structural unemployment was a permanent feature. Finally, the oil crisis, with its expected consequences on price structures, trade patterns, and growth prospects, has brought another major source of concern for employment trends.

The ability to solve employment problems by the spontaneous dynamics of growth is thus being seriously questioned; and, consequently regional, industrial, or employment policies have been increasingly discussed—both at national and EC levels—as tools for substantial improvements in the pattern of employment. With all their shortcomings these measures show that in addition to growth other policies and adjustments will be necessary to cope with the employment problems raised.

This study attempts to assess the employment trends as well as present policies of the countries of the European Community—at a time when changes now appearing on the horizon raise particular concern in the field of employment.

EMPLOYMENT IN WESTERN EUROPE: PERFORMANCE AND ASPIRATIONS

The total labor force in the EC, which has now reached about 103 million, has shown a rather slow yearly increase. Only France and the Netherlands have registered regular increases of around 1 percent per year, while Britain, Germany, and Italy have recorded a slight decrease in the size of their labor forces. The level of civilian employment in the EC has remained around 101 million, with a country pattern similar to that of the labor force.

The structure of civilian employment has undergone substantial changes. The share of agricultural labor decreased—for the Six—from 16.3 percent in 1965 to 11.5 percent in 1972 (13.2 percent to 9.6 percent for the Nine). Manufacturing, which represented 44.0 percent of the labor force in 1965 for the Six (44.7 percent for the Nine), reached 44.5 percent in 1972 (43.7 percent for the Nine). The share of the services sector increased from 39.8 percent in 1965 (42.1 percent for the Nine) to 44.0 percent in 1972 (46.7 percent).

The rate of unemployment for the six original member states as a whole was brought down from 3.4 percent in 1958 to about 1.8 percent in 1965-66. Since then it has been picking up tendentially and in 1972 it was again at 2.2 percent. The situation is different for the new members. Unemployment increased in Britain from about 1.2 percent in the early 1960s to about 3 percent in 1971-72 while Irish unemployment rose to the 5-6 percent mark during the same period. Patterns do in fact differ from country to country. Any attempt to categorize them can be criticized for oversimplification. Yet the following data may perhaps best account for the existing diversity.

Five of the EC countries have recorded a substantial flow of immigration. Among them Germany and Luxembourg have practically achieved full employment—both with a slight decline in total population and in labor force. Britain, Belgium, and France have recurrent employment problems of unequal intensity: Britain and Belgium have labor forces which are stable or declining slightly in size, while France, which has by far the lowest population density in the Community, has a labor force which has been increasing. Italy and Ireland are countries where emigration has traditionally played a significant role in the employment equilibrium. Both countries have a declining labor force and high rates of unemployment (Italy, 3 percent and Ireland, 6 percent, on the average). The Netherlands and Denmark are the only countries where cross-border flows of labor play a marginal role.

In spite of this diversity some broad features common to most EC member states can be perceived. The most striking one is the development of immigrant labor. In 1972 foreign labor accounted for 7.8 percent of the total population of wage-earners, with Luxembourg (34 percent), France (10.8 percent), and Germany (10.6 percent) having the highest percentages. In contrast, in 1960 the corresponding figure for the original Community was only 2.8 percent—with France and Belgium showing around 7 percent. All member states that have received immigrant workers participated in this increase. The Netherlands moved from a position of net emigration to one of net immigration. Even Italy—the only remaining country whose workers have emigrated to other parts of the Community—recorded a nominal increase in immigration. The bulk of this immigration has come from non-EC countries—mostly Mediterranean and African. Foreign labor originating from non-Community states increased from 620,000 in 1959 to 3,400,000 in 1972. On the other hand, foreign labor originating from partner states, principally Italy, increased more slowly. Between 1955 and 1972 it only grew by 50 percent from 560,000 to 1,100,000, in spite of the achievement of free circulation of labor, for which a 1968 Community directive established far-reaching rights.

Geographical mobility within countries is more difficult to assess. In some countries such as Italy and France there has been a steady flow from rural and peripheral areas to more central and industrial ones. An EC Commission study limited to the original Six shows that the share of the labor force of the periphera areas such as the eastern border of Germany, the Mezzogiorno, and the south and west of France decreased from 22 percent in 1960 to 20 percent in 1970. The share of the central areas, running roughly between Rotterdam, the Ruhr district, and Paris, increased from 17 percent to 19 percent. These trends existed in the 1950s before the Rome Treaty (1957) was signed and were slightly reduced in the 1960s. The combination of strong reliance on external immigration, substantial intranational mobility, and very limited intra-Community mobility thus creates a very specific problem.

Few statistics are available on sectoral and vocational mobility. Though it is generally admitted that such mobility has substantially increased since the end of the Second World War, especially from the agricultural, mining, and textile sectors, mobility often meets with considerable reluctance in view of the readaptation it requires from individual workers.

In fact, the comparatively satisfactory levels of employment reached in the 1960s by most Western European countries have given rise to some new aspirations such as job security. This is illustrated by various measures designed either to reduce the risk of worker dismissal or to finance the cost of it through public or company funds for readjustment. More recent demands include job enrichment, the improvement of the conditions of work, and better promotion prospects for all workers. However, since the end of the 1960s the development of these aspirations for better employment has coexisted with the primary concern of job creation. Immediately before the fuel crisis the situation in the Community could have been depicted as a contrast between the countries which had reached full employment or thereabouts and were aiming at better employment and those which were still trying to achieve full employment. After the shock of the fuel crisis and its threats to growth and the balance of payments the picture has become less clear. The old concern has extended to more countries and both concerns coexist within individual ones.

EMPLOYMENT POLICY: A POLICY-MIX?

Policies in the field of employment cannot be isolated from the whole economic process. They depend, first, on the overall capacity of an economy to deliver the goods required by internal demand and by the world market. Thus they rely primarily on demand management and on international trade and monetary policies. They also depend on legislation and on collective bargaining aimed at improving job security and conditions of work. These may be analyzed as constraints and costs imposed on the economy to improve the total welfare. Finally, the considerable complexity of the labor market— its geographical and vocational fragmentation—calls for specific policies to improve the flow of information on available jobs, to provide for the training of workers, and to compensate for natural and historical handicaps of a regional or sectoral character.

While there is a broad consensus in Western Europe on the need to combine all three approaches, attitudes vary as to their relative weight. There has been a long-standing debate on the ability of spontaneous forces of expansion—as they result from trade liberalization and from aggregate demand management policies—to solve the problems of structural unemployment. Should "structural policies" be of a marginal or supporting character, or should they be developed significantly in order to come to the forefront of economic policy? (This debate is, of course, closely linked to the market versus plan debate.)

Full Employment Through Overall Expansion

The progress achieved in the postwar period by the Western European economies in the field of employment has relied basically on demand management and trade liberalization.

The relationship between employment and growth is an obvious one. The level of employment is related to the level of output, and the latter is in turn controlled by the level of aggregate demand. It is, therefore, easy to conclude that a steady expansion of demand is the simplest way to improve or expand employment.

Such commonsense reasoning meets, however, with two closely interrelated problems. First, demand expansion may be damaging to other policy targets such as price stability or external equilibrium. Second, the types of goods and services for which demand will be stimulated are not necessarily those for which capacities are available at short notice.

Trade liberalization and currency convertibility provide some of the most powerful checks to avoid excessive expansion of demand. They force operators and policy-makers to take account of price and payments targets and to improve the chances of adjustment between output and demand. Also under certain conditions they increase the export of expansionary forces to other countries. Clearly, however, trade liberalization and currency convertibility are also perceived as threats to national employment. The positive effects resulting from increased exports and from the competitive pressure to put internal resources to better use may be overcompensated by the negative effects of increased imports on employment. This is particularly relevant in those cases where the negative effects are strongly concentrated in a few sectors.*

The achievements of this policy were substantial in the original six countries of the EC—particularly up to the mid-1960s. Germany and Belgium gradually reduced their unemployment. France and Italy—whose industries and unions were particularly concerned around 1958 about the competitive effects of the Common Market—recorded substantial modernization and industrialization with very few of the shutdowns that were feared. In fact the Italian rate of unemployment decreased until 1964. The reconciliation of these two traditionally protectionistic countries with trade liberalization is perhaps not the least important of the EC's achievements. The trade pattern that developed within the Community seldom led to specialization at industry level. In very few cases, as in the refrigerator industry in Italy, did firms displace the entire range of products of their competitors. Intraindustry specialization prevailed over interindustry specialization.

However, the overall performance in EC countries in terms of employment seems to have deteriorated somewhat since the mid-1960s. No further progress has been registered in the reduction of unemployment rates. The French rate has even increased from 1.5 percent to some 2 percent. In fact, policies relying basically on demand management and trade liberalization have achieved a significant success, but this calls for three important qualifications:

---

*Ever since the nineteenth century maintaining employment has been the major argument for protectionistic policies.

1. The performance has been very unequal. The successes achieved by Germany and Belgium are challenged by the shortcomings in Italy and Britain.

2. The achievements of demand management policy are certainly not unconnected to the development of inflation both in Europe and in the rest of the world. Differences in the propensity to inflate are closely related in Western Europe with the level and severity of unemployment problems. On the other hand, the U.S. payments deficit in the 1960s—generally admitted as a major cause of the breakdown of the international monetary system and the ensuing inflation—bears a close relationship to internal expansion and employment targets of this country.

3. The demand for labor generated by demand expansion has not always been of a kind suitable to the manpower resources available domestically. To a significant extent it has required resorting to external immigration. In France, for instance, the increase in the total number of wage-earners between 1971 and 1973 amounted to 320,000 units. In the same period new placements of foreign workers amounted to 230,000, while the average number of unemployed was around 500,000.

One is thus tempted to assert that an employment policy primarily geared to liberalization and demand expansion has two major shortcomings. First, it only succeeds in securing full employment where the national economy concerned has enough flexibility to adjust the supply of labor to the pattern required by final demand—particularly, but not only, with respect to exports; this flexibility is considerably facilitated by the availability of foreign labor. Second, an employment policy basically geared to demand expansion will tend to perpetuate a given structure of output and employment. When this structure becomes inadequate to deal with policy considerations such as pollution, external imbalance, or excess of immigration other instruments will be required. The changes required to meet these other targets will act slowly and create fears of unemployment. Such fears usually result in a priority for short-term targets over long-term or structural targets, and thus retard desirable changes.

The Search For Complementary Policies

The Issues

The shortcomings of past performance among EC countries with respect to employment lie mainly in the ability to achieve adequate matching of the new activities stimulated by demand with the human resources available. Since the early 1960s there has not been what one could consider an overall surplus of labor in view of the flow of immigrant workers. It is, on the other hand, quite appropriate to speak of the coexistence of job vacancies and seekers, of immigration and structural unemployment.

At first sight this seems simply a problem of structural unemployment mostly concentrated in peripheral areas and linked with declining activities. The persistence of Italian and British problems in this matter contrasts with the large-scale reduction of the German and Belgian problems of the 1950s. Geographical mobility did function but mostly within countries instead of within the Community. The resulting overall trend—if it persists—will threaten the very survival of certain areas.

However, a similar discrepancy appears in terms of the sectoral and vocational matching between jobs offered and worker redundancies within the same regions. The shortage of highly skilled workers in the machine-tool industry contrasts with the redundancies of skilled and semiskilled textile workers. Although such a situation has probably always existed it is reasonable to expect that discrepancies have increased in the period of fast growth and structural change Western Europe has known; it may be interpreted in two different ways.

According to the economic interpretation policies have failed to redeploy labor in step with structural change. Expansion implies changes in types of products and activities, and takes care of itself in regard to the creation of new demand for goods and services. But the labor market is more sluggish than the capital and goods market, and fails to supply the kind of labor required.

In social terms, however, it is difficult to expect the brunt of the adjustment to be borne by the worker. Maximizing labor market flexibility and mobility would imply that welfare targets are assessed only in terms of the total level of goods supplied, and not in terms of their distribution or of the individual cost to acquire them. It is, therefore, necessary either to socialize the cost of adjustment, or to intervene by region and industry in the spontaneous pattern of activity.

Ideally, therefore, employment policy has to find some optimal point between two extreme targets. At one end, securing the full adjustment of the labor supply to the needs of expansion would involve a considerable—and probably unbearable—amount of geographical and industrial mobility. At the other end, adapting the pattern of activities to the present pattern of labor supply would mean at the limit a quasi-stationary economy without improvement in welfare. Policies vary from country to country. It is fair to assume that the greater labor mobility in Germany and Italy places these economies more toward the first end; Britain and France are much further away from it. Labor market adjustability is also higher where there is a supply of highly mobile migrant workers.

It seems increasingly difficult to expect that such optimal combinations of labor mobility and job security will be attained spontaneously. Specific efforts are necessary to make progress toward full employment and to overcome persistent fear of unemployment—a cumulative factor of rigidity.

The Instruments Developed

Since the early 1960s the problems of structural unemployment and labor redeployment have led most countries of the enlarged Community to develop two sets of instruments. The first aims at creating new jobs by increasing the demand for labor through regional or sectoral incentives. Its most common form consists of granting public subsidies or tax reductions for the promotion of activities in less favored areas. Often introduced as a temporary remedy, it has become a more permanent feature since one-shot injections of capital incentives were found insufficient to compensate for the handicaps. The importance of this issue is enhanced by the increasing trend toward reduction of regional wage differentials in most European countries.

The second method—developed more recently—attempts to improve the quality of the labor supply. Actions of this type aim mainly at improving the flow of information between job seekers and vacancies, and at developing training facilities and incentives to mobility. The attachment of most European workers to their region and to their job makes it all the more important to offer them alternative possibilities—especially in the case of industries with poor economic prospects. Geographical mobility, which was very important in the initial conception of the Common Market, raises many problems in view of the disequilibrating effect it has in most countries. Its decline makes it all the more important to develop sectoral and vocational mobility to maintain the overall responsiveness of the economy to industrial changes. This is especially true at a time when fuel price increases are bound to bring profound transformations in the pattern of domestic and export demand.

A comparative analysis of the relative role of both types of instruments in various countries would be an interesting but lengthy task. Certain general impressions may, however, be presented here.

Regional measures rely mainly on incentives and occasionally disincentives. These were mostly developed from scratch in the 1960s. Labor market policies rely mainly on operational activities by public agencies such as employment services and training agencies. Most of these agencies had previously been in existence as virtual charitable services for the poorest sections of the population, but since the 1960s public policy has had to start modernizing these services, intensifying their operations, and making them more attractive for all categories of workers.

Furthermore, there are great differences from country to country in the size and quality of both types of measures. A French report estimated that the amount of regional aid in 1970 was 2 billion French francs in Italy and in Britain in contrast to 300 million in France.[1] If this is related to the number of unemployed as a general measure of the intensity of structural unemployment it leads to expenditure figures of about 3,600 francs per unemployed worker for Britain (about $720 at pre-1971 parity), 3,300 francs for Italy (about $660), and 1,100 francs for France (about $220).

Similar comparisons of public expenditures for labor market and re-training policies have not yet been made. An extremely rough estimate issued by the EC Commission, based on the expenditures of the respective national agencies, leads to the following results for 1970:[2]

(in European units of account = pre-1971 $)

	Total Expenditure	Per Unemployed
Belgium	64 million	840
France	135 million	370
Germany	877 million	5,800
Italy	42 million	70
The Netherlands	19 million	335

The spread is one to eighty between Italy and Germany. There is little chance that more accurate and comparable figures could alter the conclusions one can derive from these results regarding the considerable disparities in national policies in this area.

It is difficult to estimate the actual results achieved in both directions. Any causal analysis in such matters leads to uncertain results. Belgian statistics show for instance that 280,000 new jobs have been created by investments aided by regional incentives since 1959, but there are few hints as to the actual role of these aids in investment decisions. However, some surveys among large firms tend to indicate that the general business climate, tax legislation, and the availability of skilled manpower and of transportation facilities are greater determinants than investment incentives.

So-called structural policies—of a regional or an industrial character— have often been compelled to aim at retarding necessary adjustments rather than promoting new kinds of activities. The shipbuilding industry, or even agriculture, illustrates such a situation—where policy seems to be dictated by the absence of adequate employment alternatives immediately available to the workers involved. Such exceptions to a "rational" allocation of resources cannot, however, be systematically criticized because unexpected changes in industrial or economic trends may sometimes justify them. In addition, such retarding actions may be the cost that has to be paid in certain more sensitive areas in order to make the overall process of change brought about by growth and trade liberalization politically acceptable. This "umbrella" function appears clearly in the case of agriculture. A much criticized common agricultural policy coincided with a reduction of about 50 percent in the number of European farmers within 10 years.

The Impact of the European Community
on the Employment Situation
of Member Countries

Policies contributing to full and better employment are of course formulated and implemented mainly at the national level; however, the

Community, which has been charged by the Rome Treaty (1957) to assist in attaining a high level of employment, has contributed to this goal in three ways.

First, and foremost, it has provided the framework and rules for a policy of managed demand expansion and trade liberalization. Trade liberalization—both within the EC and with non-EC countries—has been negotiated and managed in an orderly way. This has had a strong influence on the efficiency achieved by the original member states; traditionally protectionistic countries or groups have reconciled themselves to its positive role.

The influence of the EC on demand management is more debatable. Coordination of economic policies up to now has achieved limited results. On the other hand, the various committees and ministerial meetings at Community level have certainly contributed to a growing awareness of the economic interdependence of the member states. (In this matter the role of the EC cannot of course be dissociated from that of the International Monetary Fund or of the Organization of Economic Cooperation and Development.) In the period of monetary instability that started after 1968 decisions made by individual countries tended to take account of the potential impact on the partner states. This is partly due to the combination of managed safeguard clauses and of control rules included in the Rome Treaty, but it is also very much due to the awareness of the strong interdependence between countries that has developed in industry and trade unions since 1958. These achievements are now of course being questioned by the disturbances resulting from inflation and from the fuel crisis. But the close trade interdependence makes most social groups on the continent aware that any attempt to "go it alone" could be suicidal.

Second, the Community is fully establishing the right of free circulation for workers. Contrary to initial expectations this has not had a very significant impact in economic or social terms. It is in fact marginal in the huge process of third-country immigration that developed. But it has a considerable political significance since it can be seen as the only political right established by the EC for individuals.

Finally, the Community has fragments of a "structural policy" for employment. Its nucleus was set up in 1953 under Article 56 of the European Coal and Steel Community Treaty which provides for grants for readjustments in these two industries. When these grants were established in the 1950s such operations were not yet a part of member states' policies. They contributed to the orderly retreat of the coal industry, mainly by the direct support they provided, but also by the incentive they gave to establish similar measures at the national level.

Two additional instruments were established by the Rome Treaty: the European Investment Bank and the European Social Fund. The bank was conceived as a relatively classical development bank in order to finance projects of common Community interest along with infrastructure and industrial projects for regional development. Its influence on employment has been indirect.

The European Social Fund, on the other hand, was specifically designed to refinance labor mobility costs and labor readjustment costs in all industries. Its automatic and unconditional character ended in unbalanced results. The countries best equipped for the establishment of readjustment programs, which meant mainly Germany, were getting the major share of the cake. The fund was thus losing its incentive role which was an essential element in the initial design. As a result the fund was entirely reformed in 1971 to allow for more selectivity and to reemphasize the incentive role. The reform has enabled the Social Fund to finance retraining and readjustment operations, either as a support to Community policies (on the basis of EC Council decisions) or as a support to national policies. Its yearly appropriation of 280 million units of account in 1973 has been used primarily to facilitate sectoral adjustments (agriculture and textiles) and to ease employment for certain less advantaged sections of the labor force (handicapped and migrant workers).

Future Prospects

Today there is a deep concern in Western Europe about future employment trends. This has been intensified by the disturbances the fuel price increases have caused in balance of payments and growth prospects. But this sudden shock should not conceal the fact that substantial problems existed earlier. Since the late 1960s the original Community as a whole has hardly made any progress in the reduction of the overall unemployment rate. It is probably not a coincidence that inflation has increasingly become a potential source of disruption.

Thus, the countries of the Community are faced with two sets of problems. For the short term, except for Germany, they are confronted with very unfavorable balance-of-payments positions. Consequently, they will have to bring inflation under control and it will be difficult to avoid restrictive policies.

In the longer term they face some more basic problems. Growth now appears as a doubtful universal panacea for existing or impending unemployment. Therefore what other policies can be developed to achieve the reduction of unemployment? Immigration was an easy solution to ensure adjustments on the labor market but as it reaches a saturation point in many places it seems bound to decline in importance. How should the pattern of activities and jobs be altered in the future to take account of this change?

The key to these questions may lie in a more earnest handling of the instruments of labor market policy. These have often been carried out with the dominant concern of achieving social targets and hence have remained peripheral in the formulation of economic policies. Perhaps the realization that labor market adjustments are crucial for the smoother operation may lead to reassessing their role and to giving them a more central place in designing strategies. Such a reassessment is certainly a precondition for any attempt to reconcile the readjustments our economies require after the fuel crisis with rising expectations for employment security and a more equitable chance for all in access to work and to promotion.

NOTES

1. Rapport "Piquart," quoted by the Commission of the EC in *"Rapport analysant les problèmes qui se posent dans le domaine régional à la Communauté élargie"* (annexe - chap. III—Objectifs et instruments des politiques régionales des Etats membres).

2. Figures taken from a Commission report: *"Les activités des services de main-d'oeuvre et de formation professionnelle dans la Communauté,"* Brussels 1971. (Unemployment benefits proper are deducted. They also show a very broad spread. The number of unemployed is given in the report).

4

TRADE UNIONS AND INDUSTRIAL POLICIES IN WESTERN EUROPE
Hans Günter

Industrial policy, if it is taken to mean a coherent set of measures intended to orient all industrial development toward a desired direction, is a relatively recent concept in Western Europe. In fact, probably no country in Western Europe has applied industrial policy in this complete sense of the term. But there is little doubt that public policy, even if a country has no indicative planning, is increasingly exerted with the aim of shaping total industrial developments. In a market economy, which is the basic economic organization of the countries in question, such policies have to take into account and are often subordinated to "autonomous economic trends." These trends are the results of decisions taken by individual enterprises in response to the opportunities and constraints of markets, competition, and the international exchange of products and capital. In addition, the existence of the European Community (EC) and the operations of multinational firms constitute other main decision-making levels for industrial policies.

It therefore appears useful to study trade union attitudes and reactions to industrial policies at these four main levels: state, enterprise, EC, and multinational corporations. This is done in an admittedly preliminary fashion in the following discussion. The paper concentrates on the main orientations (as the author sees them) rather than on variations of the theme, because in a continent like Europe a variety of policy conceptions, approaches, traditions,

---

The author is responsible for the opinions expressed in this paper; they are in no way attributable to the International Institute for Labor Studies (IILS), where the author is a senior staff associate.

cultures, and union orientations prevail. Not including them obviously entails the danger of simplifying a rather complex picture.

THE NATIONAL LEVEL

While the industrial policies pursued by the individual European governments often differ substantially because of their unequal economic structures,[1] union attitudes, despite marked variations in their industrial relations priorities, their ideologies, and their wider social goals, share one broad common denominator: assuring and maintaining full, well-remunerated, and stable employment. These employment goals were difficult to reconcile, however, in the period of especially pronounced structural economic change experienced in Western European countries since the mid-1950s.

The period of reconstruction beginning after the Second World War was much less one of structural economic change than one of rebuilding global capacities. It was characterized by the successful "management of the big economic aggregates" by public policies, which in keeping with Keynesian ideas developed in the 1930s left the orientation of economic growth in most countries mainly to private initiatives. This approach assured the Western European states full or high employment from the 1950s on, even in traditional emigration countries such as Italy. No marked differences existed in this respect in countries like France which had opted for indicative planning or countries like West Germany which espoused a neoliberal ideology and stressed the free play of market forces. However, in the latter case lavish growth incentives, for example, in the form of tax exemptions or subsidies, were given by the government and these had a definite influence on directing overall and sectoral growth performance.

Two basic premises were favored in many influential union circles as a result of the unprecedented growth experienced in Western Europe during the first two post-war decades of the "economic miracles." First, the decision-making powers of employers at the enterprise level needed to be preserved in order to enable efficient economic management. Second, power and responsibility for overall growth and employment performances were to be vested mainly in the state. As a result of this postwar experience and these convictions, despite foreseeable problems with members, enlightened union leadership had to accept the adjustment and adaptation of labor to the exigencies of economic growth and change. This orientation visibly benefited the majority of the labor force and society as a whole in terms of continuous high employment, increases in real wages, and improved standards of living. It also followed from this experience and from this division of responsibility that it was the governments which had to have the main responsibility for compensatory policies such as adjustment assistance to individual workers and to industries.

Acceptance of the position that labor had to adjust to wider economic exigencies was fostered in many union quarters for two other reasons. First, mostly as a heritage of nineteenth century labor movements, many unions in Europe do not perceive themselves exclusively as defenders of the particular economic interests of their members (that is, as "wage machines"), but also as agents of social stability that contribute to society's overall shape and direction of change. The majority of unions in Western Europe, mainly those of social and Christian orientations, understand societal change as a gradual process that also includes gradual change of industrial structures. But even most of the Marxist-oriented and Communist-led unions, which are very influential in countries such as France and Italy, have found it necessary to defer their more radical ideas of social change. In the interest of their members' more immediate concerns they have sought, as have other unions, mostly to use their influence to attenuate the social consequences of structural change in growth-oriented capitalist economies.

The second reason for the broader outlook of Western European unions on industrial policies is their growing inclusion (together with other interest groups, especially employers' associations) in national-level policy and planning institutions or in informal consultations. This is usually in an advisory capacity. Both unions and governments see advantages in these arrangements in terms of extended influence, of gaining support for policies, and of early accommodation of interests. In addition, such arrangements may serve to reduce conflicts. Unions and employers' organizations thus tend to become indispensable collaborators with governments;[2] but they often share more responsibility than influence and power.

Examples of bodies used in Western European nations for such purposes are, in France, the National Economic and Social Council and, at the technical level of the planning process, the Central Planning Council; in Belgium, the National Committee of Economic Expansion; in Britain, the National Economic Development Council; in Italy, the National Council of Economy and Labor; in Austria, the Central Council for Employment Market Policy; and in Sweden, the Economic Planning Council. In addition, in most countries there are sectoral and also regional institutions with similar functions.[3] The German unions have pressed unsuccessfully so far for the creation of a Federal Council for Economic and Social Policy, mainly because central planning is still not very respectable, due mostly to past authoritarian abuse. But as in the other countries the German unions are consulted informally in all major policy and legislative measures affecting industrial policy, and take part in the administration of public institutions that play an important role in social adjustment, such as the Federal Institute of Labor. This organization has responsibilities for worker placement, adjustment assistance, training, research, information, and counselling.[4]

From the 1960s European industrial policies focused heavily on structural changes such as rationalization, industrial concentration and the transformation of the composition of the production structure, and massive intakes of foreign labor in countries with overemployment, such as Switzerland, West Germany, and France. The concentration process tended to get out of hand in public industrial policies and became controversial not only for labor but also within the EC context. Finally, unequal distribution of industrial growth on a sectoral and geographic basis forced governments to turn their attention to regional development schemes aiming at the industrialization of backward areas with labor surpluses.

Several of these structural problems and policies put the "progressive union ideology" of adjusting labor to the requirements of economic growth to a severe test. This was especially true in those cases which involved declining industries such as coal mines and textiles. This ideology meant that short-run job insecurity had to be accepted in order to obtain long-term employment security. A substantial part of the labor force had to accept the harsh fact, as stated in the Second French Plan, that in the internationally integrated, growth-oriented, capitalist market economy, "with (its) evolving techniques and needs, it is impossible to guarantee every worker, for the whole of his life, a particular job in a particular place."[5]

The concept of active labor market policies evolved slowly during this period, in part under union pressure.[6] In Sweden the concept is most developed. It is based on better projection and planning of labor resources and skills in relationship to industrial policies and the coordination and balanced development of both. However, even in these advanced approaches labor still remains largely the dependent variable. Improved placement services, training and retraining facilities, adjustment assistance to those who change jobs, housing programs, and research undertaken for forecasting purposes all have been introduced in various degrees in the different countries and are mainly intended to facilitate labor mobility.

Fearing excessive social costs, practically all unions in Europe, with some possible exceptions, such as the Swedish and Dutch unions, have strong misgivings in principle regarding accelerated labor mobility. They prefer firms to move to areas with a surplus labor supply and redundancies in contrast to massive migration of workers to areas with growth industries. But governmental policies on the whole proved insufficient or ineffective to reverse the trend toward industrial and geographical concentration. Unions frequently complained about the insufficient decentralization of industrial policies. Examples of this have occurred in connection with French planning, the industrial development of southern Italy, British industrial settlement policies, Belgian regional development plans, and the industrialization of certain German border regions.

In light of this experience union positions were not always coherent or unanimous in the individual countries. In Britain, for instance, the Trade

Union Congress (TUC) criticized the abolition of economic planning in the early 1950s, which favored unequal development, but insisted at the same time on better training opportunities for workers and other measures improving mobility.[7] In other countries, such as Italy, high labor mobility remained suspect for the majority of the unions while a minority, for instance the *Confederazione Italiana Sindacati Lavoratori* (CISL) and the *Unione Italiana del Lavore* (UIL), soon became convinced that full employment could only be attained through extensive adaptation of the skill composition of the labor force and its geographical location.[8] This latter viewpoint by force of circumstance finally became the principal reaction of European unions to structural industrial policies.

Another industrial policy option for which trade union attitudes were decisive was the policy of massive immigration of foreign workers. This was pursued in countries such as France, West Germany, Belgium, Switzerland, Sweden, and to a certain extent Britain, where tight local labor markets seemed to endanger the projected growth patterns. The decisive reason for these immigration policies was that cost/benefit analyses made at the enterprise level showed that labor-intensive growth was to be preferred to capital-intensive growth. Not much consideration was given by public authorities, at the earlier stages of labor immigration, to cost/benefit calculations at the national level. Nor was much consideration given to the degree to which the domestic labor force would tolerate the increase in foreign labor. Such neglect led to a number of complex problems and eventually to attempts in later years to reduce or at least stabilize the foreign labor component in most of the abovementioned countries.

The lack of concern by public authorities for other than enterprise-oriented considerations may have been encouraged by the general assumption that recourse to foreign labor was only a passing phenomenon. Although subsequent developments, which confirmed economic forecasts, made it clear that foreign labor was to become an important permanent feature (it accounts in Switzerland for 30 percent of the labor force and in Germany for 10 percent), the fiction of the temporary nature of foreign labor was often officially maintained, partly as an excuse or justification for neglecting necessary social infrastructure investments.

It is possible that the unions' favorable attitudes (which on the whole prevailed in Western Europe) toward the massive intake of foreign labor were influenced somewhat by the expectation that the influx was to be short-term. But other more substantial considerations encouraged the same attitude. These included the convictions that economic growth and employment opportunities would increase rather than decrease as a result of labor immigration; the possibilities for social upgrading of domestic labor would expand as foreign labor was occupying or creating new and mainly lower-level jobs; and productivity and correlated real wage gains would remain high in sectors with high proportions of foreign workers.[9]

However, foreign labor functioned as a "buffer" in times of economic recession. Unemployment rates during periods of slower growth were several times higher with foreign than with domestic workers, the latter having moved apparently into more stable jobs which were less affected by short-term economic variations. Newcomers on the labor market, both individuals and ethnic groups, tended to replace them in less attractive and less stable jobs.[10]

Naturally, most of these developments could be appreciated only ex post facto. Therefore, the decision of Western European trade unions to accept large-scale foreign immigration entailed, in reality, a certain amount of risk for their employment and wage goals; and it was undoubtedly also international labor solidarity that motivated their positive attitudes.[11]

Risks were also taken by the unions in respect to traditional industrial relations. It was to be expected that foreign workers would bring with them different attitudes toward work, union roles, and employer/labor relations. Despite their relatively lower rate of union organization[12] and weaker economic position foreign workers influenced industrial relations in a number of respects. They often showed greater militancy in cases of labor conflict, stimulated the pressure for equal remuneration for equal work, brought the problems of low-skilled workers into the forefront of industrial concerns (for instance in the case of the Renault conflict over the *"ouvriers spécialisés"*— O.S.), and frequently defied established trade union authority in cases of labor unrest. Thus, they created challenges to union priorities and organization but they also advanced a number of traditional union claims and gave new opportunities for labor solidarity at the shop, industry, and Community levels.

It cannot be overstressed that the positive reaction of European unions to structural industrial policies in the postwar period, best characterized by the emphasis on employment security and not job security, was facilitated if not conditioned by continued high economic growth rates in most countries. It was somewhat less attractive to unions in Britain where growth rates lagged behind a number of other European countries. Conversely the greater resistance of British unions to policies affecting job security was often made responsible for the poorer growth performance. Despite labor market and social policies economic growth was by far the most important individual factor allowing the social cost of increased labor mobility to be kept at a tolerable level. High economic growth provided new employment opportunities, mostly in excess of demand, and at the same time increased the economic resources for compensatory measures that were needed to cushion the social consequences of structural changes.

Since these favorable conditions may be about to change with the present, and perhaps long-term, likelihood of reduced overall growth in Western Europe (and elsewhere), union attitudes toward industrial policies cannot remain unaffected. The determinants of this crisis are the price and supply of energy, the resulting adverse balance of payments, strains in the international monetary system, inflation combined with the menace of a general stagnation (stagflation), and specific immediate problems of key industries such as the automotive sector. These determinants together with the increased concern about the natural environment and the depletion of resources provide a fertile ground for zero- or low-growth ideologies and for defensive rather than risk-taking union attitudes.

Few industrial policies have been prepared to deal with this problem and there is considerable uncertainty regarding the policies that ought to be pursued. But selective measures and greater coordination of industrial and social policies are thought to offer on the whole greater promise than the earlier options of global demand management and accelerated structural change. As regards employment prospects there is little doubt that governments, even in Germany where inflation is dreaded, will opt for relatively high employment instead of price stability when such a trade-off is necessary. But even in the best of circumstances reemployment opportunities for redundant workers will decrease as demonstrated by the development of supply/demand ratios, while the direction of long-term structural economic change seems blurred.

Under these circumstances the basis for unions accepting pronounced labor adjustments to growth-created change is being eroded. At least in the short run job security takes priority over uncertain longer-run employment security and the improvements of real wages. Thus, resistance to change, apparently something of an outmoded reflex in recent industrial history, may once again become a tool for labor and possibly also for a lengthy "post-industrial" period.[13]

Nevertheless, governments tend now to be asked by the unions not only to secure aggregate full employment to provide adjustment assistance to workers but also to direct,[14] or even retard or stop, structural economic change in order to secure jobs. Subsidies to commercially unprofitable enterprises are now requested in the interest of employment maintenance. Public orders for noncompetitive production lines are pressed in sectors such as the aircraft industry. And in some countries, such as Britain, where it fits the ideology of the government in power, public ownership of certain enterprises menaced by shutdowns or mass dismissals is advanced as a solution to job insecurity.

These developments are bound, however, to increase the tension between the change-demanding "efficient society" (largely equated so far with economic growth, profitability and greater material welfare) and the growing desire for greater social stability in terms of employment and income. At the same time reduced growth rates tend to intensify the fight over relative shares and power positions between labor and capital and among different groups of workers and unions.

In an attempt to reduce the effects that conflicting goals of different social groups have on national policies experiments with various versions of basically voluntary *concertation* have been carried out since the mid-1950s in most European countries. Such action was sought in the past, but mostly in regard to incomes, wages, and price policies. On the whole it was not too successful, at least not in the long run. Now employment problems tend to be included in these attempts. Efforts are being made in several countries, most notably in Britain, to balance wage restraints on the part of the unions against employment guarantees by management and government, although it is still unpopular for union leaders to assert that "a wonderful wage agreement is of no value if the firm with whom we have negotiated the agreement does not employ people any more."[15] Under conditions of rapid growth the basically uncoordinated goals of different groups appeared compatible. But these conflicting directions are much more difficult to deal with under the present circumstances within which industrial policies are formulated. This may contribute to the enlargement of the "social contract" between unions and governments and lead to new experiments designed to reduce these sources of tension.

THE ENTERPRISE AND INDUSTRY LEVEL

The history of Western European trade unions leaves no doubt that most of them consider the enterprise the essential place where the fortunes of the working class are determined. More than at the other levels of industrial policy decision-making conflicting interests are directly experienced in the enterprise. Simultaneously, in line with the functional exigencies of market economies ultimate decision-making power in the enterprise remains the prerogative of the employer. Apart from consultation requirements in certain cases the processes of production, location of industry, investment, and expansion and contraction of activities, all of which have far-reaching consequences for workers, remain almost undisputedly in the hands of management except in a few notable exceptions, especially the codetermination scheme in the West German iron and steel industry. In some countries, the more important dismissals must be taken up with the unions; thus in Sweden, where one month's notice is required before termination or extended layoffs, employers must meet with the unions if the unions desire such discussion. In Italy terminations have to be suspended if a union protests.

Furthermore, in most countries better coordination between important managerial employment decisions and public authorities has resulted from regulations which require employers to notify in advance, or consult with, or in rarer cases obtain the approval of, public institutions (labor inspectorates, ministries, labor offices, or tripartite bodies) before undertaking dismissals. In Sweden, for instance, employers have to submit reports to a County Administrative Board with information concerning planned or expected extensions or limitations in production, employment, or operations. In France a governmental agency can delay a plan to reduce the labor force in a particular sector. In West Germany notice must be given and approval obtained from the national employment office in cases of large-scale dismissals, and such approval is obtained subject to a number of delaying procedures. Because of these regulations employers have to provide justifications for their actions, alternatives can be explored, and compensatory governmental measures can be set in motion.[16] But employers maintain to a large extent their decision-making prerogatives.

In most continental Western European countries it is not the unions but the general bodies for employee representation within the plants and enterprises that are mainly involved in decision-making about dismissals—particularly in regard to their social impact. These bodies, such as works councils and staff delegates, have their authority as a result of legislation or collective arrangements. The cooperation of works councils in the preparation of so-called "social plans" in West Germany is an example of such involvement. The social plans were foreseen by the Workers' Constitution Act and comprise all measures that must be negotiated between management and works councils that involve assistance to personnel affected by staff reductions or shutdowns. These include the delaying of dismissals, provision of facilities for occupational retraining, and provision and amounts of severance allowances.

Works councils and similar bodies have been established to facilitate peaceful cooperation with management while simultaneously taking into account the economic purposes and efficient functioning of firms. The unions have generally succeeded, however, in penetrating these bodies with their own members. But in many countries they have felt obliged also to reinforce their plant representation outside the framework of these organs. In part, against heavy employer resistance they have created their own enterprise-level organizations that can also deal with management. In several countries, such as the Netherlands and West Germany, this has led to a certain duplication of worker representation within enterprises. In the latter case union spokesmen now exist in many enterprises in addition to the traditional works council; but their functions are still ill-defined. Plant-level organization of unions has also been a theme of union action in Italy as evidenced by the labor conflicts there in 1969.[17] In major Italian enterprises union sections now coexist for each of the three major unions together with an assembly of department delegates appointed by them and the traditional works council.[18] And in France trade union sections were introduced by legislation at the plant level in 1968. In addition, the position of shop stewards or trade union delegates has been strengthened in recent years in Scandinavian countries and in Belgium.[19]

These developments have brought increased union control over working conditions and dismissals, mainly in regard to employer-initiated changes of labor organization in firms. In Britain in recent years shop stewards affiliated with various unions were able, through pressure and strikes, to increase their influence on enterprise decisions affecting employment, especially in the big enterprises where they formed "combine committees."[20]

Parallel to and in part preceding these moves to increase "workers' control" the unions in various countries have concluded special agreements in various sectors of industry to regulate the social consequences of employment problems stemming from entrepreneurial productivity policies and rationalization measures. These agreements can be seen as a kind of partnership.

Thus, starting with the famous agreement at the Fawley Refinery near Southampton in 1960, thousands of so-called "productivity agreements" have been concluded in Britain, essentially at the plant and enterprise level but also occasionally for a whole industry. Although the main purpose of these productivity agreements was, at least for the employers, the abolition of "restrictive working practices" to create higher efficiency through greater flexibility for management in manpower utilization, most of these agreements also address themselves to employment and reemployment questions. In regard to this last aspect they include provisions covering reductions in overtime, redeployment conditions, and encouragement of voluntary departures with appropriate compensation and redundancy payments. The British unions are not unanimous about productivity bargaining. Some reject it because of the loss it entails in worker control, the loss of status for craftsmen and skilled workers, the execution of shift work, and the loss of overtime resulting from the reorganization of work.[21]

Since the early 1960s special collective agreements covering problems of employment security have been concluded in France. This occurred first at the industry level and eventually also at the national level. Similar to the British arrangements, they include regulations for redeployment, early retirement, internal transfers, and occasionally retraining and severance pay. Frequently these agreements are based on the principle that dismissals should only be carried out as a last resort. Naturally, this is little more than a recommendation. The industries in which such agreements are principally found are textiles, sugar, iron, and steel—that is, sectors in which problems of restructuring due to industrial concentration are particularly pronounced. Under the dual pressures of the labor unrest of 1968 and government influence a national agreement on security of employment was signed in February 1969 between the French National Employers Association and nearly all major union confederations. The agreement instituted joint employment committees for the different industries to "examine in the event of collective dismissals the difficulties in the application of redeployment and training facilities." The object of the deliberation of these joint committees concerns the worker who has already lost his job; the committees cannot interfere in managerial policies leading to such dismissals. The national-level agreement also enlarged the consultation rights of the workers' committees and certain guarantees for workers menaced by dismissals on economic grounds.

In October 1974 the five main French unions concluded a new nationwide agreement with the employers' association. It has been hailed as the most far-reaching accord of its kind ever signed in France or any other European country. Under its provisions employees of all grades made redundant are assured full payment of their salary for a year if they remain out of work.[22] Similarly in the early 1960s in West Germany special collective agreements for the protection of workers against the social consequences of rationalization measures were concluded for various regions in such industries as textiles, metal, and chemicals. In fact there now also exists a national-level agreement for the West German metal industry.

The West German rationalization protection agreements stipulate in particular an active participation by works councils and trade union representatives in the study of the consequences for workers of rationalization measures planned by management, the transfer of workers to other jobs, and the conditions under which these should take place. They also provide increased protection for workers affected by dismissals, including an extension of the period of notice, the provision for continued salary payments for a certain time at the original level in the case of a transfer involving downgrading, and the granting of substantial financial compensation in the case of dismissal.[23] The unions were unable in practically all countries to obtain through these special agreements guarantees for advance personnel planning. This is apparently still a relatively uncommon concept in European entrepreneurial practice.

Compared with the prior situation the special agreements for the protection of workers in cases of rationalization certainly provide substantial advantages. Nevertheless, they do not affect the essence of managerial decision making. Subject mainly to monetary compensation, increased consultations with workers' representatives or unions, and their fuller involvement in the implementation of policies regulating the social consequences of managerial decisions, management remains free to decide on such rationalization measures as it deems necessary. Thus "the special responsibility or prerogatives of management are not called in question by agreements of this type."[24]

Provisions for increased protection of workers regarding the social consequences of industrial policy have also been increasingly incorporated in ordinary collective agreements. Traditionally, in Europe these agreements have been restricted mainly to wages and labor conditions. A good example is the one adopted in November 1973 for the metal industry in the German region of North Wurttemberg/North Baden. Apart from including a number of participation and control rights of workers and unions regarding shift-work regulations, speed of assembly lines, rest periods, and other aspects of the industrial work environment, this agreement contains clauses which make it extremely difficult to dismiss workers over the age of 55. (The agreement has been hailed by the German unions as a model approach to the "humanization" of work.)

In some European countries, in particular Sweden, the unions do not consider collective agreements a major instrument for protecting workers against the social ill-effects of enterprise-level industrial policies. Although there is a national agreement in Sweden regulating compensation payments for dismissed workers the Swedish unions assert, even more than their counterparts in the rest of Europe, that the protection of workers against the adverse effects of technological change is primarily the responsibility of government.

In the early 1970s employer-initiated experiments with alternative forms of work organization such as autonomous work groups, job enlargement, and job rotation, have begun to spread particularly in the Scandinavian countries, Italy, and France. These developments have given the unions occasion to also sharpen their position on employment questions.[25] They have been concerned about achieving a mixture of high employment and good work conditions, both of which are characteristic of present industrial relations in Europe.

While the reactions of unions and their propensity to cooperate in such experiments differ somewhat from country to country and among various union organizations, they all tend to take the line that new work organization and leadership styles should by no means lead to reduction of personnel and intensification of work. Collective agreements concluded in the early 1970s at the plant and industry level in the North Italian metal industry contain such assurances. They stipulate further that alternative forms of work organization, introduced by employers, must go hand in hand with upgrading, retraining, and improved pay schemes.[26] In the same vein a far-reaching collective agreement was signed by Fiat in December 1974, providing for the participation of unions in program development, investments, and the related problems of labor redundancy and redeployment. At the same time Fiat management committed itself not to effectuate any dismissals during 1975 despite sales problems.[27]

Will industrial policies at the enterprise level substantially change if union strength at the plant continues to increase? Two basic options seem available in this regard and both are in line with present tendencies. One emphasizes partnership through worker participation in decision making, the other emphasizes conflict by contesting the distribution of managerial functions through workers' control. The West German codetermination formula, introduced by law in 1952 under specific historic conditions in the coal and steel industry, provides a limited test case for the first option. Thus the supervisory boards of enterprises subject to codetermination now include an equal number of representatives of workers and unions with those of shareholders together with a neutral member. Thus at least in theory worker representatives could have initiated very different employment policies as a result of their strategic part on these boards. Empirical studies do not however confirm this proposition.

In fact a report of independent experts (the so-called Biedenkopf report, named after the chairman of a Bundestag committee of inquiry) found that rationalization measures, take-overs, mergers, and shutdowns of enterprises were not prevented or blocked by the labor representation, although such decisions had obvious negative effects on job security and employment. Without exception (according to the Biedenkopf report), the worker representatives respected the need for profitability of the enterprise, including the adjustments required for labor that were implied. But the acceptance of dismissals or redeployment of workers was often retarded and always tied expressly by work representatives to a satisfactory regulation of their social repercussions. The Biedenkopf report was quick to add, however, that proper attention to the social aspects of enterprise decisions has nowadays become an "established general pattern of managerial behavior."[28] The German case may thus tend to suggest that at least with integrated (institutional) forms, even of equal worker participation, there is no certainty that enterprise-level industrial policies will be basically modified under the conceptions and constraints prevailing in market economies.

There can be no doubt, however, that for unions the acceptance of managerial decisions and reasoning in capitalist societies is often a painful and by no means conflict-free process, irrespective of the procedures through which they may be involved in these policies. Strike records in declining industries speak a clear language in this respect. In addition to employment problems quite a number of strikes in these industries were also prompted by the desire of workers to remain at the same place in the occupational and industrial pay hierarchy. By and large these attempts were unsuccessful.[29]

In the case of coal mining, an industry with a traditionally strong labor organization union, action was frequent and violent. However, the unions mainly attempted to impress governments with the need to slow down pit closures, to undertake large-scale reconversion measures for firms and workers, and to encourage the creation of new industries.

This insistence of unions on compensatory government measures rather than on defying decisions taken at enterprise level was common to all countries during the main period of postwar restructuring. This was true irrespective of whether coal mines were mainly in public hands as in France and Britain or privately owned as in West Germany. Union pressure had a very definite influence on the large-scale public reconversion programs which were initiated in the late 1950s and early 1960s in all coal producing European countries and were assisted by measures of the European Coal and Steel Community (ECSC).

In the West German case a massive public program of industrial reconversion, including subsidies for shutdowns and for coal prices, tariff protection, large-scale social assistance, and retraining for workers, practically brought private enterprises under the tutelage of the state. In the Ruhr this development forced them to merge into one major concern.

In the British case coal mines were nationalized between 1945 and 1950 and managed by a state-appointed Coal Board which together with the successive governments underwrote a vast program of pit closures. Unlike their German counterparts, which have parity codetermination arrangements in all major enterprises, the British workers only had a consultative role in this process. Judging by the German experience, however, it seems doubtful that effective worker representation in the British Coal Board would have led to radically different policies, as some analysts appear to believe.[30] On the other hand, the Coal Board's policy of pit closures was denounced in various union documents as lacking economic justification as well as a sound social cost/benefit analysis; and trade union militancy, which had been tempered by dismissals and resulting unemployment problems, increased after 1968.[31]

In France too pit closures, mechanization, and reduction of employment in the mines were implemented in line with comprehensive governmental plans. Strike action did achieve delays of one or two years in the "rundown" of the industry and spurred efforts for the accelerated introduction of new industries. These were often not sufficient to remove all unemployment problems in the regions in question. The effects of the new "energy crisis" have now led the government to envisage delaying the phasing out of production in the Pas de Calais region to 1985-86—instead of the original dates of 1980-82—and to interrupt dismissals through early retirement schemes.[32] In the changed circumstances of the energy markets the unions seem also to have found a more ambitious rhetoric. Thus, a French mining federation of the *Confédération Française Démocratique du Travail* (CFDI) (a partner of the interunion strike coalition composed of the CGT, CFDT, FO, and CFTC for the autumn 1974 strikes in the Lorraine region) recently announced in November 1974 that it would "impose on government a new coal mines policy" on a national scale.[33]

In any case the classic conception of strikes as a simple refusal to work is no longer the ultimate expression of worker discontent over managerial employment decisions. Instead, counterstrategies in the form of factory occupations ("sit-ins") and "active strikes" ("work-ins") have attained considerable prominence in recent years, although the number of these cases where workers have been successful is small so far. It would be premature, therefore, to speak of a new stage of worker reaction. At any rate these actions are signals of a new worker resistance against enterprise-level industrial policies that endanger job security. At the same time they demonstrate the fragility of postwar social partnership ideologies in economically difficult times for the new generation of workers.

Practically all cases of factory occupation started spontaneously on the shop floor. However, union organization at the plant or higher levels—for instance, where multinational firms are involved at the level of the international union federation—tend to channel or direct the movement and to mediate among workers, employers, and governments. Furthermore, together with action on the shop floor unions obtain wide publicity of the cases in the hope of generating public support. Inevitably, on the other hand, as the strikes continue the positions of different unions tend to diverge, coalitions break down, and problems arise in balancing group against general worker interest.

Three well-known recent examples of active worker resistance to managerial employment decisions are the cases of the Scottish Upper Clyde Ship Builders (1971), the French watch factory, LIP (summer 1973 to January 1974), and the Dutch-based multinational synthetic fiber producer, AKZO (April to September 1972).

Both in the Upper Clyde Ship Builders and LIP cases the workers not only occupied the factories but continued production under their own direction ("active strike" or "work-in"). They did not intend, however, to definitely introduce "workers' self-management," a concept which does not seem to be viable in the long run within the present organization of capitalist market economies. Rather their goals were to show up the inability of management to maintain employment of the work force and to win time for mobilizing public opinion and for the longer-term reorganization measures with the help of the government.

As one of the main union leaders in the LIP factory put it, the major single value of the "active strike" was the desire "to demonstrate that dismissals have no ineluctable character" and that "today workers must reject the fatality of being dismissed."[34] In line with the concept of workers' control the idea was to "remove the employers' decision-making rights through the struggle."[35]

In the AKZO case strike action and factory occupations were successfully coordinated on a cross-frontier basis; management had to give up rationalization plans which would have reduced employment in several European subsidiaries, even though these plans had been considered indispensable by an independent group of experts called in at one phase of the conflict. Aided by perhaps special and unforeseen economic prospects the AKZO concern now seems to be once again functioning. This furnishes support for the critics of the unique competence of management in particular and experts in general as well as support for the increasing claims of unions everywhere in Europe to "open the books" to them.

EC LEVEL

The European trade unions with Socialist and Christian orientations have committed themselves in various programs to European unification and integration. They have been favorably, disposed, therefore from the beginning toward collaboration within the EC (and even before that within the ECSC), although they are dissatisfied with the relatively small degree of influence which the EC structure offers them regarding European industrial and other policies.[36] The Communist-led unions were basically hostile to the idea of the "Europe of capital" and saw the ECSC and the EC as only furnishing an institutional setting for capitalism. They have also been refused working contacts by the non-Communist unions for many years. Since the mid-1960s a more realistic appreciation of the "objective reality" of European economic integration has developed among the Communist-led unions and, helped by East-West detente, they have successfully pressed for access to EC consultative organs. Thus in September 1970 five representatives of the Communist-led *Confederazione Generale Italiana del Lavore* (CGIL, of Italy) and the *Confédération Générale du Travail* (CGI, of France) were appointed members of the Economic and Social Committee of the EC. This tendency for greater cooperation among unions of different political orientations could increase in the future as the possibility for a rapprochement between the European Community and COMECON increases.

Several analysts have argued that the absence of the Communist-led unions from the European scene in the past may have adversely affected the influence which the unions could have wielded within the framework of European institutions and at the European level in general,[37] for instance by pressing for European collective bargaining. This concept has been violently opposed so far by the employers[38] and their EC-level association (UNICE), which to be sure does not have authority for this area. At the same time it is evident that national economic and social problems and related national policies have always been looked at by the unions as priority matters. The main reason for this is that the essential locus for decision making in regard to industrial policies still remains within the confines of the nation states.[39] Furthermore, union communication channels for influence on industrial policies are much more efficient at the national than at the European level. Therefore, despite the progress which has been attained in European economic integration and harmonization—also reflected in a greater amount of social levelling especially regarding wages and labor conditions—the European level is undoubtedly secondary to both the national and enterprise levels.

Because of the unions' weak status in the Community institutional structure and the problem of forging solidarity on an EC-wide basis it is not surprising that most union influence on EC (and earlier ECSC) decisions seems to have been achieved as a result of pressure on the national governments which are represented on the Council of Ministers. The Council together with the Commission is the most influential organ of the European Community. Formal union representation in Community institutions is limited to membership in consultative bodies such as the Economic and Social Committee and to the mixed committees established for a number of specific industries; in the Economic and Social Committee unions occupy seats together with employers and representatives from other social groups such as consumers. The mixed committees are mainly concerned with the "upward harmonization" of labor and social conditions. In the preparation of important policies the Commission also requests advice and collaboration from influential national and international (European) union organizations outside these bodies regarding such industrial policy matters as productivity, wages, and regional economic development.

The relatively limited possibilities for unions to participate in European institutions was one of the reasons why practically all prominent leaders of the British TUC have raised their voices against British entry into the European Community. The TUC pointed out that "the Commission makes the policy and the Council takes the decisions, and that trade unions have very little part in either function."[40]

Concerned above all with national priorities the unions have rarely acted as a class-conscious entity within the ECSC or the EC. For instance, in the important question of industrial restructuring they have tended rather to enter into coalitions with governments or their national employer counterparts. French trade unionists have been very interested, for instance, in defending French industry against competition by working for an equalization of social security contributions throughout the Community. Belgian trade unionists together with employers opposed the closing of unprofitable coal mines. And the West German trade unionists have been very concerned with the general competitiveness of their country's industry.[41] This does not imply, however, the absence of common union action programs or of attempts at European social harmonization.

A prominent example of the latter is the European Miners' Charter. This charter was discussed between 1964 and 1966 in the Mixed Committee for Mining of the ECSC. It would have provided miners in the member countries with improved and harmonized labor conditions and fringe benefits. But the initiative was thwarted by the employers—and by several governments— which invoked the competence of national governments for decision making on these matters and the economic difficulties of introducing such a scheme in a declining industry where national policies were being implemented to further curtail production.

Apart from the broader questions of industrial and social policy decision making, the interest of trade unions has centered on attempts to influence those EC institutions that facilitate the social adaptation of workers to industrial policies. A major institution of this type is the European Social Fund. It provides financial and training assistance mainly to workers affected by structural industrial changes in the various countries. However, its relatively modest impact has generally been out of proportion to the hopes it raised in union quarters. Thus the trend is for the number of workers retrained and resettled to fall.[42] This has led to recent union demands to make the fund more effective, including the suggestion of bringing it into a closer relationship with the activities of the European Investment Bank. Other EC institutions in which the unions cooperate in an advisory capacity are the Committee for Free Movement for Workers and the Committee for Vocational Training. Furthermore, the unions are very interested in the proposed European Regional Fund, the establishment of which is still being delayed by controversy among member governments regarding its financing and use. In the opinion of most European unions it could provide an instrument for a certain amount of European industrial planning for areas within the Community displaying manpower surpluses and thus reduce the need for excessive labor mobility. Benefits from the fund would be concentrated to a great extent on the three countries with the most severe regional problems in the EC—Britain, Italy, and Ireland.[43] Finally, the recently established Permanent Employment Committee, in which unions have equal representation with employers, could become a new focal point for the discussion of employment-oriented industrial policies.

While the influence of trade unions within the EC has not developed in line with their expectations the existence of European economic institutions has provided a tremendous stimulus toward greater European unity. In addition, the similar social concerns of the unions in the various countries have had a clear spillover on a number of policies prepared by the European bureaucracy. This is true especially of the new Social Action Program of the Commission that includes among other things a draft directive recommending to member governments the improvement and harmonization of worker protection in cases of mass dismissals—for example through notification of the competent public authority that could oppose dismissals if the reasons invoked are found to be nonexistent.[44] The program responds mainly to job security problems raised by increased capital concentration, takeovers, and transnational mergers within the Community. In the same vein an "Acquired Rights Directive" is proposed by the Commission regarding the transfer of accumulated rights, protective provisions, and guarantees from an old job to a new one.[45] Another case in point is the so-called Fifth Directive, which recommends enhanced participation rights of workers in enterprise decisions.

Since the inception of European economic institutions, more particularly the Common Market, both the Socialist and Christian unions have established a number of European-level organizations. These have mainly been for the exchange of information, for the development of common policy positions and action programs, and for liaison with the EC.[46] A major step for the Socialist unions was the founding of the ECFTUC in April 1969. This organization is in addition to the national member unions of the EC countries, the European counterpart of the International Confederation of Free Trade Unions (ICFTU), and the International Trade Secretariats (ITS's).

A European counterpart of the WCL (the international organization of mainly Christian unions whose European strongholds are predominantly in the Benelux countries) was also founded in 1969; it is called the European Confederation of Christian Trade Unions. And the Communist-led CFT (of France) and the CGI (of Italy) have set up a permanent coordination committee in Brussels.

Free (Socialist) and Christian union organizations have evolved the practice of developing common positions on European and EC matters. Within the context of industrial policies this includes agrarian, regional, and migration issues. The European Confederation of Christian Trade Unions proposed a united trade union organization for Europe at several of its congresses. Such a development is not yet in sight. So far institutionalized cooperation between the free and Christian unions has not developed, and noninstitutionalized cooperation has been rather irregular.[47]

In February 1973 the Socialist trade unions from 15 European countries joined together to form the European Trade Union Confederation (ETUC). In effect this was a merger of ECFTUC and the European Free Trade Association's (EFTA's) Trade Union Committee. This organization includes unions from EC member countries and unions from Scandinavia, Austria, Switzerland, and Spain. Such an enlarged geographical basis has undoubtedly facilitated the affiliation of the TUC. In fact, the former TUC general secretary was elected president of the ETUC.

The trade unions have thus managed to create well-constructed European organizations although these organizations reflect their ideological diversity. But at present despite these organizational efforts and increased cross-frontier cooperation their low influence on European matters compares unfavorably with their national influence. This makes them advocates for a revision of the European institutional structure.[48]

MULTINATIONAL CORPORATIONS

In contrast to the situation in the United States the policies of multinational corporations (MNCs) and their effects on employment have not yet become a major issue for European unions. This does not mean that unions are unconcerned about the seemingly discretionary power of multinational headquarters. These powers are beyond the reach of their usual influence and appear to enable the managers of the multinationals to shift production capacity from one country to another. This may influence the process of capital concentration in ways which unions feel will turn out to be detrimental to job security, employment levels, and the relevance of workers' job skills.

The unions also denounce the investment decisions of multinational corporations because they may be uncoordinated with national-level industrial policies. As has been seen, such policies are at least conceived with some degree of union and worker participation. In contrast to these possibilities of participation the unions are not consulted about the policies of the corporation as a whole. The unions' basic aim in Europe as elsewhere is, therefore, to reduce the power of multinational headquarters to make unilateral decisions on matters of interest to labor.

Whether or not the industrial policies of multinational corporations have on balance had negative social effects has been attenuated by the pronounced economic growth typical for postwar Europe and by the modern labor market policies of the governments. The labor market, as well as social policies, acted as early warning systems for public policy and formed a compensatory remedy especially for the social problems of structural change no matter what their origins may have been. Finally, the transfer of production lines and "job exports" to low-wage countries by multinational firms, which under union pressure has become a public concern in the United States, has not as yet taken on substantial proportions in Western Europe.

Consequently, industrial policies in Europe did not need to look at the foreign multinational corporation as an agent of general employment creation. Multinational firms were mainly considered by public authorities as instruments of industrial modernization and were also preferably called upon, usually with trade union support, to play a role in the job-creating industrialization of backward areas. Foreign firms were on the whole more responsive to government incentives intended to attract investments in depressed areas, and contributed successfully to regional development in the cases of Britain, France, and Belgium.[49] Southern Italy, on the other hand, is an example of a less successful interaction between government and multinational corporations in respect to regional policy, and an illustrative case also of the more general failure of international capital movements to make a substantial contribution to diminishing the need for large-scale intracountry and intra-European migration.

For the reasons mentioned previously, especially the diminished prospects for growth, industrial policies of multinational firms in the future should become a much bigger problem for the European unions. The increase in cross-frontier mergers, fusions, and take-overs in Western Europe will be an added factor. The attempts of European trade unions to win influence on the industrial policies of multinational corporations will undoubtedly become intensified by these tendencies. Present positions and some possible perspectives on these problems are sketched out in the following analysis.

Union responses and strategies in Western Europe regarding industrial policies of multinational corporations have developed in rather a specific environment. This is in part due to European integration but also to fairly liberal policies in most countries regarding trade and capital movements. This is also shown by the fact that many are both host and home countries of multinational corporations. On the social side the highly developed national labor legislation and industrial relations systems tend to integrate multinational corporations, whatever their origin, fairly well in the existing national context.

Furthermore, the headquarters of the International Trade Secretariats is located in Western Europe. In cooperation with or through their European committees or counterparts the ITS have found the Western European scene very favorable for developing strategies regarding multinational corporations. At present these are concentrated on corporations in the metal, chemicals, and food industries, sectors in which international capital concentration is greatest.

World councils for individual multinationals have been created especially for European-based firms. These represent a structural innovation. It seems unlikely even in Europe that these councils alone could counterbalance multinational management from within. But in addition to their regular function of exchanging information they provide a structural innovation which facilitates the coordination of action by the ITS's.

A particular feature of such action on the European scene are the repeated negotiations mainly between the European trade secretariats and the headquarters of a number of firms including Philips, Brown-Boveric, and Nestlé. Coordinated strike action over frontiers and other solidarity measures of unions also have their main strong points in Western Europe. This has been demonstrated by the cases of AKZO, Dunlop-Pirelli, Ford, etc.[50]

With partnership-type negotiations, such as the various talks between International Monetary Fund/European Monetary Fund (IMF/EMF) officials and Philips management, the unions' essential goal is to reach similar rights of consultation and information on a European level as they already have in the individual countries. These are sought particularly in regard to the firms' investment and employment policies in view of their social consequences, such as job changes and dismissals, for members in various countries.

On the other hand, relations with multinational firms seem mainly to have been concerned with wage problems, not with the industrial policies of the corporations. But this is somewhat superficial. In practically all dealings with multinational management industrial and employment policies come up as essential issues at a certain stage. For instance, unions may fear that their wage claims might make multinational management look for production alternatives in lower-wage countries. Management, as in the Ford case, may threaten to expand production in other than the strike-prone country or to close down the factory. For a number of economic, technical, and political reasons the latter case seems to occur extremely rarely in Europe. Nevertheless, multinational corporations in Europe and elsewhere still have retained great liberty regarding their transnational investment decisions. Union action on the whole has not had a decisive influence on their industrial policies and it is doubtful whether such action alone will ever develop into a real countervailing force. Current research tends also to suggest that industrial relations problems, at least those experienced so far by the multinationals, are merely second-line considerations for corporate industrial policies.[51] These policies appear to be determined primarily by the goals of market penetration, optimum resource utilization, profits, tax considerations, and other economic criteria.

It would also appear that European unions, like unions in general, cannot easily conceive and put into practice a global counterconcept to the global industrial planning of the multinational firms. This involves, among other questions, which jobs should be protected by international action, especially if there are options among different countries of location. How far does international union solidarity go? Currently, the guideline is to try to safeguard jobs everywhere when they are endangered by the industrial policies of multinational firms. The few successful examples of unions having opposed industrial policies of multinational corporations, such as in the AKZO case, followed this simple principle.

The chances of success of union action seem to be greatest when there is a special combination of factors and circumstances. These include significant mobilization on the shop-floor level over national frontiers, efficient guiding action by the International Trade Secretariats, mobilization of public opinion, and governments' parallel interest in maintaining employment where it exists. In the AKZO case the Dutch government was opposed to the company's plans at a period of economic recession. The alliance with national governments—and with their regional extension, the EC—seems to be one of the more promising conditions for extending union influence on the industrial policies of multinational firms. As in other cases of structural economic change it will also be the governments which will have to devise compensatory policies for any investment/employment decisions of multinational firms where they may negatively affect labor markets and job security.

CONCLUSIONS

Union responses in Western Europe toward industrial policies involving structural change are in a state of reorientation. Pressing mainly for a satisfactory regulation of the social consequences of such change, and participation in it, appear insufficient in times of reduced economic growth. Although such pressure by unions will certainly continue, they will intensify action to obtain more direct influence on industrial decision making at the four levels which have been described. This appears to be required in the interest of greater social security for workers—in the largest sense of the word—in times of increasing economic insecurity. Both partnership and conflictive procedures will be used in this process, which in essence is one aspect of the question of power and control in society.

NOTES

1. R. Toulemon and J. Flory, *Une politique industrielle pour l'europe* (Paris: Presses Universitaires de France, 1974), p. 6.

2. R. W. Cox, "Trade Unions, Employers and the Formation of National Economic Policy," in A. M. Ross, ed., *Industrial Relations and Economic Development* (London: Macmillan, 1967), p. 232.

3. See International Labour Office, *Participation by Employers' and Workers' Organisations in Economic and Social Planning* (Geneva, 1971).

4. Gerhard Leminsky, "Trade Union Policies Concerning Structural Change in the Labour Market and Technical Progress", in *International Conference on Trends in Industrial and Labour Relations*, Jerusalem Academic Press, 1972, pp. 507-515.

5. Quoted by Laurent Lucas in "Case study—France," in *International Trade Union Seminar on Active Manpower Policy*, Vienna, September 17-20, 1963, *Supplement to the Final Report*, OECD, 1964, p. 20 (hereafter cited as *OECD Supplement*).

6. P. Holmberg, "Background of Public Labour Market Actions," *OECD Supplement*, p. 170.

7. R. Boyfield, "Case study—Great Britain," *OECD Supplement*, p. 47.

8. Pietro Merli-Brandini, "Case study—Italy," *OECD Supplement*, p. 86.

9. See for instance, Bundesanstalt für Arbeit, *Überlegungen zu einer vorausschauenden Arbeitsmarktpolitik* (Nuremberg, 1974), p. 83.

10. Hans Günter, Paper prepared for Meeting on Labor Migration and the Economy, Ford Foundation, Paris, April 5-6, 1974, pp. 2-3.

11. Both the concern about growth and full employment on one side and practical international union solidarity are specifically referred to, for instance, in a statement on foreign workers by the German DGB. See DGB, *Die deutschen Gewerkschaften und die ausländischen Arbeitnehmer*, (Frankfurt, 2.11.1971), pp. 9 and 10.

12. See G. Gosack, S. Castle, "Gewerkschaften und ausländische Arbeiter," in O. Jacobi, W. Müller-Jentsch, and E. Schmidt, eds., *Gewerkschaften und Klassenkampf-Kritisches Jahrbuch, 1974*, p. 183. With consideration to the diverse and often agricultural background of foreign workers their rates of unionization, while lower than those of nationals, are higher for instance in West Germany than usually assumed.

13. Hans Gunter, "Social Policy and Post-industrial Society", *IILS Bulletin*, no. 10, p. 132.

14. See in this context M. Krüper, ed., *Investitionskontrolle gegen die Konzerne?*, ro-ro-ro aktuell, (Hamburg, 1974).

15. Statement by Jack Jones, leader of the biggest union in Britain, the

Transport and General Workers' Union, reported in "Jack's Right," *The Economist*, October 19, 1974, p. 119.

16. For more details see International Labour Office, *Termination of Employment*, Report III to International Labour Conference, 69th sess., Geneva, 1974.

17. D. Albers, W. Goldschmidt, P. Oehlke, *Klassenkämpfe in Westeuropa*, (ro-ro-ro aktuell, Hamburg, 1971), pp. 109-191.

18. Ibid., p. 145.

19. Johannes Schregle, "Labour Relations in Western Europe: Some Topical Issues, *International Labour Review*, January 1974, p. 7.

20. D. Albers, W. Goldschmidt, P. Oehlke, *OECD Supplement*, p. 225.

21. Ben Hooberman, *An Introduction to British Trade Unions*, (Harmondsworth, England: Penguin Books, 1974), pp. 71-72.

22. "Top Unions Walk Out on Patronate," *Financial Times*, November 22, 1974.

23. The data on productivity and other agreements draw heavily on Y. Delamotte, *The Social Partners Face the Problems of Productivity and Employment*, (OECD, Paris, 1971).

24. Ibid., p. 150, referring more specifically to the French and German agreements.

25. For a wide-ranging analysis of these developments see Y. Delamotte and K. F. Walker, "Humanisation of Work and the Quality of Working Life—Trends and Issues", *IILS Bulletin*, no. 11 (Geneva): 3-14.

26. Y. Delamotte, *Die Auffassungen der französischen und italienischen Gewerkschaften zur Humanisierung der Arbeitswelt* (Paper prepared on behalf of the IILS for a DGB Conference on Humanisation of Work (Munich, 16-17 May, 1974), (mimeographed).

27. Also "L'Accord réalisé chez Fiat pourrait faire école en Italie," *Journal de Genève*, December 3, 1974.

28. *Mitbestimmung im Unternehmen, Bericht der Sachverständigenkommission* (Stuttgart, Kohlhammerverlag, January 1970), p. 81.

29. Hans Günter, "Changes in Occupational Wage Differentials," *International Labour Review*, February 1974, pp. 136-155.

30. See Ken Coates and Tony Topham, *The New Unionism: the Case for Workers' Control*, (Harmondsworth, England: Penguin Books, 1974), pp. 120-123.

31. D. Albers, W. Goldschmidt, P. Oehlke, *OECD Supplement*, pp. 244-246.

32. "Une région qui porte les stigmates de la mine," *Journal de Genève*, November 2-3, 1974.

33. "Le gouvernement cherche à prévenir une extension des conflits du secteur public," *Le Monde*, November 2, 1974.

34. Quoted by Marcel Pouchard, "Securité de l'emploi et mutations industrielles," *Droit Social*, January 1974, p. 7.

35. Charles Piaget, *LIP, Charles Piaget et les Lip racontent* (Paris: Editions Stock, 1973), p. 27.

36. E. M. Bussey, "Organized Labor and the EEC," *Industrial Relations* 7 (1967-68): 160.

37. Pierre Traimond, "Le syndicalisme ouvrier face à la communauté économique européenne," *Droit Social*, June 1968, pp. 354-359.

38. The employers reject the unions' "abstract theory of social harmonization," *Arbeitgeber*, Annual Report for 1968 of the Confederation of German Employers' Association, p. 139.

39. Hans Günter, "International Collective Bargaining and Regional Economic Integration: Some Reflections on Experience in the EEC," in Hans Gunter, ed., *Transnational Industrial Relations* (London: Macmillan, 1972), p. 333.

40. B. Hooberman, op. cit., p. 136.

41. E. Haas, *The Uniting of Europe* (Stanford, Calif.: Stanford University Press, 1958), p. 355.

42. D. Swann, *The Economics of the Common Market* (Harmondsworth, England: Penguin Books, 1973 ed.), p. 142.

43. *Financial Times*, November 1, 1974.

44. International Labour Office, *Termination of Employment*, op. cit., p. 68.

45. See "The 'Acquired Rights' Directive: A Full Explanation," *European Industrial Relations Review*, May 1974, pp. 9-13.

46. For an account of the evolution until 1969 see R. Blanpain, "Efforts to Bring About Community-level Collective Bargaining in the Coal and Steel Community and the EEC," in Hans Günter, ed., *Transnational Industrial Relations*, op. cit., pp. 275-308.

47. M. Bouvard, *Labor Movements in the Common Market Countries, the Growth of a Pressure Group* (New York: Praeger, 1972). The part on recent European union developments draws on this volume.

48. Ibid., p. 261.

49. Gordon Richard Thomas, *Foreign Investment and Belgian Regional Development*, Geneva, Graduate Institute of International Studies, 1971 (mimeographed).

50. For a union-oriented analysis of these strategies see E. Piehl, *Multinationale Konzerne und internationale Gewerkschaftschaftsbewegung* (Frankfurt: Europäische Verlagsanstalt, 1973).

51. N. G. McCrea, *Industrial Relations and the Organisation of Industrial Relations Management in Multinational Companies*, forthcoming.

CHAPTER

5

EMPLOYER ASSOCIATIONS AND THE STATE IN FRANCE AND BRITAIN

Jack Hayward

In trying to penetrate into the murky area generally designated as the interface between government and industry it is natural to focus attention first on sorting out the component elements of these two conglomerates and to explore in depth the representative bodies through which firms and government departments have conducted many of their formal contacts. Our aim will be to secure, through a comparison between the arrangements that exist in France and Britain, some preliminary answers to the following questions. Are there some overall cultural determinants of government-industry relationships? How have the government's economic agencies and the employer associations evolved in recent years in a context where their interdependence has appeared to be unavoidable but in which each side has pursued a separate strategy? How has power shifted within government and within industry? What is the relative importance of indirect contacts at the level of the peak organization, of the trade association or chamber of commerce, as compared with direct contacts open to large firms? Do the cases of national planning and a policy of industrial restructuring help us to offer tentative answers to such problems? Given that we start with a minimal knowledge of both sides of the relationship, a preliminary description and analysis of such data as are available must be made. Our initial hypothesis will be that employer associations are not in practice as important a mediating link in government-industry relations as either their public image or the tendency of political scientists in liberal democracies to overstate the role of representative institutions would lead one to believe.

Traditionally, the two approaches to the analysis of relationships between government agencies and business organizations have been in terms of state intervention in the activities of business or pressure by firms and employer associations on the political and administrative executive. Emphasis on state intervention has been characteristic of those countries where the legal norm of sovereignty held sway and where a *dirigiste* tradition has involved the active and direct participation of the public authorities in the working of the economic system. Such *étatisme* has been a notorious characteristic of France, where paternalistic government officials have generally regarded the private sector as composed at best of "partners" and at worst of satellites. The agencies of the state enjoy a monopoly of legitimate authority with which private bodies may be associated at the behest of the government. The relationship between the public authorities and business is conceived primarily in hierarchical and unilateral terms, with government bodies exercising regulatory tutelage over their private sector clientele.

This approach, which until recently was not merely a normative description of what the government-business relationship should be but a fairly realistic description of what it actually was in France, has not been confined to that country. In Britain, which has subscribed to a less authoritarian conception of government-business relations, private business is regarded by S. E. Finer as "only a sub-species of public administration" and, Finer notes, "economic management (so-called *free enterprise*) is nothing else than a *very highly decentralised form of public administration*"; while Finer does not suggest that in Britain this surrogate relationship of private business to the government necessarily implies the French kind of coercive state idealism in practice, his suggestion that "private enterprise is a system of public management by private persons" undoubtedly makes the authority of business derivative from a state which chooses to delegate certain functions to private agents.[1] In the special circumstances of the First and Second World Wars the relationship may in practice have seemed to approximate such a "surrogateship" and it is also true that it was not possible simply to revert to the prewar "normalcy." The employer associations in both France and Britain received a great fillip during the First World War, their respective peak organizations being created either during or immediately after it thanks to assistance from government.[2] The Second World War further strengthened the trade associations as the main links between business and government; they became agents of the latter in controlling and coordinating the former. However, the postwar disengagement of business representative organizations from this administrative embrace went much further in Britain, both out of reluctance to collaborate closely with a Labour government and because Conservative governments were ideologically committed to restoring an "arm's length" relationship.

Despite the fact that "the man in Whitehall," unlike the man in the Rue de Rivoli, is not assumed to know best, it has been claimed that in Britain business has been dominated by a civil service elite and has accepted "a Whitehall consensus."[3] While such assertions have the attractions of paradox, their implausibility becomes apparent as soon as the contrast with France is made. The process of *pantouflage*, which peoples the top managerial posts in the French public and private corporations and creates an interlocking economic directorate trained in the *grandes écoles* and apprenticed in the public service, has no equivalent in Britain. Insofar as there is any "colonization" of big firms by Whitehall, it takes the form—apart from tax inspectors—of a trickle of senior officials at the end of their career into posts that utilize their Whitehall knowledge and contacts in the service of their firm, rather than the occupancy of key managerial positions. The whole image of Whitehall as "unbusinesslike," requiring if anything an injection of private sector entrepreneurs to enable the government to discharge its industrial functions adequately, downgrades the standing of the bureaucracy in a society where the profit motive has traditionally enjoyed a prestige and legitimacy that it is painfully seeking to acquire in France. Insofar as the business world seeks to borrow luster from other elites it would seem from the large number of peers of the realm gracing British boards of directors[4] that pride of officially conferred rank rather than school-made merit is regarded as an asset.

A rival approach, emphasizing the pressure exerted by powerful groups upon a government that is relatively passive, responding to impulses from its environment rather than itself taking the initiative, tends to be more characteristic of pluralistic countries such as the United States or Britain. The government, rather than being conceived of as the supreme coercive power, is regarded as the creature of the consent of private bodies, elevated as a result into the position of veto groups. Compromise and a reluctance to exert public power characterize a relationship in which intervention is regarded as a piecemeal, incremental, intermittent phenomenon responding to particular pressures in a context where matters are normally resolved by market forces. While in the United States the influence on government that business organizations enjoy would seem to outweigh by far the pressures exerted by labor, in Britain the situation has become a more tripartite one, with the trade unions, at first in a mainly negative sense and more recently in a more positive way, seeking to share in the making of the major industrial policy decisions and in 1974 having attributed to them the responsibility for toppling a Conservative government.

In Britain, where the implicit norms owe more to *laissez-faire* than to *dirigisme*, the presumption has been that government agencies should avoid interfering with market forces as far as possible. This view was reflected in the Conservative government's 1970 description of the function of the new Department of Trade and Industry (DTI): "It is the Department's task to establish a general framework of requirements, incentives and restraints within which firms can operate as freely as possible to their own individual advantage."[5] However, the anachronistic assumption that such activities would be pursued solely through the market process rather than by securing the DTI's help to manipulate the market to their advantage was rapidly exposed as an illusion. Far from being able to content itself with the unselective, nondiscriminatory construction of a general framework within which competition could be left to operate freely, both Labour and Conservative governments have felt compelled to come to the assistance of a series of firms in poor financial shape. Such an ad hoc attitude is a natural consequence of the sponsorship role which has been the salient feature of government-business relations in Britain.

While the chairman of the Trade and Industry Subcommittee of the House of Commons Expenditure Committee bluntly described sponsorship as "holding the hand of the private sector at the expense of the taxpayer,"[6] the DTI preferred to describe it as "partly a responsibility for handling the problems which these industries present to the Government and partly for assisting them to strengthen their economic and export performance and technological strength."[7] This characterization of official sponsorship suggests its duality, reflecting both the traditional passive willingness to respond to requests for help by business and the newer, more interventionist activities. The House of Commons Expenditure Committee's report for 1970-71 brought out the reluctance to adopt the second type of sponsorship: "DTI said in March 1971 that in the field of financial aid to industry the Department might on occasions take the initiative, but it was primarily for firms to come to the Government with proposals. If a particular part of private industry said to the Government that within the existing framework it could not make ends meet, the Government could take one of three courses. It could alter the framework; it could let the firm or sector of industry go under; or it could offer special assistance provided that a plan could be put forward demonstrating that there was a likelihood of commercial viability in the end."[8]

The increased interdependence of business and government has meant that both in France and Britain a system of de facto power sharing has developed within an institutionalized system of reciprocal influence. Rather than a one-sided emphasis upon either state intervention or business pressure, which although they can be identified as distinct activities are part of a complex system of reciprocal relationships, it will be necessary to explore both the major governmental economic agencies and the employer associations involved in the system before we can assess their contribution to industrial policy in the two countries.

THE ECONOMIC AGENCIES OF GOVERNMENT

The increasingly extensive and intimate involvement of government agencies in the industrial life of liberal democratic polities, which may go as far as nationalization but usually stops short of it, has led both to institutional changes and shifts in the distribution of power within the executive and among its interest group interlocutors. There have also been concomitant changes in the formal and informal channels through which reciprocal influence has been exerted and representations have been made. Because there has been anxiety that these developments lack liberal democratic legitimacy, formal representative arrangements have been on a consultative basis, but this precaution has still not averted attacks on the "corporatist" nature of the relations between government and business. In any case it is generally recognized that attempts to overcome the compartmentalized verticality within and between both administration and industry are more important at the unofficial level which is decisive as far as the actual implementation of formal changes is concerned. Whereas a traditional style of government-industry relationship directed primarily at preserving stability could rely largely on formal and indirect links with the mass of firms through their representative associations, an industrial policy directed at securing specific changes tends to favor informal and direct contacts with the large firms who have the real power to take the relevant decisions.

Given the traditionally bilateral nature of links between sponsor departments and particular industries, matched by the "vertical" structure of both government and business organization, it has been natural for both "intervention" and "pressure" to be piecemeal. However, attempts have been made to secure ad hoc political coordination through interministerial committees and administrative coordination through interdepartmental committees, while a Cabinet Economic Policy Standing Committee under the chairmanship of the Prime Minister provides a forum for general economic oversight. In France the Prime Minister has a better equipped private office to help in this task, while the Planning Commissariat provides him with a more effective instrument for advising on the strategic definition of objections and the arbitration of disputes than is the case with the Central Policy Review Staff attached to the Cabinet Office in Britain (since 1970). Despite the fact that an interventionist Prime Minister (and President of the Republic in France) may on occasion overrule the Treasury and Finance Ministry, the normal "horizontal" corrective to the verticalism of the sponsor ministries is provided by the macroeconomic department primarily concerned with controlling public expenditure and monetary policy.

In both countries left-wing governments twice attempted to avoid the subordination of overall economic policy to a ministry with predominantly financial concerns that had been accustomed to deal with industry only through the sponsor ministries. All four attempts failed, although one could argue that the Treasury and Finance Ministry did not emerge unscathed once they had absorbed their rivals. The successive reorganizations of the Treasury in the 1960s, particularly in conjunction with the development of five-year planning of public expenditure, have extended its perspectives, while it developed new arrangements (discussed below) with the Ministry of Technology (MinTech) partially to avoid the kind of detailed control over day-to-day transactions that deprived the sponsor ministry of responsibility for its own activities. However, whereas in France the Prime Minister had at his disposal the Planning Commissariat, which gave him an independent capability vis a vis the Finance Ministry, in Britain the weakness of the National Economic Development Office—it is very much in the shadow of its Council—the NEDO provided no such countervailing capability. The survival, despite its vicissitudes, of national economic planning in France, exercised some pressure upon the Finance Ministry to go beyond a purely case-by-case approach to requests for public money, but its tendency to operate increasingly by offering incentives to particular firms has, if anything, accentuated its propensity to a piecemeal, incremental approach. Another factor reinforcing the piecemeal character of negotiations between business and government is the tendency for *cabinets ministériels* and even ministers to become involved in support of particular industrial projects so that political rather than economic considerations become of foremost importance.

Symmetrical with the compartmentalization of the sponsor ministries, there is a great fragmentation of employer associations which are the clientele of particular divisions within the central administration. The peak organizations have the widest range of contacts, but like the other employer associations their regular access to government is through the major industrial ministry: the Department of Industry (DOI) in Britain and the Ministry of Industrial and Scientific Development (MISD) in France. The DOI has had a particularly protean past. Until the creation of MinTech in October 1964 by an incoming Labour government the Board of Trade (BOT) dating back to and still representing the ultra-laissez-faire attitudes of the late eighteenth century, was the ministry mainly responsible for relations with business. Just as it was felt that the new macroeconomic policies to be pursued would be better discharged if the Treasury were partially circumvented by a new Department of Economic Affairs, MinTech was established to supplement the negative, regulatory BOT approach (working primarily through the trade associations) with a positive, modernizing role carried out through the new Economic Development Committees (EDCs) and directly with large firms. MinTech, after a slow start, proved to be the rather more successful innovation.

Sir Richard Clarke, Permanent Secretary of MinTech from 1966 to 1970, has described how his department evolved through a series of mergers into what in practice was a Ministry of Engineering and then a Ministry of Industry. In the process MinTech acquired new functions, including the sponsorship of industries hitherto undertaken by the BOT, while according to Clarke, "Aircraft and atomic energy, much the biggest recipients of government industrial money (and in departmental enclaves of their own) were brought within the main stream of industrial and economic policy."[9] Clarke diagnosed the central political predicament of trying to formulate and implement an industrial policy in Britain as one of imposing a responsibility on government while denying it the correlative knowledge and power. To the extent that government then fell back on the provision of financial support, detailed intervention had meant that in some cases "the top management find it easier to seek the company's income by bringing pressure on the department instead of by developing the competitive power of the business."[10]

Given the obvious financial dangers involved and the threat that Treasury public expenditure control would as a consequence become particularly constricting, MinTech negotiated a "concordat" with the Treasury in July 1968;[11] this action is rather interesting, given the extent to which the French industrial ministry has been crippled as an agency of industrial policy owing to its servitude to the Ministry of Finance. The main purpose of this agreement was to replace the detailed scrutiny of MinTech's expenditure by a "continuing dialogue" in terms of totals, not of items or day-to-day transactions. Treasury consent to such a relaxation of control could only be obtained by MinTech's preparing a strategy covering all its expenditure, which was then subdivided into three categories. First, expenditures susceptible to effective departmental control, which could be programmed as much as ten years ahead, would be covered by a "ration," with provision for negotiated annual changes. This embraced a large part of civil expenditure, including grants to industrial research associations, development contracts for industry, preproduction orders for machine tools, and so forth. The ministry made its own assessment of the priority to be accorded each of its expenditures within this category. Second, there were the expenditures that could not be programmed five years ahead because of uncertainty and therefore had to be settled ad hoc between MinTech and the Treasury. Projects like Concorde, shipbuilding and industrial reorganization schemes, and advances to the Industrial Reorganization Corporation (IRC), were within this category. Lastly came MinTech's expenditures under open-ended statutory commitments, such as investment grants, which were not susceptible to Treasury restraint. Provided the Treasury could be satisfied that MinTech had developed a system of economic appraisal, adopting consistent criteria covering all its expenditure decisions, it was prepared to concede a degree of freedom from detailed supervision that was the envy of the French Ministry of Industry, which sought to remodel itself in 1969 on MinTech lines. MinTech was amalgamated with the BOT by the Conservatives in 1970 into a vast Department of Trade and Industry combining the government's responsibility for relations with both public and private enterprise and simplifying communication between industry and the administration. This merger was unscrambled, however, by the 1974 Labour government, the incoming Secretary of State for Industry recognizing his department as very much like the MinTech he had left in 1970.

The French Ministry of Industrial and Scientific Development (MISD) was the successor to the traditionally feeble Ministry of Industry, split between "vertical" divisions having strong clientele relations with particular industries and acting as their spokesman within the administration. The only thorough investigator of this area of French public administration, Erhard Friedberg, has suggested that the traditional pattern involved close ties between a highly segmentalized bureaucratic structure "partnered" by a symmetrical set of trade associations. Each side was extremely weak: the bureaucrats because it was the Finance Ministry that wielded the state banking power, and the trade associations because they usually had little authority over their member firms. Yet they were interdependent in that contact with the trade associations "gave the ministry officials the illusion that they were in touch with industrial reality," while the employers' associations could impress their member firms with an equally illusory access to the government.[12] The only exceptions to this stable but dysfunctional system of government-industry relations are provided by a few powerful divisions that enjoy ties with major firms in the public or private sector thanks to their common membership in the prestigious corps of mining engineers.

The attempt to create a more powerful and integrated MISD failed. Although it was backed by the establishment in 1969 of an Industrial Policy Interministerial Committee to improve coordination, this committee seldom met. Just as the specialized divisions of MISD destroyed the attempt to centralize power in an Industrial Policy Division, so the Finance Ministry prevented MISD from loosening its grip over the disbursement of public funds. The result of this failure to make the MISD the instrument of a more integrated industrial policy decision-making process has been to undermine the position of the employer association mediators between the government and the firms. There has been recourse to informal negotiations between the large firms and the government, relying increasingly on the *corps des mines* and more generally on the *polytechnicien* network of senior officials scattered throughout the relevant ministries and in *cabinets ministériels*, as well as in top positions in leading companies.[13] The frequent involvement of ministers in such matters, including the   Prime Minister and even the President of the Republic, encourages a highly politicized, case-by-case approach to industrial policy, depending very much on circumstances, such as the likelihood of substantial unemployment in sensitive areas or the proximity of an election. Thus the horizontal coordination which the traditional administration has shown itself incapable of fulfilling has meant that the ministries have to some extent been superseded, although in certain concentrated sectors like steel the trade association has controlled the interface between government and the firms.

As in Britain, government solicitude has been attracted by the weakness of a major firm or more often of an entire industry, so that industrial decisions are more a collection of expedients than the consequences of a deliberate policy. Although no common strategy has inspired the actions of the French government, it is possible to discern three categories of industry with which it has especially close relations.[14] First, rearguard action has been taken to slow down the regression of declining industries prior to a reallocation of resources to more resilient sectors. Both in France and Britain, shipbuilding has been a leading example in the private sector, while until recently coal has been a notable example in the public sector. Political pressure to cushion the shock of redundancy is especially great when the problem is localized in areas with little alternative employment. Even in industries such as steel, which are not actually declining but where technological advance has meant that less labor is required and production is shifting from inland Lorraine to the coastal plants of Dunkirk and Fos, state support is sought and secured in France, while in Britain intense pressure is exerted on the nationalized British Steel Corporation not to close down an obsolete plant. This type of geriatric treatment for ailing industrial combatants can be described as offering them the succor of *Les Invalides* or the Chelsea Pensioners in their old age.

Second, to protect national independence and prestige, particularly in areas where military considerations arise, the French and British governments have sought to preserve and to promote the development of technologically advanced industries. The main industries where this policy of securing the survival of a favored firm through the input of public funds and purchases have operated are nuclear power, computers, and the aerospace industry. In each case the attempt to back or create national champions has run into difficulties, compelling the firms to have reluctant recourse to collaboration with foreign firms. Third, this leads naturally to attempts to help industries that are especially exposed to foreign competition, usually by a crisis intervention when a major firm or industry appears about to succumb to overwhelming financial difficulties. In both countries the machine tools industry has had to receive such fire brigade assistance on more than one occasion.

Whether or not the firm or industry working with the government is in public or private ownership seems to have had little effect on the closeness of their collaboration. Paradoxically in Britain, where business hostility to nationalization has taken a far more vociferous and doctrinaire form than in France, public corporations were welcomed into membership by the Confederation of British Industries (CBI) at its inception in 1965, although it was only in 1969 that corporations exchanged the status of associate without voting rights for that of full member, The French *Conseil National du Patronat Français* (CNPF) has no such links and none are contemplated (if only because they would doubtless raise problems of jurisprudence), while in Italy and Sweden the public corporations have actually been ordered by the government to leave the peak business organization and form their own association. In Britain, the new ecumenism has not been without its problems, symbolized by the existence of two CBI committees dealing respectively with state intervention in private industry and private and public sector relationships. The Central Bank in both countries has provided an equivocal link between the public and private sectors, although the much greater

autonomy and strength of the City of London has meant that the Governor of
the Bank of England is more the spokesman of the private financial interests,
whereas the Governor of the Bank of France is subject to closer Treasury
control.

EMPLOYER ASSOCIATIONS

Whereas British business emerged from the Second World War enjoying
a virtuous identification with patriotic work for victory, most French business
suffered from guilt by association with Vichy and even collaboration with the
enemy. In any case, business and its values have traditionally had much lower
public standing in France than in Britain. A private opinion poll
commissioned in France by the CNPF on the public attitudes toward business
yielded results so horrific that they were never published. There is scant
information of a similar nature available in Britain, although when asked
about the distribution of power in the country the public considers that the
trade unions are the most powerful organizations. Particularly when the term
"large firms" is substituted for "big business," the employers are (rather
curiously) considered to have less influence on the way the country is run than
do the trade unions.[15] The poor image of big business in France is doubtless
due in part to the survival of an immense small business sector. French
microenterprise is far more assertive than its modest British counterpart,
which more readily accepts the hegemony of the large firms. In France the
mass of small shopkeepers and artisans have been willing to resort to direct
action when the representations made on their behalf have been unsuccessful,
and the government has frequently yielded to their demands, not merely in the
fiscal and social security spheres but in the matter of avoiding competition
from bigger business. The 1973 Royer Act, for instance, gave the small
shopkeepers a virtual veto over the intrusion of supermarket chains into their
preserves, threatening to stop the clock as far as the modernization of French
distribution is concerned.

However, whereas Poujade in the 1950s and Nicoud in the late 1960s and
early 1970s have been the vociferous advocates of the usually self-employed
mass of those who are struggling to survive in an era with an emphasis on
large-scale industry, it is the CGPME, or General Confederation of Small and
Medium Sized Firms, dominated for thirty years (1944-73) by Léon
Gingembre, that is the most representative organization of smaller industrial
business. Gingembre, like Poujade and Nicoud, fits well into R. H.
Salisbury's version of an exchange theory explanation of the origin of interest
groups in terms of an entrepreneur-organizer. Although he also played an
active part in the 1946 creation of the CNPF, having as early as 1929 been
responsible for liaison between the Paris Chamber of Commerce and the

CGPF (the CNPF's predecessor), Gengembre was a firm proponent of the separate identity of small business, denouncing "the myth of the private sector's unity." Having deliberately drafted Article 2 of the CNPF's rules to ensure that it would be a weak liaison committee between trade associations, regional associations, and his CGPME, he effectively withdrew his organization from the CNPF in 1948. Explaining his declaration of independence from the CNPF, Gingembre asserted: "I became aware that when we went to see government bodies, it was always the problems of the chemical, steel or other big business sectors that were discussed. When I tried to raise the problems of small and medium sized firms, this was treated as inopportune."[16] As far as tactics are concerned Gingembre stressed that, to gain official recognition, he had first to engage in "brutal" direct action before winning permanent consultative status. However, increasingly the CGPME has turned away from pure pressure group action of the type exemplified in the 1960s by Nicoud's *Comité d'Information et de Défense* (CID), and concentrated on the provisions of services, thereby diverging from the view (discussed below) that pressure group action is the by-product of an organization offering selective incentives to membership.

In Britain the Smaller Businesses Association is a pale shadow of the CGPME. Set up because it rightly feared that the CBI would be dominated by big business and would be inclined to work closely with the government of the day, it has failed to impress either civil servants or ministers, a living testimony to the ineffectiveness of small business as a pressure group in Britain.[17] The CBI, in its desire to avoid identification as a purely big business institution, created a Smaller Firms Council but this has not materially increased the influence of small business. Lacking public law status and the funds that come with it, appealing to tradesmen rather than industrialists, British chambers of commerce have not played the representative role on behalf of provincial smaller business that the French chambers have fulfilled—so much so that the CNPF's regional associations are rather weak as a consequence. In Britain firms attach only limited importance to the representational work—either at national or local level—of the chambers of commerce, but their services in export documentation and promotion are valued highly.[18]

TRADE ASSOCIATIONS

The relatively large number of small firms that have survived in France compared to Britain has not encouraged an intensely competitive relationship between them. This is not due simply to governmental toleration or active promotion of cartels. J. H. McArthur and B. R. Scott have shown that the prevalence of market sharing by agreement, frequently extended to cover agreements on the timing of investments or joint ventures to achieve the scale of operations required by modern technology,[19] has tended to favor the preservation of the existing industrial structure and to find its institutional expression in the trade associations (TA's). Henry Ehrmann and other observers have stressed the importance of the Organization Committees during the Vichy period in fostering the development of TA's, which as voluntary organizations had generally not made much headway. Employers became accustomed to paying dues and providing statistical information, while the TA's in a new guise acquired the funds, knowledge, and staff that made many of them effective for the first time.[20] This wartime period of detailed state intervention and virtual incorporation of employer associations into the government apparatus brought out the complementary nature of trade associations and government regulation. TA's flourished mainly at times when member firms looked to them for help vis à vis administrative constraint. To the extent that market forces are free to operate, what divides the firms in a particular industry becomes more important than what unites them. The leaders and staff of the TA's, therefore, have a vested interest in the preservation of an extensive system of state regulation, which enables them to provide the multitude of specific personal services that attract the support of member firms, in the same way that a deputy or mayor secures the votes of his constituents. The semipermanent character of price control in France ensures that firms frequently rely on their TA for help in obtaining exemption or favorable treatment.

The symmetry between the structure of TA's and that of their supervisory-cum-sponsor ministries is very great, divisions within the ministry corresponding fairly closely to the clientele of a major TA. Taken in conjunction with the fact that the permanent staff of these associations tend to be recruited by *pantouflage* from the public service, a symbiosis develops between particular subdivisions of the MISD and individual TA's. The increased status of the top association officials, engaged in semipermanent dealings with their opposite numbers in government departments, means that they cannot be confined to the role of mere spokesmen but enjoy the freedom of action necessary for the conduct of successful negotiations on behalf of their members. Most important TA's tend to be dominated by a "tandem made up of a businessman and an association official," respectively holding the office of president and director general.[21] In part the former confers the necessary legitimacy on the actions of the latter, but when the president is able to remain in day-to-day contact with the association's activities he may be in effective personal control or at least in joint control with the senior business bureaucrat. A particularly striking example of such a tandem relationship has existed for a decade in the CBI between the president and the director general, as we shall see below.

Jacques Lautman has usefully distinguished four types of French TA presidents.[22] First, there is the traditional business notable, usually the elderly head of a medium-sized family business with time on his hands, who can represent and mediate on behalf of all the heterogeneous firms in the trade, for example mechanical engineering. Second, there is the business bureaucrat who is promoted from the management of a large firm to a TA presidency as an apotheosis preliminary to retirement. His modest role is to coordinate the specialized activities of diversified groups, for example in electronics and chemicals. Third comes the big business managing director, with the status that the market power of this firm confers. The smaller firms accept his leadership because they do not challenge his firm's share of the market, or else have become mere subcontractors. As the process of industrial mergers develops, this type of TA leader will become increasingly common. Lastly there is the TA official who after many years as director general becomes the association's president. Although these are often former *polytechniciens*, two of the most striking examples of this type—Jacques Ferry, president of the steel trade association (CSSF) and head of the biggest business group (see below), and François Ceyrac, who became president of the CNPF after working his way to the top of the Engineering Employers Confederation (UIMM)—were both products of *Sciences Po*. They have to make up in *grande école* prestige and experience what they lack in legitimacy as "genuine" businessmen. In exceptional cases a TA director general may, like Pierre de Calan, start in the public service as an *inspecteur de finance* and then head the cotton industry TA for fourteen years before becoming managing director in a major nontextile firm and a powerful voice inside the CNPF.

That the CSSF and UIMM should both have been headed by TA officials is interesting, since they are descendants of the *Comité des Forges*, which from the mid-nineteenth century was the dominant employer association in France.[23] While the UIMM (like the Engineering Employers Federation in Britain) is concerned primarily with industrial relations (that is, with trade unions) and is an employers' organization rather than a trade association, embracing the engineering industry in general and not just the steel industry, the CSSF provides a rare example of a TA not merely offering traditional services but guiding the strategies of its member firms. It has dealings with the executive, the judiciary, and the legislature on behalf of its members. It exchanges information with the MISD's Iron and Steel Division and has frequent dealings with the Finance Ministry's Taxation Divisions. It tests in court tax cases affecting its member firms. It does public relations work with members of Parliament and makes representations to parliamentary groups on its own or with CNPF delegations. Its president frequently gives evidence to the Production Commissions of the Assembly and Senate. The services it offers to member firms include comparative studies of costs, centralized purchasing of raw materials and fuel, common research, and above all collective financing of investment. In 1950 the CSSF set the pattern, followed subsequently and less effectively by the chemicals, electrical engineering, and metalworking industries among others, of joint borrowing through the *Groupement des Industries Sidérurgiques* (GIS), which enabled the CSSF both to know the investment plans of the major steel firms in detail and to influence them. The CSSF was also involved in close dealings with the steel division of MISD—which approves each firm's share in a loan—and with the Finance Ministry, which fixes the total amount that GIS is allowed to raise in the capital market. "This pyramiding of authorizations to borrow money opened the way for negotiations at each level—between company and industrial association, association and (MISD) directorate, and directorate and Ministry of Finance."[24] The CSSF under Ferry's leadership was thereby able to play a pivotal role in shaping the industry's strategy.

The problem of securing cohesion in business organizations has led to the proliferation of a plurality of organizations servicing the same sector. A trio of American scholars have argued that, to avoid splitting over controversial issues, TA's give expression to unresolved differences through a multiplicity of specialized associations designed to cope with specific problems while preserving "quasi-unanimity."[25] The Devlin Report on industrial representation in Britain made some harshly frank comments on the fragmented structure of TA's that is said to lead to an excessive number of "disconnected associations, each serving its own limited purposes," encouraging "the parochial outlook of businessmen who do not see beyond their own particular product."[26] Whereas most critics of British industrial representation have concentrated their fire on the trade union movement's inadequate structure, lack of centralized authority, and inability to enforce discipline, the Devlin Report made it abundantly clear that these failings are present to at least the same extent in employer associations. While the report's spectacular proposal to create a comprehensive Confederation of British Business attracted the greatest public attention, it was its more mundane suggestion about the rationalization of TA structure that promised the most fundamental change toward effective industrial representation. Four kinds of TA's were distinguished in the report. In some industries there was one dominant organization, such as the Society of Motor Manufacturers and Traders or the Chemical Industries Association. In others, like textiles, electronics, and the distributive trades, there was a consortium. In a third type, such as construction, food and drink, or nonferrous metals, there were several effective associations. And the last and most numerous category of highly fragmented representation included mechanical engineering, clothing, footwear, mining, and fishing. The Devlin Report recommended that the CBI should seek to reduce the number of affiliated TA's and EO's (employer organizations which negotiate with trade unions on industrial relations rather than with the government) from some 200 to about 40. However, it tempered the severity of its diagnosis with a stress on the voluntary nature of mergers and a hope that a combination of foreign competition with more attention by firms to the associations of which they are members would speed the rationalization of TA structure.[27]

The Devlin Report estimated that British TA's had only half the income of their continental counterparts, and this was reflected by the fact that most of them were understaffed and overworked. The report noted that 311 out of the 865 associations surveyed had only part-time staff; 100 boasted a full-time staff of one; 231 had more than one official; and 223 indicated no staff at all and were usually serviced by an accountant or a solicitor. Although like French TA's the more prestigious British associations attract a number of senior civil servants, the general caliber of staffs is low because of the low salaries that they are paid. The report noted: "The DTI considers that within its coverage only a relatively small number of the hundreds of trade associations with which it deals can be considered fully effective. The overwhelming majority adopt a highly cooperative attitude towards the Department's work but many are limited by the resources available."[28] It was found that the TA's seldom disposed of the information necessary to support their case in dealings with the government, or were unable to provide it with rapid and full replies to its requests for information. Unlike France, where until recently the government depended for its industrial statistics on the TA's, in Britain "more often than not, these associations had to rely upon government for information about industry."[29]

Although the report showed four-fifths of the TA's had dealings with both the central government and nationalized industries, while three-fifths had contact with local authorities, government departments are more inclined to approach large firms directly rather than through the TA's, which are more representative of the views and interests of the smaller firms. The big companies have easy access to the ministries and do not need an introduction from their TA. As for the small firms, they place "representation to government" after "the opportunity to make social contact with other companies in the sector" and "the provision of general market or technical information."[30] These and other more technical functions like standards and export promotion have been developed to supplement the price fixing and market sharing activities which continue covertly to play an important role in the life of TA's despite the passage of the 1956 Restrictive Trade Practices Act. The large firms generally tolerate the TA's because the latters' support or cover lends legitimacy and openness to the formers' backstairs dealings with the government, while the TA's depend on the financial support and power of the large firms to give them such credibility as they enjoy with government bodies.

PEAK ORGANIZATIONS

We saw above that one way in which employer associations deal with the problem of ensuring their survival is to diversify into a large number of specialized bodies, but this does not meet the need for a multipurpose peak organization (PO) to express a collective standpoint. Given the axiom, "The broader and more heterogeneous the organization, the greater the problem that some sub-groups will dissent on a given issue," it is natural for the PO to take refuge in the evasion of controversial matters and, where it has to formulate a precise policy, to avoid internal friction by simply not enforcing it on its own members.[31] These tactics enable it to keep up the pretense of unanimity and are a common feature of the behavior of PO's not merely in the United States but also in Britain and France. Such pusillanimous conduct is frequently the subject of caustic comment, but it might be presented as elementary prudence by leaders conscious of the fragility of their hold over members united in a voluntary association. In his *Reflections on the Revolution in France*, Edmund Burke argued, "In all bodies, those who will lead, must also, in a considerable degree, follow. They must conform their propositions to the taste, talent and disposition of those whom they wish to conduct."[32] This is a view which has been put more paradoxically in the common French witticism, "As I was their leader, I had to follow them." As we shall see, following the reorganization in the 1960s of the PO's in the two countries—a similar attempt in Italy having failed—a more assertive style of leadership developed. However, in Britain the CBI has suffered internal stresses because its leadership has sought to act in a way that it believes best serves the interests of business rather than reflecting the "quasi-unanimity" of organized business opinion, while in France the more cautious approach of the CNPF has meant that its leaders have generally preserved a better facade of organizational placidity.

In his influential study, *The Logic of Collective Action*, M. Olson argues that in large organizations "the rational individual . . . will not be willing to make any sacrifices to achieve the objectives he shares with others. There is accordingly no presumption that large groups will organize to act in their common interests."[33] To explain why people nevertheless join associations Olson stresses their ability to offer "selective incentives," that is, benefits restricted to members which offset the cost of belonging to a group and which can be withdrawn as a selective sanction. Selective incentives are available to organizations having "the authority and the capacity to be coercive" or "*positive inducements* that they can offer the individuals in a latent group."[34] The lobbying activities of such associations are dismissed as a by-product of the provision of services, given the limited coercive power of PO's. Yet the evidence suggests that although members of such bodies may not rate them sufficiently highly to warrant paying more than a pittance toward their running costs, and despite the fact that the activities of such associations often reflect the purposes of small, self-recruiting, and self-perpetuating oligarchies rather than those of the membership, Olson does not provide a satisfactory explanation of the creation and duration of employer associations. We have already observed that small business PO's in France are started by entrepreneur-organizers concentrating on securing collective benefits through pressure for changes in public policy, although they later tend to place increased emphasis on the provision of selective services. A forthcoming study of the CBI by David Marsh and Wyn Grant, which attempts to test the Olson thesis, suggests that in Britain, while small firms place greater stress on the services offered, collective benefits offered in dealings with government constitute the main incentives.

Because the membership charges are very modest and benefits are difficult to calculate, few firms have made "a cost-benefit analysis of CBI membership. Most felt they should join or were persuaded to join and the costs involved were not sufficiently high to impel them towards the rationality threshold."[35] Many firms were found not familiar with the services that the CBI could offer and, in the case of the large firms who were more likely to have this information, they seldom had such need and were more likely to come to the help of the CBI than vice versa. Although they have private access to the relevant ministries, the big firms place particular emphasis on their PO spokesman function vis à vis the government and as a counterweight to the TUC. Thus in Olsonian terms CBI members appear to act irrationally. "They make little use of services and other selective incentives yet the collective incentives they claim to value would be available to them even if they were non-members."[36] While Salisbury's economic model shares with Olson the view (misleading as far as PO's are concerned) that "most group activity has little to do with efforts to affect public policy decisions but is concerned rather with the internal exchange of benefits by which the group is organized and sustained," Salisbury places greater emphasis on nonmaterial benefits, particularly sociability and normative or ideological benefits,[37] which seems to correspond more closely with such empirical investigation of French and British PO's as has been made. The pressure to join exerted by group opinion is also a potent incentive, particularly when the cost of membership in terms of subscription fee and discipline to be endured is not high.

Both the CBI and the CNPF have managed to attract a large part of their potential constituency into membership, particularly the larger firms. Thus the CBI—which unlike the CNPF has firms as direct members—embraced in mid-1952 146 of the 200 largest companies listed in the *Times* (London), including 85 percent of the 153 industrial firms but only a third of the 47 commercial firms. At that time 50 percent of the 1,000 largest firms were members, as well as almost all the major TA's and employer organizations.[38] While the CBI practice of having firms as direct members is less tidy than the CNPF arrangement, it provides greater scope for large firms to exert their influence and avoids domination of the PO by TA's that generally give undue weight to the views of smaller firms. The CNPF's weakness is that it is more of a confederation of TA's, and this prompted Jacques Ferry in 1969—the year in which the CNPF was reorganized to increase its effectiveness—to set up AGREF (*Association des grandes enterprises françaises faisant appel à l'épargne*) specifically to speak out for big business. TA's have a majority of seats on the CNPF Permanent Assembly and General Council, but they are in a minority on the CBI Council.

Figure 5.1 sets out the formal organization structures of both the CBI and CNPF. The most important omission is any reference to the role of PO officials, which is particularly serious in the case of the CBI director general. In its first ten years of existence the CBI has had only two incumbents: John Davies, who left in 1970 to become Secretary of State for Trade and Industry in the Conservative government, and Campbell Adamson, a long-standing nationalized steel industry executive who served as coordinator of industrial affairs at the Department of Economic Affairs under the Labour government. Although the president and the director general generally go together to see ministers and officials, because the CBI presidency changes hands every two years, it is the director general who tends to personify the organization. On the other hand the CNPF president is elected for a three-year term and can be reelected once with the possibility of a year's further extension, which partly accounts for his stronger position vis à vis his business bureaucrats Adamson's position was seriously weakened when he made a bitter attack on the Conservative government's Industrial Relations Act just before the February 1974 General Election. Already suspected by many of his owner-manager members of being too avant-garde in his views, the damage he inflicted on the political friends of business was taken as a pretext for curbing his freedom of action. The internal pressures are now for the CBI to concentrate more attention on industrial opinion and become less of an adjunct of government.

The CNPF Executive Council and the CBI's General Purpose Committee are both a sort of "general staff" or PO Cabinet. The CNPF Executive Council consists of the heads of the major French employer associations—steel, chemicals, automobiles, petroleum, textiles—which pay most of the CNPF's running costs. UIMM alone accounts for 22 percent of the CNPF's income, so it is perhaps not surprising that Ceyrac, elected president of CNPF unopposed in December 1972, was then head of UIMM. Three of the CNPF's vice-presidents chair its key commissions dealing with economic policy, industrial relations, and international economic relations. The chairmen of CBI committees—usually the directors of large firms—are appointed by the president, who chairs the General Purpose Committee himself.[39] The other two especially important CBI committees deal with economic and employment policy. Unlike the CNPF, the CBI has not developed an active role in negotiation with the trade unions on industrial relations matters.

While the CBI came into existence thanks in part to business's need to have a more authoritative exponent of its views in the planning-cum-interventionist context of Britain in the mid-1960s, the CNPF's 1969 reorganization was its response to the general strike of May-June 1968.

FIGURE 5.1: Employer Peak Organization Structures in Britain and France*

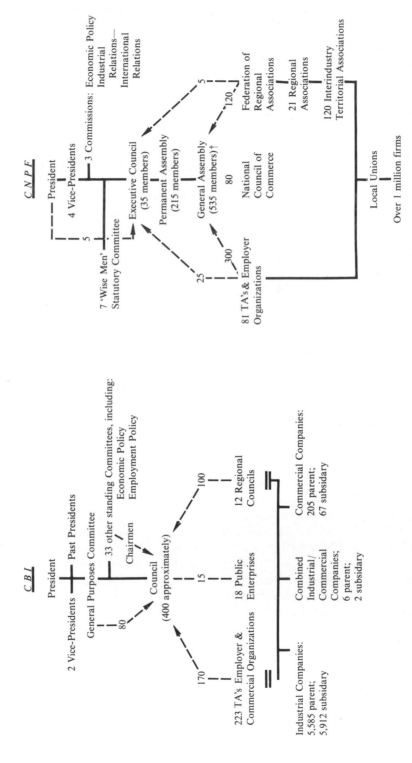

* Most of this data relates to the situation as at mid-1972
† There are 30 associate and 5 coopted members

136

Conscious that its negative attitude toward the trade unions and government had contributed materially to the crisis, it sought increased strength and responsibility to act on behalf of its members and not merely seek the protection and assistance of government. This meant changing the traditional tactics described by Michel Crozier in these terms: "Paradoxically, it is by resisting change that the entrepreneurial class is able to extract the most profit from its role as change agent. By sitting tight until a real emergency develops, it obliges the State to come to terms with it and reinforce the privileges of the bourgeois dynasties."[40] The traumatic experience of the Grenelle negotiations in May 1968 produced not the retreat into introversion that followed the 1936 Matignon Agreement, but rather an increased willingness to accept rather than avoid negotiated commitments. The extent to which the CNPF has carried its rank and file with it is evidenced by an opinion poll of 426 businessmen in November 1970 (see Table 5.1). As one would expect, it is especially among the larger, Paris-based firms that the new CNPF enjoys its greatest support, but even if it is less inclined to lead from behind it spends much of its time looking over its shoulder. Although it has a slightly higher income than the CBI, the CNPF nevertheless only attracts about a fortieth of

TABLE 5.1

**Concordance of Organizational Positions with Those
of French Businessmen in General
(percentages)**

	How Business Views CNPF			
	Accurately Represents	Too Innovative	Too Conservative	No Opinion
Number of Wage Earners Employed				
20-100	44	19	14	23
100-500	45	16	20	19
500 or more	52	7	19	22
Location				
Paris	52	11	19	18
Province	42	17	16	25
Total	47	15	17	21

Source: Sondages, nos. 1-2 (1971), p. 135.

the money spent by French firms on employer associations. Both PO's leave political contributions to other business organizations and thus do not enjoy the leverage that comes from acting as paymaster to political parties or candidates.

While the CNPF, increasingly enamored of market forces, whose verdict the big firms could manipulate rather than be compelled to endure, secured increased freedom from price controls and successfully resisted the adoption of a statutory incomes policy, the CBI launched a successful voluntary price restraint policy which most of its members loyally observed from August 1971 to October 1972. Like wage restraint policies patronized by the TUC when a Labour government is in office, this policy got off to a good start and certainly was an excellent piece of public relations, improving the image of business and strengthening its position vis à vis government by demonstrating its ability to secure sacrifices from its members. The strain on the loyalty of its members grew as they came to consider that their PO was becoming a pliable instrument in the service of the government. Succumbing to the temptations to win Whitehall approval by assuming their share of the burdens of national economic management, the CBI leaders often expressed views before they were able to canvass grassroots business opinion. Had the CBI-backed gamble on growth succeeded, no doubt much would have been forgiven; but its failure meant that Enoch Powell's advice—that the safest posture for an industry confronted by an interventionist government would be not to have an organization or spokesman at all—found a sympathetic audience even if few firms actually resigned from the CBI.

A number of fringe business organizations exist in the two countries, tending in Britain to represent right-wing ideological standpoints, like the Industrial Policy Group or the Institute of Directors, and in France mildly left-wing (by business standards) bodies, such as the Young Managers' movement (*Centre des Jeunes Dirigeants d'Entreprise,* ex-*Centre des Jeunes Patrons*), the Catholic Employers Centre (CFPC), or the currently most lively organization, *Entreprise et Progrès*. Disappointed at the lack of change in the CNPF before 1968—leading to his exclusion from its hierarchy from 1966 to 1968—*Enterprise et Progrès'* director general, José Bidegain, has sought to bring pressure on the CNPF from outside as well as from within. In 1965 he gave up running his family shoe firm to concentrate on making the footwear TA more effective. He has been a force prodding the CNPF forward; witness his 1973 efforts to get the CNPF to accept responsibility for finding a solution to the crisis following the bankruptcy of the Besançon firm of Lip. The fate of change agents like Adamson and Bidegain will be indicators of the readiness with which PO's in the two countries accept new responsibilities vis à vis the trade unions and the government.

Employer Associations and National Planning

Britain and France have borrowed from each other in the matter of industrial planning institutions. And there are instructive differences in what was adopted, how it was transformed, and what the practical results of the operation were. Britain was first in the field in 1945 with the establishment by the Labour president of the Board of Trade of working parties whose role was to investigate industries that were not to be nationalized. They were constituted by equal numbers of employer and trade union members from the industry with the addition of independent members and were operated under an independent chairman. This device was quickly imitated by Jean Monnet in the form of the French modernization commissions which set to work in 1946. All but one of the British working parties recommended the establishment of a permanent body, and the 1947 Industrial Development and Organization Act provided for the establishment of Development Councils. However, partly owing to the late 1940s reaction against the neocorporatist consensus that had developed in the 1930s, and partly because of the fear among the TA's that the proposed councils would take over some of their functions at the same time as they would broaden the basis of "industrial self-government" by including trade unionists, the general creation of such councils was resisted as threatening "backdoor nationalization."[41] Meanwhile in France the Modernization Commissions were presented as the centerpiece of consensus-building in support of the French Plan's objectives. Although TA members accounted for only 12 percent of the total membership in the First Plan compared to 22 percent among business executives, they had overtaken business executives by the Third Plan (16 percent as against 13 percent) and continued to precede them in the Fifth Plan (21 percent against 19 percent).[42] In a country where relations between business and the civil service had been characterized by a mutually reinforcing antagonistic irresponsibility on the part of the former and authoritarian distrust by the latter, the collaborative face-to-face contact secured by the Modernization Commission meetings helped to socialize both sides to new relationships thanks to the mediatory role of the planners.[43]

The disastrous consequences of the British attempt to imitate French planning in the 1960s can be more directly attributed to British business interests and attitudes. Some of the blame must be laid at the door of a public relations presentation of French experience that stressed the persuasive rather than the coercive aspects of planning, calculated to appeal to British businessmen, politicians, and civil servants at a time when a Conservative Britain (that embraced planning and was a candidate for Common Market membership) would have been a useful ally in overcoming German resistance to the Common Market's medium-term planning. However, the main responsibility must be laid at the door of those in Britain—notably a small group within the CBI leadership—who believed that French-style planning would both increase business influence on economic policy and reduce piecemeal government intervention in industry. The claim that industrial planning could be secured by voluntary agreements between employer associations and the government was specious, as we have seen that the peak business association and TA's in Britain—like their equivalents in France—did not have planned policies but reacted to problems after they presented themselves.[44]

Unlike British business which blocked planning at its inception in the late 1940s and promoted its revival in the early 1960s, French business for a long time cooperated with reticence, avoiding precise and binding commitments so as to allow itself freedom to secure a financial quid pro quo in bilateral bargaining with the finance and industry ministries. McArthur and Scott rated the influence of planning on industry as modest, its main function being to provide legitimizing cover for cartel arrangements through the modernization commission *groupes de travail* meetings. With the presence of trade union members, however, inhibiting such activities, only in their absence could the phasing of investment plans be extended to the discussion of allocation of market shares, sources of supply, and pricing policy. The piecemeal, ad hoc, bilateral character of industrial policy making betokened the lack of comprehensive industrial planning. The resulting collection of expedients was decorated with the euphemism of selective intervention but as McArthur and Scott note, "The overall impression is one of a fire-fighting approach: the timing of state actions, the remedial measures, and the industries selected for attention . . . all seemed related to special crises rather than to a predeveloped plan. . . ."[45] Defense, advanced technology, regionally concentrated unemployment due to declining industries, import-saving or export-earning: these were some of the factors motivating state intervention. Because of their representative character the modernization commissions, like TA's, were seldom capable of being truly selective by making choices between conflicting interests, much less doing this in planned fashion.

Even in the case of French planning, which worked far more successfully than its British counterpart, the plans merely stated the government's economic strategy; they did not necessarily or usually initiate it. The nature of the planning dialogue varied a great deal from sector to sector but there was always a marked divergence between the formal, open, consultative planning process symbolized by the Modernization Commissions in France and the Economic Development Committees (EDC's) in Britain, and the real, secret, and decisive bilateral bargaining with the major firms. Two leading French public servants have asserted that French economic policy operates at two levels: the affirmation of principles and day-to-day action, where the means are sought of "implementing exceptions to the affirmed principles."[46] In some cases, such as energy policy in France, the strictly economic aspects were subordinated to defense and foreign policy considerations, the government building up a national, state-controlled oil industry and forcing the multinational oil companies onto the defensive by a vigorous assertion of national regulatory power.[47] The contrast with the passive role of British governments in this policy area is marked. In the process the Energy Modernization Commission sessions were reduced to a fruitless discussion of technicalities, the businessmen being constrained to the frustrated impotence which trade unionists have usually had to accept. In other areas, such as the General Manufacturing Commission covering some 240 industries, the businessmen lost interest in the proceedings because no planning was being undertaken. The civil servants were allowed to get their way on paper. In a very few cases, such as steel, the trade association (CSSF) is so powerful and well-led that the government chooses to work through it but even here "the real 'planning' in steel was done by a handful of people, in private and outside the planning process."[48]

In Britain the EDC's have worked best in terms of identifying the problems of their industry and suggesting solutions when a very small number of representative and well organized TA's existed. The EDC tended to become a mere extension of the TA in industries like electrical engineering or chemicals, which were dominated by a single TA. This was especially the case because the National Economic Development Office left it to the TA to collect the data on the basis of which the EDC's discussions took place. At the other extreme, in the Distributive Trades EDC, where about 150 small and weak TA's existed, it was necessary to reduce the fragmentation and this led to the creation of the Retail Consortium.[49] Most of the EDC's survived the demise of the National Plan in 1966, but there was a reduction of commitment by some leading industrialists and a reluctance either to participate actively or to pay attention to EDC report. This attempt to circumvent the TA-sponsor ministry relationship based upon lobbying by vested interests has not proved to be an effective instrument of public industrial innovation.

Both in Britain and France dissatisfaction with arrangements for industrial planning has led to reorganization. We have already described the institutional changes made in the ministries primarily responsible for industrial policy. Under CNPF pressure and following the work of official committees examining both the public and private sectors, most of the French modernization commissions concerned with particular industries were downgraded in August 1969 to committees under the aegis of an Industry Commission which it was hoped would be better able to formulate an overall policy for industry in the context of the Sixth Plan (1971-75). The new arrangements appear to have given a broader "economic policy" slant to the traditionally more parochial "market research" emphasis, and allowed the more dynamic firms to secure acceptance for their conception of accelerated industrial development as the centerpiece of the Sixth Plan. This may be regarded as the logical conclusion of a planning process described by Crozier as having as its most original feature the planners' intuition that "they would only succeed if they placed themselves at the service of the business world and the civil service and sought, in return, to secure their help instead of trying to compel their obedience."[50] Under these circumstances it is no surprise that, of all occupational groups, businessmen in large firms attach the most importance to planning.[51] The Sixth Plan's attempt to develop a public enterprise policy rather than a conflation of separate policies was largely a failure. In Britain after the contradictory gropings of the Conservative government of 1970-74, the Labour government has sought to open up new ground by proposing the creation of an IRI-like National Enterprise Board to pull the public sector together, while "planning agreements" are to be offered to the hundred largest firms, along the lines of French "program contracts."

Government and Industrial Restructuring

A striking feature of the 1960s vogue for restructuring industry was the virtual absence of TA's and PO's from any significant part in the process. Paralyzed by their preoccupation with preserving quasi-unanimity, they left it to the more dynamic firms to initiate mergers or take-overs, with governments either ignoring, promoting, or preventing the process that shifted power on a grand scale within the private sector. (For example the CBI and the Association of British Chambers of Commerce were strongly opposed to the creation of the Industrial Reorganisation Corporation, discussed below). In France, which traditionally had attributed to the state responsibility for controlling industrial organization, the task of industrial reorganization was delegated to a few large firms whose creation was a salient feature of public policy. In Britain, with its deep-rooted liberal tradition favoring competition, there was a more ambiguous attitude, with governments scrutinizing and regulating the emergence of private monopoly power rather than restraining it. The deputy chairman of the textile combine Courtaulds has stated that the Monopolies Commission investigations "made it clear that government concern was much more with restrictive agreements of one sort or another which might be endangering competition, than with dominant enterprises."[52] Furthermore as Douglas Jay (Labour president of the Board of Trade in the 1964 Labour government) said in 1961, the Monopolies Commission-inspired 1956 Restrictive Trade Practices Act itself has actually in some degree incited the rush towards monopoly, because big firms now find that they cannot make price agreements but can amalgamate."[53] So in both countries governments undertook a policy of concentrating economic power in the boards of a few big firms at the expense of the TA's, which had hitherto been their officially acknowledged interlocutors.

Following up the Monopolies and Mergers Act of 1965, the main instrument of the public promotion of mergers in Britain from 1966 to 1971 was the IRC. "The Industrial Reorganisation Corporation was perhaps the most novel, most high-powered, most entrepreneurial, most publicised, most controversial, but ultimately the most significant and successful of the innovations in economic management introduced by the Labour Government," noted the director of the Manchester Business School (and a former IRC director).[54] Operating more like a state merchant bank than the Italian state holding company (IRI) with which it was usually compared, the IRC generally made loans without acquiring a shareholding, or where it acquired shares did not intend to hold them permanently. Its main purpose was in any case to improve management as well as structure, to avoid some of Britain's firms becoming "lame ducks" by sponsoring or initiating nonbureaucratic, discretionary intervention to promote international competitiveness. Harold Wilson has somewhat incautiously described IRC's function as being to take British industry "by the scruff of its neck and drag it into the twentieth century." This entrepreneurial and modernizing purpose was reflected in the membership of the IRC board—consisting mainly of go-ahead industrialists and merchant bankers—and in its lively full-time staff, but also in its autonomous status as a paragovernmental agency. The latter has been defined as a body acting under the general direction of the government, using public funds, but "at arm's length from Whitehall departments" and having some independence in day-to-day operations.[55] Such freedom from close accountability commended itself to beneficiary businessmen who wanted IRC to have freedom to use its commercial judgment, but the Conservatives resented the substitution of a public agency for the City of London and were obsessed with their fear of "trap-door nationalization." When in 1972 they created an Industrial Development Executive they made it part of the industry ministry.

IRC's task was to identify the industries requiring reorganization and the companies upon or through which it would act. To make international comparisons of industry structure and performance, it first required domestic aggregate industrial data for which it depended mainly on MinTech. There was very close contact between IRC and MinTech, but after the early innovative phase the civil service view favoring integration within the administrative system and the parliamentary stress on accountability reasserted themselves against an IRC that was moving "towards involvement in strategic management decision-making on a continuous basis."[56] (The strength of British ministries and the insistence of the House of Commons on at least the semblance of accountability are the major obstacles in the way of transposing an IRI-like agency to Britain from Italy, where the bureaucracy and Parliament have to be bypassed because they are so indecisive.) The IRC's ability to increase its independence from MinTech by its access to confidential company information and its ability to conceal its subjective appraisals behind the shroud of secret bilateral dealings with particular firms[57] undoubtedly aroused suspicion and hostility. Although only 4 percent of the mergers that went through in the 1966-70 period were promoted by IRC they involved leading companies in key sectors such as motor vehicles (the British-Layland merger of BMC and Leyland Motors), computers (ICL, formed in 1968 out of English Electric Computers—which had been helped to absorb Elliott Automation in 1967—ICT and Plessey's Computer Division), electrical and electronic engineering (GEC's absorption of AEI and subsequent merger with English Electric), and lent the merger mania an aura of public interest sanctity.[58]

The French Fifth Plan (1966-70) stated that the primary objective of French industrial policy was "the establishment or reinforcement where they exist already of a small number of firms or groups of international size;" and the plan added that "in most industrial sectors (aluminum, steel, mechanical and electrical engineering, electronics, motor cars, aircraft, chemicals, pharmaceutical products, etc.) the number of these groups should be very small, often even reduced to one or two."[59] It went on to assert: "In a market economy, guided by a plan, the prime responsibility for industrial development belongs to the industrialists. On their initiative depends the success of the policy whose objectives and the means of attaining them have been explained. But these initiatives should be worked out in conjunction with trade associations and the state. . . . It is indispensable that the trade associations keep their member firms informed on the situation by preparing or having prepared economic studies of their industrial structure and that of competing foreign industries. The diagnosis arrived at might subsequently, with the help of the public authorities, provide the basis for defining and implementing a policy of improving structures. Relatively old examples (the cotton industry) and recent ones (steel) confirm the utility of such intervention by trade associations."[60] However, in France as in Britain most mergers came about without public intervention, including such notable ones as the chemical and aluminum industry giant Pechiney-Ugine-Kuhlmann. Even in the case of the 1966 Steel *Plan Professionnel*, which owed much to state intervention, it has been noted: "Printing the results of dramatic industry reorganizations in the plan, as though these had developed as part of the planning process, helped obscure the fact that these dramatic changes were planned in secret, on an ad hoc basis, with disregard sometimes amounting to contempt for the consultative planning process."[61]

The 1969 creation in France of the Industrial Development Institute (IDI) was directly modeled on the IRC, although the Nora Report on Public Enterprise had advocated a holding company along IRI lines. Thanks particularly to the influence of the Minister of Industrial Development, Pompidou's confidant François Ortoli (former planning commissioner and future chairman of the EC Commission), it was decided instead to set up a state development bank-cum-industrial marriage bureau, which would concern itself primarily with helping small and medium-sized firms. In fact the IDI has been more an industrial consultant than a supplier of funds, and was compelled to use a disproportionately large part of its limited resources to keep the French computer national champion (CII) financially afloat on terms which suggest that the definition of a mixed economy as one where profits are private and losses are public is strictly applicable.[62] It has also been handicapped by the fact that the state and private banks that supplied part of its capital have been reluctant to encourage a rival. Although unlike the IRC it has survived, the IDI has not fulfilled the hopes of its progenitors.

The textile industry in the two countries provides an interesting case of the problems of restructuring a traditional industry exposed to foreign competition. In Britain it was the head of a leading man-made fiber-textile firm, Lord Kearton of Courtaulds—described as "the fastest-talking and one of the fastest-moving autocrats in the whole of British industry"[63]—who was chosen as the first IRC chairman. His firm, after successfully defeating a takeover bid in 1961 by its leading rival, ICI, followed a strategy of acquiring a large number of textile firms to build up a powerful vertical fiber-textile group. This objective was carried out in close consultation with Board of Trade officials to ensure that there were no objections on monopoly grounds and to secure greater tariff protection in return for rescuing parts of the ailing Lancashire textile industry. Rather than relying on its fragmented TA's the British textile industry had set up in 1957 the informal "Derby Group" to work out a common policy in its dealings with the government. They tried to secure a protected home market as a condition for positive new regrouping initiatives, instead of the old organization of contraction followed under the aegis of the Cotton Board, a pioneer development council of EDC established in 1939. The board had since 1965 invited representatives from the three firms mainly responsible for restructuring—Courtaulds, ICI, and Viyella—to attend all its policy-making meetings, recognizing the need for a change in the industry's traditional strategy and methods. Following a 1966 initiative of the permanent secretary of the Board of Trade the Cotton Board—reconstituted as the Textile Council in 1967—published a report in 1969 that had a major influence on government textile industry policy both on tariff and mergers.[64]

Such a shift from the old fragmented TA-ministry relations, via a quasi-corporatist Textile Council, toward a situation in which the reorganized industrial ministry dealt largely with the few dynamic firms capable of implementing the restructuring policy it favored, was also tried in France at about the same time and basically for the same reasons. (However, in the French case the competitive pressures came from the EC reduction of tariffs rather than the British 1932 commitment to lower tariffs and Commonwealth textiles.) Textiles had a relatively low priority in French industrial policy, not being regarded as prestigious or important and having few links with the *grands corps*: "Most of the industry, trade association and administration officials connected with textiles are clear outsiders in the national power structure."[65] For the government to circumvent the TA barrier to direct contact with the major firms it was necessary to secure the legitimizing cover of a representative body capable of imposing compulsory levies on the textile firms for the purpose of reorganizing the industry. In France the role of the Textile Council was played by the *Comité Interprofessionnel pour la Restructuration de l'industrie Textile* (CIRIT), set up in 1966. However, as well as excluding trade union representatives and including representatives of state banks, CIRIT was essentially an instrument of the Ministry of Industrial Development, whose representative has a veto over the committee's decisions and whose officials report on requests by firms for financial support. An investigation of CIRIT's activities in relation to wool textiles has nevertheless shown that the firms still turn to their TA, the Central Wool Committee, as mediator in their dealings with CIRIT and that there is a close correlation between active membership or a leading role in the TA and receipt of a CIRIT subsidy.[66] As in the case of the French steel industry, some TA's have shown a capacity to adapt successfully to the new environment of government-business relations.

An Area of Mixed Authority

It has been noted in regard to modern industrial society: "What characterizes modern industrial society is less a one-sided movement of public authority into the private sector than an interpenetration of public and private powers that has led to the creation of a broad area of mixed or shared authority."[67] This has involved a substantially increased participation in the political process by private interests both in pluralist countries like Britain and statist countries like France. Both business and trade union organizations have been under pressure to accept more intimate involvement with government and to make some sacrifice of their independence in exchange for more influence. However, the peak organizations have been conscious that they do not have the authority to commit their members to agreements entered into with the government. So despite window-dressing discussions at the summit between the representatives of political and economic power the real bargaining takes place between the actual holders of power, who are more closely interconnected in France than in Britain. In matters of industrial policy-making, it is increasingly a matter of contacts between a few leading businessmen on the one side and a few senior civil servants and ministers on the other.

In making some general concluding contrasts between the relationships of employer associations and governments in France and Britain, as seen in the industrial policy context, the dimensions of state versus business domination and of arm's length autonomy versus corporatist collusion must both be borne in mind. The traditional French position was one in which the state both dominated business and tended to be in a corporate relationship with it, while in Britain business traditionally enjoyed much more freedom from government, which was likely to trust business implicitly. However, there has been considerable change in recent years, as the French appear to have departed from state capitalism and corporatism in a liberal direction whereas the British seem to have felt compelled to move toward a more corporatist and *étatiste* type of capitalism. In both countries the resistance to such changes continues to be strong, and it is often difficult to ascertain to what extent political, administrative, and business rhetoric should be given credence. In neither country does the existing state of knowledge suggest that categorical answers can be given to questions about how decision-making power is shared within the nucleus of policy makers at the highest levels of government and business. What appears clear is that more knowledge about the activities of the employer associations as such will not provide the answers.

NOTES

1. S. E. Finer, "The Political Power of Organized Labor," *Government and Opposition* 8, no. 4 (Autumn 1973): 395-396; see also S. E. Finer, "The Political Power of Private Capital, Part I," *The Sociological Review* 3, no. 2 (December 1955): 285.

2. See H. W. Ehrmann, *Organized Business in France* (Princeton, N.J.: Princeton University Press, 1957), pp. 19-20; and S. Blank, *Industry and Government in Britain: The Federation of British Industries in Politics, 1945-65* (London, 1973), pp. 14-15.

3. J. P. Nettl, "Consensus or Elite Domination: the Case of Business," *Political Studies* 13, no. 1 (February 1965): 41 and 29-33.

4. See A. Roth, *Lord on the Board* (London: Parliamentary Profiles, 1972).

5. Britain, *The Reorganisation of Central Government* (White Paper), Cmnd. 4506, 1970, para. 23.

6. "Public Money in the Private Sector," *Sixth Report from the Expenditure Committee of the House of Commons Minutes of Evidence*, 1970-71, HC 546, p. 42, para. 206.

7. Ibid., p. 370.

8. Ibid., pp. 78-79.

9. "MinTech in Retrospect—I," *Omega* 1, no. 1 (1973): 34.

10. "MinTech in Retrospect—II," *Omega* 1, no. 2 (1973): 151.

11. The details of the Treasury-MinTech concordat are derived from Sir Richard Clarke, *New Trends in Government* (London: HMSO, 1971), pp. 48-53. Although this "concordat"—which was the only one of its kind—was carried over into the DTI, it succumbed in 1972 to the Treasury desire to recover more effective control over financial support for industry. Informal "understandings" between Treasury divisions and spending departments were favored instead. See Sir Samuel Goldman, *The Developing System of Public Expenditure Management and Control* (London: HSMO, Civil Service College Studies, no. 2, 1973).

12. "Le Ministère de L'Industrie et son Environnement," mimeographed, January 1970, p. 22. Erhard Friedberg has developed this standpoint in a series of remarkable research reports: "Le systeme d'intervention de l'état en matière industrielle" (Paris: Publications de l'A.U.D.I.R., Hachette, 1973); 'L'internationalisation de l'économie et modalités d'intervention de l'Etat: la 'politique industrielle' " (paper delivered at the Uriage Conference on *La Planification dans la Societé Française*, October 1973. For a more official view see R. Catherine, *L'Industrie* (Paris: Presses Universitaires de France, 1965), pp. 115, 121ff.

13. E. Friedberg and D. Desjeux, "Fonction de l'Etat et rôle des Grands Corps: le cas du Corps des Mines," *Annuaire International de la Fonction Publique*, Autumn 1972, *passim*, and J. A. Kosciusko-Morizet, *La 'Mafia' Polytechnicienne* (Paris: Editions du Seuil, 1973), pp. 100-103, 106-107, 136-139.

14. For this tripartite division and many of the examples mentioned I am indebted to the chapter on France by C. A. Michalet in R. Vernon, *Big Business and the State, Changing Relations in Western Europe* (Cambridge, Mass.: Harvard University Press, 1974). See also J. H. McArthur and B. R. Scott, *Industrial Planning in France* (Cambridge, Mass.: Harvard Graduate School of Business Administration, 1969), chap. 10 *passim*.

15. See *Gallup Political Index*, no. 37, January 1963 and *Sunday Times* (London), July 15, 1973.

16. R. Priouret, "Face à face avec Léon Gingembre," *L'Expansion*, November 1973, pp. 211-221. See also G. Lavau, "Note sur un 'pressure group' français. La CGPME," *Revue Française de Science Politique*, April-June 1955, pp. 370-383, and Ehrmann, *Organized Business in France*, op. cit., pp. 172-184. On the entrepreneur group initiator see Ehrmann, "An Exchange Theory of Interest Groups," in R. H. Salisbury, ed., *Interest Group Politics in America* (New York: Harper and Row, 1970), pp. 43-45.

17. See Britain's *Report of the Bolton Committee of Inquiry on Small Firms*, 1971, Cmnd. 4811.

18. *Report of the Commission of Inquiry into Industrial and Commercial Representation*, ABCC/CBI, November 1972, p. 126.

19. McArthur and Scott, op. cit., p. 183.

20. Ehrmann, "An Exchange Theory of Interest Groups," op. cit., p. 89; cf. p. 76 ff. and pp. 371-372. See also J. Lautman and A. Jacob, "Rôles du syndicalisme patronal et évolution économique," in J. D. Reynaud, ed., *Tendances et Volontés de la Société Française* (Paris, 1966), pp. 269-270.

21. P. de Calan, *Les Professions* (Paris: Editions France-Empire, 1965), p. 262; cf. p. 58, pp. 95-101. See also Ehrmann, pp. 258-270.

22. J. Lautman, "La construction de l'intérêt de profession dans les syndicats patronauz," *Sociologie du Travail* 9, no. 4 (October/December 1967): 410-412.

23. See R. Priouret, *Origines du Patronat Français* (Paris: Grasset, 1966).

24. McArthur and Scott, op. cit., p. 200; cf. pp. 134, 199-201, 220; see also B. Catherine, *La Chambre Syndicale de la Sidérurgie Française et la Convention Etat-Sidérurgie ou l'action d'un syndicat professionnel aujourd'hui*, unpublished memoire, Institut d'Etudes Politiques, University of Grenoble, 1966-1967, pp. 25-41.

25. R. A. Bauer, I. de Sola Pool, and L. A. Dexter, *American Business and Public Policy* (Chicago: Aldine, 1964), chap. 22 *passim*, especially pp. 332, 339.

26. *Report of the Commission of Inquiry into Industrial and Commercial Representation*, op. cit., pp. 5, 40.

27. Ibid., pp. 65-70; cf. pp. 25-39 and app. 9, p. 127.

28. Ibid., p. 63; cf. p. 64, pp. 75-77 and app. 7, p. 123.

29. Blank, op. cit., p. 69. However, as firms are concerned, they are more inclined to use TA rather than government publications to obtain official statistics. See *Government Statistical Services*, fourth report from the Estimates Committee of the House of Commons, Cmnd. 246 of 1966-67, 1968 app. 8.

30. *Report of the Commission of Inquiry into Industrial and Commercial Representation*, op. cit., app. 8, pp. 125-26.

31. Bauer, *de Sola Pool*, and Dexter, op. cit., p. 339 and pp. 333-337.

32. E. Burke, *Select Works*, vol. II (Clarendon Press ed. 1888), pp. 47-48.

33. M. Olson, op. cit., pp. 166-167.

34. Ibid., p. 133.

35. "On Joining Interest Groups," part of a forthcoming book on the CBI by D. Marsh and W. Grant. I am very much indebted to the authors for an opportunity to consult unpublished drafts of some chapters of their book.

36. Ibid.

37. R. H. Salisbury, op. cit., p. 53 and pp. 48-52. Salisbury's terms are "solidary" and "expressive" benefits.

38. *Report of the Commission of Inquiry into Industrial and Commercial Representation*, op. cit., pp. 21, 78.

39. Wyn Grant and David Marsh, "The Confederation of British Industry," *Political Studies* 19, no. 4, p. 404.

40. M. Crozier, *The Bureaucratic Phenomenon*, (Chicago: University of Chicago Press, 1964), p. 284.

41. Blank, op. cit., pp. 85-88; cf. also J. W. Grove, *Government and Industry in Britain* (London: Longman, 1962), pp. 289-292; and PEP, *Growth in the British Economy* (London: Allen and Unwin, 1960), pp. 222-223.

42. H. Schollhammer, "National Economic Planning and Business Decision-Making: the French Experience," *California Management Review* 13, no. 2 (Winter 1969): 77.

43. M. Crozier, 'Analyse sociologique de la planification française', *Revue française de sociologie* 6 (April-June 1965): 157; see also L. Nizard, 'Administration et société: planification et régulations bureaucratiques,'

Revue francaise de science politique 23, no. 2, (April 1973): 223-227.

44. See Jack Hayward and Michael Watson, *Planning, Politics and Public Policy: The British, French and Italian Experience* (London: Cambridge University Press, 1975) and S. Blank op. cit., pp. 148-156, 168-169, 213, chap. 6 *passim*. It is worthy of note that prominent Conservatives like Lord Eccles could assert in 1946 that "the better the plan, the fewer the controls"; quoted by N. Harris, *Competition and the Corporate Society: British Conservatives, the State and Industry, 1945-1964* (London: Methuen, 1973), p. 132.

45. McArthur and Scott, op. cit., p. 471; cf. also pp. 413-414, 439-441, 468-472. For a more optimistic picture of the influence of French national planning on business decisions see the subjective assessments based on a survey and interviews in Schollhammer, op. cit.

46. Ehrmann, op. cit., p. 293.

47. McArthur and Scott, op. cit., pp. 341-357, 421-424.

48. Ibid., p. 434. See also Jack Hayward, in R. Vernon, op. cit., and J. Saint-Geours, "L'actualité du Plan en France," *Droit Social*, 1964, p. 604.

49. G. D. Vaughan, "Economic Development Committees," *Public Administration*, December 1971, p. 374, and T. Smith, "Industrial Planning in Britain," in Hayward and Watson, op. cit. See also Grant and Marsh, "The Representation of Retail Interests in Britain," *Political Studies*, forthcoming.

50. Crozier, "Analyse sociologique de la planification française," op. cit., p. 154. See also R. Priouret, *Les Français Mystifiés* (Paris: Grasset, 1973), pp. 104-109, 121-122, 254-257, and J.-J. Bonnaud, "Planning and Industry in France," in Hayward and Watson, op. cit.

51. Sofres, *Les Français et l'Etat*, Spring 1970, p. 87; cf. Jack Hayward, *The One and Indivisible French Republic* (London: Weidenfeld and Nicholson, 1973), p. 181.

52. A. Knight, *Private Enterprise and Public Intervention: The Courtaulds Experience* (London: Allen and Unwin, 1974), p. 129.

53. Quoted in ibid., p. 130.

54. W. G. McClelland, "The Industrial Reorganisation Corporation 1966/71: an experimental prod," *The Three Banks Review*, June 1972, p. 29.

55. "Public Money in the Private Sector," *Sixth Report from the Expenditure Committee*, H. C. 347 of 1971-1972, July 1972, p. 58.

56. S. Holland, ed., *The State as Entrepreneur—New Dimensions for Public Enterprise: The IRI State Shareholding Formula* (London: Weidenfeld and Nicolson, 1972), p. 245; Holland was a specialist adviser to the Commons Expenditure Subcommittee for Trade and Industry.

57. M. E. Beesley and G. M. White, "The Industrial Reorganization Corporation: a study in choice of public management," *Public Administration* 51 (Spring 1973): 71-81. For a MinTech view see Sir Richard Clarke, "MinTech in Retrospect—II," op. cit., p. 154.

58. Holland, op. cit., p. 247 and G. Turner, *Business in Britain* (Boston: Little Brown & Co., 1970), pp. 75-79. On the 1964-1970 Labour Government's

relations with the motor and computer industries see M. Hodges, *Multinational Corporations and National Government: A case study of the United Kingdom's experience, 1964-1970* (Lexington, Ky.: Lexington Books, 1974), chaps. 5 and 6.

59. France, *Vme Plan de Développement Economique et Social*, 1965, pp. 68-69.

60. Ibid., pp. 72-73.

61. McArthur and Scott, op. cit., p. 501.

62. See R. Priouret, *Les Français Mystifiés*, pp. 91-93, 154, and "Public Money in the Private Sector," op. cit., p. 747-748.

63. G. Turner, op. cit., p. 451 and chap. 13 *passim*.

64. A. Knight, op. cit., chap. 6 *passim*.

65. McArthur and Scott, op. cit., p. 399.

66. E. Friedberg and D. Desjeux, *L'Industrie Lainière et ses relations avec le Ministère du Développement Industriel et Scientifique*, unpublished interim report, sec. 2 *passim*. On the failure of the IRC's attempt to restructure the British wool textile industry see W. Davis, *Three Years Hard Labor* (London: Andre Deutsch, 1968), p. 53.

67. S. Blank, op. cit., p. 3.

PART

III

THE EUROPEAN
COMMUNITY

6

INDUSTRIAL POLICY
AND THE EUROPEAN
COMMUNITY
Steven J. Warnecke

As a result of the establishment of the Common Market in 1957 many proponents of a supranational European Community had hoped that the gradual implementation of a regional customs union would produce conditions facilitating the development of a "European" industrial base.[1] Although the network that was supposed to evolve would result from cross-frontier restructuring of small and medium-sized firms, the principal component would be the large-scale European corporations that were to be established in lead industries. These firms which would be "European" in ownership, control, and character were considered indispensable for simultaneously forming an irreversible foundation for economic union, and, consequently, political union.[2] Moreover, they would be formed from smaller, inefficient national industries and be large enough to challenge the international predominance of the American multinational.

From the beginning, the successful outcome of the interrelationship posited between the evolution of industrial planning, development and restructuring (whether on a public or private basis) and the consolidation of the EC's geopolitical and geoeconomic base has depended upon several unexamined assumptions. First, both the private and public sectors would find it in their interests to pursue policies to build a Common Market industrial network. Second, if such a network could evolve it would significantly diminish the importance of national boundaries as well as contribute to the establishment of a regional political and economic union. Third, the Community did constitute a large enough area for pursuing the kinds of policies toward industry which the proponents of European cooperation have believed desirable.

For a variety of reasons all of these assumptions have not corresponded to the political and economic realities of the Community nor to the dynamics of a multistate customs union. Since the signing of the Rome Treaty, (1957), industry has been caught between the contending political perspectives of the member states and the Commission concerning the preferred evolution of the EC. On the one hand, although the states have viewed membership as advantageous, their participation, by and large, has reflected a view of the EC as being a bloc composed of competing members held together by intergovernmental bargaining. On the other hand, the Commission has advanced the view that the Community would rapidly move beyond a customs union to a new supranational entity. The former has led to national policies emphasizing the strengthening of the domestic industrial base, and the latter to efforts to influence industry to contribute to the economic and political integration of the Common Market.

If governmental cross-pressures have impeded intra-Community industrial development in many sectors, the capacity of public authorities, whether on the national or European level to influence industry has been restricted because of: the existing distribution of power between the public and private sectors. The combination of the relative decision-making autonomy of business and the pressure of market forces has limited the feasibility of public intervention in the private sector as well as allowed corporations the freedom to pursue policies which at times have run counter to the political and economic goals of their national governments and the EC. In addition, the capacity of the private sector to pursue policies that support either national or Community goals has also been weakened by the politics and economics of the Atlantic Alliance. As a result of the U.S. pursuit of trans-Atlantic trade liberalization, the impact of the American economy on European business has reduced its potential contribution to the integration of the EC. American corporations, whether through direct investments, the operation of affiliates in Europe, or agreements between Community and U.S. firms, have all too often provided EC businesses with more attractive opportunities for cooperation than have competing member state firms. Furthermore, American technological predominance in NATO has been an impediment to the development of European policies on research, development, and procurement in defense equipment.

In this context the Commission, as the main administrative institution of the Common Market, has obviously been restricted to a subordinate role regarding industry. Its principal influence has been indirect through its responsibilities for the implementation of the internal customs union and the negotiation of the common external tariff. Politically it is the dependent creature of the member states and this further reduces its capacity to successfully influence industry. Consequently, the Commission has pressed the Council of Ministers for more interventionist powers to augment the impact it can have on industry through the customs union. However, in trying to formulate sectoral policies the Commission has confronted a further restriction on its power as a result of the internationalization of production and capital. Thus, in many ways, the Common Market is an economically and politically limited unit for public sectoral policies and even for private planning. This is all the more ironic since one of the reasons for establishing it was to overcome similar limitations on the national level.

In spite of these problems the Commission has continued to attempt to develop policies toward industry on the assumption that the Community does constitute a relatively self-contained entity for restructuring declining sectors and establishing internationally competitive firms in lead industries. Therefore, three fundamental questions stand behind all the issues discussed in this chapter: first, whether the political decision to impose a new geo-economic boundary can have the desired economic and political implications; second, whether Community-level efforts to develop a model for influencing the private sector have repeated the mistakes of similar national attempts; and, third, whether Community efforts to influence industry have subordinated economic considerations to the achievement of political goals.

In this regard, since neither a supranational Europe nor a "European" industrial network have developed, it is of great interest why the establishment of the Common Market has not led to the kinds of cross-frontier restructuring, concentration and development expected from the private sector. An examination of this process will not only reveal much about the dynamics of the European Community and the difficulties of managing a multistate Common Market, but the results will also be of relevance to the efforts of other customs unions, such as the Andean Group, to use industry for similar purposes. This chapter will deal with the Commission's attempts to encourage industrial restructuring and development, the responses of the member states' governments and private sectors to these initiatives, and the problems which have emerged for delineating viable regional-level policies to achieve Community-oriented goals. Many of the unrealistic expectations about the contributions government and business could make to the consolidation of the EC have been a result of the static, apolitical nature of customs union theory and the legalistic approach of the supporters of some form of European union to the transfer of power from the member states to Brussels. These perspectives have resulted in an incomplete and at times incorrect understanding of the nature, dynamics, and relationship of the public and private sectors in a multinational regional association and the possible role of the Commission in relation to the member states and their industries. Thus the various approaches to industry and integration will be examined. However, if there are major limitations in the way of the Commission intervening directly through sectoral policies this should not divert attention from two areas through which the Commission has had a substantial impact on the general environment to which the private sector must respond: regional and international trade liberalization. Although policies in these areas lead to the necessity for some Communitywide and national policies concerning industry and employment the Commission's

responsibilities for related aspects of industrial development have lagged far
behind its responsibilities for managing the customs union.

Moreover since the Community is a multinational association the
industrial policies of its member states must be understood as part of the
modified foreign policies the member states pursue toward one another and
the rest of the world. One dimension of this is reflected in the fact that if the
states have joined the EC to influence the international distribution of
industry and trade between themselves and the world, they are also engaged in
a regional competition to influence both among themselves. In this regard the
price policies of the Organization of Petroleum Exporting Countries (OPEC)
have intensified the contradictory forces inherent within the Common
Market. On the one hand, the Nine have felt compelled to pursue national
policies to expand their exports on the basis of their existing industries and to
begin to adjust their patterns of production to future expectations about the
changing determinants of international competition. On the other hand, they
have found a collective interest in pursuing some common foreign political
and economic policies—such as the Euro-Arab dialogue and the negotiations
with African, Caribbean, and Pacific countries—in order to stabilize the
impact of these forces on their industries as far as possible and to improve the
competitive prospects for their industries in world trade.

THE ROME TREATY AND INDUSTRIAL POLICY

An understanding of the contribution expected from industry to the construction of the Common Market requires some discussion of the reasons for
the establishment of the Community. Such a discussion will elucidate the
extent to which political decisions have imposed upon and determined the
geographic framework within which economic activity is supposed to evolve
as well as the mechanisms which are supposed to influence and guide this
activity.

The most immediate reason for the formation of the Common Market
was the effort to salvage trans-European cooperation after the collapse of the
European Defense Community.[3] This defense community, in response to the
causes of World War II, would have set Europe in a supranational direction,
thus fulfilling the political dreams of those who wished nation-states to be
merged into a larger political entity. Once efforts to launch this political and
security Community came to naught it seemed that the momentum generated
by the experience of cooperation in the Marshall Plan, NATO, the
Organization for European Economic Cooperation, the European Payments
Union and the European Coal and Steel Community would be lost. However,
the *relance* which led to the drafting of the Rome Treaty establishing the
European Community took advantage of the remaining momentum, though
at a cost. The costs of gaining sufficient political support for the Common
Market entailed not only limiting trans-European cooperation to closely
defined economic dimensions but hedging and submerging the question of the

EC's political structure—particularly the strident debate between the supranationalists and the nationalists.

Consequently, the Spaak Report,[4] which provided the rationale for drafting the Treaty of Rome, avoided these basic issues by focusing on the economic benefits that would be derived for private sector activity from the establishment of a common market based on liberal customs union theory.[5] The justification for forming a Europeanwide customs union was that the national markets of the member states were too small for private economic activity as well as too limited for effective national policies toward trade and industry.[6]

Thus this theory was incorporated in those sections of the Rome Treaty which limited the powers of the Commission to the implementation of policies to remove the formal legal and structural obstacles to the integration of national markets and the free circulation of the factors of production. Among these obstacles are tariffs and quotas, tax barriers, state trading monopolies, subsidies and cartels which distort competition, transport barriers, restrictions on the free establishment of businesses and on the movement of capital, discrimination in patent regulations, and disparities in company law and in laws regulating competition. It was assumed that in proportion as such barriers were removed individual firms in their voluntary efforts to pursue policies to exploit a larger market and meet increased competition would derive a number of benefits.[7] These included increased output due to better opportunities to exploit economies of scale, increased production due to specialization according to static comparative advantage, gains from improvement in the terms of trade of the Community in regard to other countries, and forced changes in efficiency arising from increased competition.[8] Moreover, the regrouping, restructuring, and merging of firms that would occur should take place on a cross-frontier basis, thus simultaneously contributing to the establishment of a "European" industrial network distinct from national networks. From the perspective of the supporters of European union the political virtue of the liberal model was that private producers exploiting market forces would incrementally contribute to the increased economic interdependence of the member states and this interdependence in turn would contain a logic about the increased necessity for member states to cede power to the Community.

Walter Hallstein, the first President of the European Community's Commission, described this evolution as a process with three interrelated stages.[9] One component, according to Hallstein, would be the merging of the private sectors of the economy, and this would be the responsibility of those operating in this sector. Another part would involve the elimination of state intervention at internal borders, and this would logically be a matter for the public authorities of the member states. And a third step would be the fusion of national economic policies into a Community policy, and this would be accomplished by the institutions of the Community. In addition to this liberal model there is another approach, which will be discussed below, that is based on the Commission taking a much more active role in encouraging concentrations and mergers.

Although the freedom for private sector activity would be expanded by the establishment of a customs union the agreement among the six original signatory states to set up the Common Market represented a compromise between those who wanted the Rome Treaty to be intergovernmental and those who wanted it to be the outline for a supranational Europe.[10] As a result of these conflicting directions the treaty incorporated one other basic approach for regulating and guiding interstate economic relations. If the Commission was to be responsible for the implementation of liberal policies leading toward integrated markets, the Council of Ministers, representing the member states, was to insure that the effects of such policies did not detrimentally affect national interests or lead to an incremental strengthening of the Commission's authority at the expense of the national governments. Therefore, the scope of private sector activity would be determined by the competing goals of the Commission and the national governments.

Finally, the treaties establishing the European Coal and Steel Community (ECSC) and the European Atomic Community (Euratom) embodied yet a third approach to intra-European industrial cooperation: the sectoral or functionalist approach. In selected cases member states could delegate powers to a European-level administration to formulate and implement policies for key industrial sectors. If cooperation could occur in a sufficiently large number of sectors contributions would be made simultaneously to the establishment of a European industrial network as well as administrative bodies with some supranational powers.

The Colonna Report on an
EC Industrial Policy

It was only in 1970, thirteen years after the signing of the Rome Treaty, that the Commission undertook a study to examine the impact of the integration of national markets on private sector industrial activity. This study, *Industrial Policy in the Community*,[11] was prepared under the direction of the Commissioner responsible for this area, Guido Colonna di Paliano. It contained statistics which indicated that reliance on the private sector had led neither to industrial restructuring and concentration and patterns of ownership and control that supported the integrative process nor to the development of large-scale firms in key sectors which could effectively challenge American and Japanese firms. The data, which was compiled by Opera Mundi Europe, covered developments in fifteen important industrial sectors through the analysis of fifteen thousand cases.[12]

Drawn from these data, the statistics in Table 6.1 show that between 1961 and the first half of 1969 there were 1,861 mergers and take-overs within individual Community countries and only 257 between companies from different Community countries. During the same period Community companies in their turn made only 215 acquisitions outside the Common

TABLE 6.1

Establishment of Subsidiaries, Cooperation Agreements, Holdings and Mergers, in the European Community, 1961-69, by Year

Years	Unilateral Establishment of Subsidiaries in Other Countries			Cooperation—Minority and Reciprocal Holdings, Common Subsidiaries, Common Parent Companies			Mergers, Take-Overs, or Controlling Minority				Totals
	From Member Country to Member Country	From Third Country to Member Country	From Member Country to Third Country	Between Firms in the Same Country	Between Common Market Firms	Between Member Country and Third Country Firms	Same Member Country	Different Member Countries	By a Member Country in a Third Country	By a Third Country in a Member Country	
1961	241	351	71	100	104	362	131	19	26	102	1,507
1962	232	348	76	141	114	343	162	11	21	85	1,533
1963	195	379	63	55	61	228	157	28	9	82	1,257
1964	273	476	139	132	123	335	172	34	18	110	1,812
1965	247	409	142	177	140	364	228	17	20	70	1,814
1966	320	467	154	205	112	289	221	31	20	93	1,912
1967	320	496	196	166	104	292	253	32	36	115	2,018
1968	304	381	191	231	160	387	272	35	29	106	2,096
1969	160	239	126	145	83	197	265	50	36	57	1,358
Totals	2,300	3,546	1,158	1,352	1,001	2,797	1,861	257	215	820	15,307

Source: Data compiled by Opera Mundi Europe.

Market. In the case of more limited forms of cooperation there were 1,352 agreements between national companies, 1,001 between EC companies with different nationalities, and 2,797 between EC firms and firms in other countries. The ideal of mergers between companies of equal stature to create large-scale, transnational European companies was rarely achieved during this period; the three examples of this are the Agfa-Gaevert merger in 1964 which linked German and Belgian firms, the Vereinigte Flugtechnische Werke-Fokker merger in 1969 which linked German and Dutch firms, and the Dunlop-Pirelli merger in 1970 which linked British and Italian firms and which subsequently fell apart in 1973.

Consequently, industrial concentrations and mergers have apparently had very little connection with the movement toward European unity. The most important mergers and take-overs have occurred within member states and not between them. When company mergers and take-overs have occurred they have mostly been between Community and non-Community companies. The same observation applies to more limited forms of cooperation such as the establishment of shared subsidies and reciprocal shareholding. Table 6.2 presents these statistics according to the fifteen industrial sectors analyzed. It is important to note that in the case of "lead" industries, such as aerospace and electronics, mergers and agreements between Community firms and those of other countries far outweighed mergers and agreements among firms in different EC member states.

Why has the gradual implementation of the Common Market not led to the kinds of business restructuring desired by the Commission, particularly in advanced sectors?

PUBLIC AND PRIVATE RESPONSES
TO THE COMMON MARKET

National Governments

The formation of the Community on a liberal basis immediately triggered an intensive and ongoing effort by national governments to intervene in the private sector.[13] It was quickly evident from 1957 that the public authorities of the member states would not resign themselves to the play of market forces to determine the direction of national industrial development. Market integration without some national intervention would have simply increased the strength of the strongest member states. This was most apparent in the French case where government efforts to modernize the domestic industrial structure were basically a reaction against the industrial power of the United States and West Germany.[14] In the Italian case national policies also involved the effort to reduce regional disparities between the northern and southern parts of the country.[15]

TABLE 6.2

Establishment of Subsidiaries, Cooperation Agreements, Holdings and Mergers, in the European Community, 1961-69, by Sector

Sectors	Unilateral Establishment of Subsidiaries in Other Countries			Cooperation—Minority and Reciprocal Holdings, Common Subsidiaries, Common Parent Companies			Mergers, Take-overs, or Controlling Minority				Totals
	From Member Country to Member Country	From Third Country to Member Country	From Member Country to Third Country	Between Firms in the Same Country	Between Common Market Firms	Between Member Country and Third Country Firms	Same Member Country	Different Member Countries	By a Member Country in a Third Country	By a Third Country in a Third Country	
Food and drink industry	226	224	69	173	95	210	227	21	12	81	1,388
Textiles	238	200	94	129	63	184	225	20	11	49	1,213
Paper industry	34	101	13	37	18	70	59	4	9	29	364
Chemicals	478	772	271	238	217	581	352	66	86	199	3,260
Petrochemicals and plastics	(148)	(192)	(66)	(70)	(53)	(180)	(80)	(26)	(27)	(45)	(892)
Pharmaceuticals	(77)	(138)	(40)	(17)	(32)	(51)	(55)	(11)	(11)	(56)	(494)
Petroleum and derivatives	86	115	45	63	34	119	41	18	8	32	561
Building materials	140	159	49	120	90	106	132	13	8	17	834
Glass	16	21	5	15	18	30	30	5	2	5	147
Mechanical engineering	542	927	310	244	221	660	284	46	24	181	3,439
Metal works and foundries	210	290	93	149	81	279	194	28	18	73	1,415
Iron and steel	16	17	3	19	8	26	42	3	3	3	140
Electrical and electro-mechanical engineering	239	332	138	97	101	243	146	18	24	94	1,432
Electronic engineering	72	369	67	50	32	192	56	11	10	56	915
Aerospace industries	3	19	1	28	23	97	23	4	—	1	199
Totals	2,300	3,546	1,158	1,352	1,001	2,797	1,861	257	215	820	15,307

Source: Data complied by Opera Mundi Europe.

Thus member state governments have frequently intervened to limit rather than to increase the possibilities for significant cross-frontier restructuring of industries. One reason for such action has been their concern that important sectors already largely in foreign hands would be controlled or dominated from abroad if foreign firms were allowed to expand their ownership even further.[16] Therefore, the French resisted American investments in the French economy during the early 1960s. Moreover, even though it was not yet a member of the Community, Britain pursued similar policies. In the mid-1960s the Industrial Reorganisation Corporation prevented the Swedish firm SKF from increasing its already large share of the UK ball bearing market by bringing about a merger among British firms.[17]

In addition, fear of foreign control has been intensified when governments believe strategic reasons justify opposition to national firms being run from abroad. In the energy sector in the early 1960s the German government blocked efforts by the Companie Française des Petroles to gain control of the Gelsenkirchner Bergwerkaktiengesellschaft (GBAG), not only because the government wanted to maintain the national identity of a firm in an area considered to be of national importance, but also because German-owned firms in this sector were rare. At the time of the merger talks 75 percent of sales of oil refineries and 80 percent of crude oil sales were being made in Germany by foreign-owned companies and GBAG represented the vast majority of the remaining 25 percent and 20 percent. GBAG finally combined with the Rheinisch-Westfaelisches Electrizitätswerk.[18] The full implications of this policy emerged under the impact of the OPEC price increases in December 1974. On the basis of the combination, the West German government now initiated efforts to create an oil company big enough to compete internationally for petroleum supplies. VEBA, an oil, electricity, and chemical firm 43 percent owned by the government, offered to acquire the 52 percent interest that it does not already control in GBAG.[19]

The EC member states have also opposed transnational take-overs and agreements if they have pursued nationally oriented science and technology policies.[20] This is particularly true if they fear a dilution of national economic strength by failure to establish capacities in key areas. This has led to competitive policies which have fragmented Community markets and impeded the development of internationally viable firms in lead industries. Thus the French government opposed the efforts of Westinghouse to take over the French computer firm Machine Bull, and encouraged the merger of several French firms to form Companie Internationale Informatique. This concentration was reinforced and supported by the national *Plan Calcul* (see Chapter 9). The German government has also sought to develop a national computer capacity through a series of *Datenverarbeitungsprogramme*, and the British government encouraged the establishment of International Computers Limited, which was formed from nine different companies. Limited intra-EC cooperation is occurring through Unidata, which is composed of Philips, Siemens, and CII. A similar pattern has evolved in the development of nuclear reactors, although the Euratom Treaty was based on the hope that the Community would play the major role in this area.

In the case of aircraft, important projects such as Concorde, the Airbus, and the development of a European space satellite and rocket launcher have been pursued on an exclusively intergovernmental basis. Governments have sought a *juste retour* from their participation, and this has lead at times to an arbitrary distribution of activities to satisfy national demands. This has been reflected in the management patterns, distribution of contracts, and intrusion of political considerations into the development of the now-scrapped European II booster rocket and the European "space lab" projects. National resistance to cooperation and mergers is most intense where economic and defense considerations coincide. This has occurred in such areas as weapons procurement, aircraft, telecommunications, and computers.[21]

Finally, governments often find they prefer to encourage national industries for foreign political and economic reasons to seek partners beyond the Community context. Such preferences bring them into conflict with their obligations to facilitate intra-European industrial cooperation. This has been most visible in the aircraft industry.

The Private Sector

While government policies which have emphasized the national context have clearly placed constraints on cross-frontier cooperation, political influence is limited because the major responsibility for such cooperation still remains in the hands of the private sector.[22] Why then have national industries failed to take advantage of the opportunities offered by the Common Market for cross-frontier mergers and concentrations?

The conclusions drawn from the Opera Mundi study about the failure of national companies to restructure are not entirely correct, if a distinction is made between the forms through which industries have preferred to take advantage of the Common Market and those forms which would involve changes in the locus of industrial ownership, decision making, and location, and consequently would support a change in the locus of political authority. As the statistics illustrate, the establishment of the Community has produced considerable concentration on a national basis either to take advantage of the enlarged market or to form defensive alliances to withstand competition from other EC firms as well as companies located in other countries.

However, cross-frontier mergers have not been the principal means, or even the preferred means, for industrial cooperation among European firms. Joint subsidies and reciprocal shareholding are more freqently used to gain some of the advantages of mergers while retaining company independence and separate identity. A 1972 Harvard Business Review article contains a partial but representative list of the kinds of large-scale agreements among Community firms that range from nationally based concentrations to cross-frontier cooperative manufacturing and marketing agreements.[23] Moreover, the existence of the EC has provided little incentive or necessity for transnational mergers in a wide range of sectors, since nationally based firms have been able frequently to improve their competitive capacity first through concentrating on a domestic basis and then by expanding into the markets of other member states through direct sales and the establishment of wholly owned subsidiaries. Thus there are a significant number of large-scale nationally based firms which operate across Europe as though it were a homogeneous market. Among them are the Swiss firms Ciba-Geigy, Nestlé, and Brown-Boveri; the Dutch Philips; and the binational firms Unilever and Royal Dutch/Shell. This is in contrast to the American international corporation which has had to break into the Common Market rather than expand from an already existing base. An analysis of the firms listed in the 1972 continental and British editions of *Who Owns Whom* not only illustrates the European preference for using direct sales or subsidiaries, but also provides information on the extent to which there is considerable trans-European business activity, even if it is conducted by firms organized primarily on a national basis.

Even the examples of "successful" cross-frontier mergers have necessitated legal and organizational forms in which the question of control was avoided or hidden. Thus the problems of distribution of power and preservation of some independence and autonomy not only affect relations between the Community and the member states but also the relations among managers and boards of directors when mergers occur. These considerations arise because the principal objectives of large-scale mergers are to increase profits, competitiveness, and efficiency. The pursuit of these ends frequently means pooling resources, cutting out duplication of activities, closing down redundant plants, and reducing the number of staff at all levels. This is bound to create difficulties among company directors, managers, shareholders, and governments.

In addition, cross-frontier mergers and agreements have been affected by macroeconomic uncertainty on a national, Community, and global level. Thus cooperation between Dunlop and Pirelli was eroded as a result of inflation and stagnation in the Italian economy. Similarly efforts of Fiat and Citroen to merge have been superceded by the successful merger of Citroen with Peugeot as a result of substantial financial aid by the French government.

Finally, firms, particularly in lead industries, in their efforts to remain autonomous, have pursued counterproductive policies in terms of the European-oriented goals of the Commission. They have implemented policies which reduce their complementary, and, consequently, the points of affinity which might bring them together in the future. The best illustration of this is provided by the aircraft industry.[24] In this sector the possibility for nationally based development and production of new planes has declined as funding requirements and market size for new projects has increased. Consequently, almost all European companies have signed cooperative agreements with different partners for different projects. This has led to a network of cooperative agreements which restrict the possibilities for companies to concentrate on a Communitywide basis because of their patchwork nature and because in the aircraft industry such agreements usually cover several decades. Moreover, as the case of the aircraft industry reveals, agreements with non-EC firms, particularly the American giants, are more attractive than similar agreements with member state firms. In the case of the development of a new engine, Rolls Royce and Snecma, instead of collaborating with each other, have turned respectively to Lockheed and General Electric.[25] The explanation, in part, is that U.S. firms often have more to offer their European partners in terms of new technology and financial resources. In part, the French have apparently been concerned about becoming overly involved through bilateral cooperative agreements with British aircraft and engine firms. While this would foster intra European cooperation it would lead to limitations being placed upon the French in using their aircraft industry for bargaining purposes within the Community and in pursuing a relatively independent foreign policy. Therefore, cooperation with the United States is preferred since it can be used tactically in intra-EC negotiations.

The Community Response

Since there was neither a sufficient number of significant cross-frontier mergers nor European capacities developed in lead industries, the Commission was prompted to seek new instruments for inducing industrial evolution it felt to be both economically and politically desirable. Thus on July 1, 1967, when the Commission was reorganized and expanded as a result of the merger of Euratom, the ECSC, and the EEC, a new Directorate General for Industrial Policy was created. It retained a part of the activities of the former Directorate General for Internal Markets and received specific responsibilities for the development of the Community's industries. It was placed under the jurisdiction of Commissioner Colonna.

The ten-year delay after the signing of the Rome Treaty in establishing a directorate for industrial policy as well as the lack of an explicit sectoral policy at the EC-level can be explained by the initial reliance on competition and other general liberal market-oriented policies which alone were available to the Commission to influence desirable intra-EC industrial developments and also to contribute to the political strengthening of the Community. Moreover, industry and technology policies did not seem quite as pressing in a time of rapid economic expansion as they had been during the reconstruction period after World War II or were becoming in the face of increased international competition.

In trying to formulate a mandate for the new directorate Colonna had to face a number of difficulties. The Treaty of Rome had neither mentioned the area of industrial policy nor granted the Commission those instruments through which national governments can exercise an influence over their own industries, such as public contracts, tax rebates, or funds for granting subsidies, and long-term credits for export financing. Moreover, the treaty had made the Commission dependent upon approval of its proposals by the Council of Ministers, and even in those cases where states have concurred in a Council decision they have been able to circumvent the decision because of their control over the implementation of Community policies. This is possible because the Commission neither has subordinate political and administrative levels directly responsible to itself nor the authority and direct influence over national administrations.[26] Finally, because of the existing distribution of power between governments and the private sector the Commission, with its far more limited powers, is even at a greater disadvantage than national authorities in trying to influence the private sector.

The Colonna Report, with its constant comparisons to American industry organized on a continentwide basis, analyzed the obstacles which stood in the way of European industrial concentrations and mergers—particularly in lead industries.[27] What was dramatically clear in the references to U.S. corporations was the extent to which the impact of the American customs union on the development of a national industrial network was the primary model for EC policies. In addition, the insistence on European firms achieving the size of huge American corporations is a reflection of the assumption that large-scale firms are more efficient and more productive. This has been increasingly modified by research which has shown in fact that medium-size firms are extremely important sources for research and development that lead to innovations in industrial technology and products.

The Colonna Report reached a number of conclusions for improving the conditions for industrial development on an intra-Community basis as well as for redefining the role of the Commission. They rested by and large on the assumption that from the perspective of EC political and economic goals the weaknesses of Community industrial evolution were, in part, a result of the negative effect on the private sector of the still-imperfect realization of the customs union. Thus the report reemphasized the necessity of general policies for creating a uniform European legal and administrative infrastructure for the private sector. This included the continued removal of formal obstacles to the free circulation of the factors of production such as the elimination of remaining technical barriers to trade, the harmonization of national company laws and the creation of a European company statute, and the elimination of tax barriers to cross-frontier linkups.

Although the Commission already had authority to implement the general policies necessary for removing these "negative" barriers to trade its reliance on voluntary industrial cooperation, particularly to create a European advanced technology as well as to modernize sectors in a state of crisis, were to be augmented through a variety of new instruments. Thus the Colonna Report proposed that the Commission pursue policies to open up national public markets to competitive bidding throughout the EC,[28] expand the coordination of state aid and subsidy policies to foster complementary rather than competitive industrial developments in key sectors,[29] and encourage intra-EC bank consortia to finance cross-frontier industrial ventures in key sectors. In addition, it also proposed that the Commission request authority to grant EC development contracts, coordinate Community-level science and technology policy more closely with industrial policy,[30] and develop sectoral policies for lead industries.

The possibility of sectoral policies had already been raised in the Second Medium-Term Economic Program, of 1966,[31] and to a large extent the European Coal and Steel Community, Euratom, and French indicative planning served as models or points of departure for development of similar policies on the Community level. The connection between these models and the activities of the industrial policy directorate are discussed in great detail in *Une politique industrielle pour l'europe*,[32] written by Robert Toulemon and Jean Flory, who were, respectively, Director General for Industrial, Technology, and Science Policy and Director General for Industrial and Technology Policy at the Commission from 1967 to 1973.

While the general instruments seek to create a geographic preference for business by establishing uniform regulations for the internal market, the latter are decidedly political and interventionist. If authorized they would give the Commission some of the levers necessary for exerting pressure on the direction of industrial development, mergers, and concentrations. Thus Commission officials believe open bidding for public contracts could have a twofold effect.[33] On the one hand, it would allow public authorities to coordinate their decisions on what equipment they need and to use their purchasing power to stimulate concentrations in key sectors such as nuclear reactors, computers, airplanes, and telecommunications. On the other hand, firms might be encouraged to concentrate because of the larger public contracts available. In addition, the capitalization of the European Investment Bank could be expanded and it could be used more directly to develop the "European" industrial network sought by the Commission.[34] Therefore, these instruments would not only allow the Commission to lay the foundation for European political and economic union, but also to define its own powers in this future polity.

There are many obstacles that confront the Commission in its efforts to further elaborate the powers it has in areas such as company law and to obtain new authority in order to become more active in its initiatives for lead industries and declining sectors. In the case of company law many national governments fear that a Community corporate law would further weaken their control over domestic firms and contribute to the shift of some power from the national capitals to Brussels. In regard to public markets some member state governments want special exceptions because public contracts are used for regional development, to support national industries or to deal with short-run political and economic problems.[35] In addition, it is unclear from the Commission's proposal how the coordination of public contracts could be achieved to facilitate industrial concentrations as well as what role the Commission would play in this process. As for development contracts, delay in the adoption of this proposal has resulted largely from the insistence of certain states—Britain and France in particular—that it should be up to the Nine to decide which projects should be awarded Community support. The Commission however feels this should be its responsibility in conjunction with the European Investment Bank.

Although the Colonna Report set the stage for future discussion it had little immediate practical impact until the Paris summit of October 21, 1972; the EC leaders who participated at this meeting issued a joint communique in which among other things they called for "the creation of a common industrial base." Almost one year later the Commission adopted a general draft resolution on Community industrial policy based upon a memorandum prepared by the Commissioner then responsible for industrial policy, Altiero Spinelli. This memorandum, entitled *Toward the Establishment of a European Industrial Base*, reemphasized the areas proposed as suitable for Community policy in the Colonna Report.[36] It also enumerated those sectors in which EC action would be desirable to facilitate concentrations, mergers, and modernization. These included lead industries such as aircraft, data processing, heavy mechanical and electrical equipment, nuclear energy, and uranium enrichment, plus industries in a state of crisis such as shipbuilding, textiles, and pulp and paper.

This memorandum was presented by the Commission to the Council of Ministers on May 7, 1973, with the request that the Council implement a variety of Commission proposals. When the Council adopted this draft action program on December 17, 1973, it was the first time since the establishment of the Community that an EC industrial policy general program was given formal status. However, future developments now depend on whether the nine member states are as committed to adopting the specific policy measures contained in the program as they were in agreeing on the general goals of the program itself. Even then the program was no more than a series of hastily contrived deadlines for future action in a variety of areas, some of which are highly charged politically such as Community-level sectoral planning. Moreover, the program was adopted a few days before the quadrupling of petroleum prices, an event which has subsequently cast a shadow on

Community action in many areas.[37]

Customs Union Theory, European
Union and Industry

It is obvious that the Commission's efforts to develop a Community role in industrial policy as well as in other areas have been severely hampered by the lack of adequate political powers and administrative and financial institutions. (In addition, the Commission also has contributed to its own weakness; in the case of the Directorate General for Industrial Policy some of the key mechanisms for formulating and implementing policies are controlled by other divisions such as competition policy, internal markets, science, and technology.) Its attempts to expand its powers have continued to be caught in the political and legal tensions between the member states and the Community on the distribution of sovereignty among them. EC proponents have tended to regard these features of the Rome Treaty as well as the resistance of the member states as manifestations of the retrograde nationalism of governments which wish to prevent the absorption of their nations into a larger EC political entity. In addition, they have looked upon the failure of industries to merge and concentrate on a cross-frontier basis as economically inefficient and politically counterproductive because of the relationship between industrial restructuring and the establishment of a European political and economic union.

However, to assert that nationally oriented public policies toward industry and private patterns of concentration and mergers limited to one nation would not have evolved if sufficient political and economic power had been transferred to the EC begs the question of why such a Europe has not come about. While it is correct that progress on a Community industrial policy cannot be separated from the future evolution of Community institutions, the models proposed by the supranationalists or federalists are unrealistic.

In this regard much of the disappointment among supporters of political and economic union about the political evolution of the EC in general and industry in particular is a result of their programmatic approach to the Community. By focusing on the policies and processes which have been deductively determined as essential to support some form of European union they have diverted attention from an examination of the real, as against the ideologically predetermined, dynamics of a multinational regional association composed of established political economies. This has led to an underestimation of the difficulties of establishing a Community political economy distinct from those of the member states as well as a misunderstanding about why the nation-state has persisted as the basic unit for political and economic organization.

While customs union theory has provided a firm basis for predicting and encouraging a significant increase in intra-Community trade and investment, it has been a poor guide for predicting how states would respond, how firms would restructure, and the impact such reorganization could have on shifting authority from the member states to the Community. Since this theory in combination with proposals for establishing European political and economic institutions has influenced policies toward industry, it is important to explain why this approach has contributed to a misunderstanding of the dynamics of the public and private sectors and the implications of a customs union for EC institutions. In order to accomplish this, customs union theory and the general problems of political union will be examined separately and then in relation to each other to illustrate the full range of the assumptions upon which they are based.[38]

Customs union theory seemed to offer an attractive rationale for facilitating political and economic integration of nation-states by improving the environment for private sector activity. In formulations such as Hallstein's the Common Market appeared to be nothing more than an enlargement of the national market, and in turn only required Community public institutions which were simply enlargements of national institutions. However, the theory contained inherent limitations if overextended for ideological reasons beyond its immediate economic implications for private sector activity to support the transfer of political authority from the member states to the Community. This resulted because it is essentially formulated in apolitical and ahistorical terms, since it only deals with the competitive response of atomistic firms in a liberal market. Consequently, it excludes the nation as a relevant unit of analysis. Therefore, the range of interests—even the role—of the state is hidden because much of the discussion of private decision making and public industrial policy is conducted in the apolitical language of the managerial and production-oriented perspective of customs union theory. From this viewpoint the firm's decisions on where to locate, its organizational structure, and its patterns of investment are significant principally in terms of how these decisions affect its contribution to aggregate Community welfare. But aggregate Community welfare only becomes meaningful when translated into how business activities affect the interests of specific EC member states and their citizens.

To the extent that a role for government can be understood in terms of this model the interests of the state are identified with insuring the efficiency of firms by facilitating market integration. However, this is an incomplete basis for justifying the transfer of national political authority to the EC as national markets are merged into a common market, since the EC is not simply to be the guarantor of a liberal capitalist system. This by no means exhausts the range of functions the state performs. In fact, the proponents of European union are well aware that the expansion of the geographic radius of private sector activity requires the transfer of adequate authority to a political level which can take responsibility for this extended geographic scope of industry.[39] This will not only require policies to assist industries but also a wide range of measures such as regional and social policies to balance the adverse effects of the private sector on different regions and classes. Consequently, while this view is essentially correct and logical there may be limits to the extent to which the Community can assume many of the functions now performed by the nation-state. Moreover, the existing EC institutions now reflect the liberal capitalist view of the Common Market. If the Community were to have its responsibilities expanded this would require a further evolution of its institutions to reflect a much wider range of political, social, and economic interests.

Although there is a traditional reluctance of sovereign states to cede power to other entities this is only one of the motives at play in the EC. What is equally as important for explaining national resistance to transferring power to Brussels is the risk attached to the experiment of constructing common European institutions and a communitywide political economy. The certainty shared by the supporters of a supranational or federal Europe concerning the shape of such institutions, the distribution of powers and responsibilities, and the capacity of the EC to insure national interests is not generally shared by the member states.[40] While it is possible through treaty arrangements to distribute power between the member states and the Community, this is a rather formalistic and mechanical way to establish a new and legitimate political authority. It is open to question whether this could lead to an effective political and administrative infrastructure to formulate policies and resolve conflicts among the new constellation of regions, classes, parties, and economic interests it would bring into existence. The assumption that the establishment of a European union is analogous to the process that has taken place in countries which are federations like the United States is ill-taken. The Community's relationship to its nine member nations is not similar to that of the United States to its own states. The dynamics of a multistate regional association are very different from federations like America. Thus the governments of the Community member states fear that efforts to establish a union of some kind would only serve to undermine the legitimate authority which now exists without an adequate authority being created to either replace or augment it. This has led to a quandary. While national governments recognize that many problems now transcend national boundaries they resist relying on Community solutions to assist them in fulfilling their responsibilities for their own citizens.

Therefore, the difficulties standing in the way of establishing EC institutions, in part, explain why the Community is a unique regional association still composed of national political economies and not a fully integrated market in which national boundaries are only of secondary importance. Thus the role of the firm cannot be understood only in terms of its relationship to the customs union and the abstract consumer. It is also an integral part of the national political economy where it is one of the major bases for national political and social stability. Consequently, governments are not indifferent to the decisions made by firms or the decisions which affect them. Reliance on an imperfectly realized liberal economic market and the nebulous institutions of the EC for allowing private decision making to influence the patterns and distribution of investment and production from the firm's perspective intersect with how the operation of such a model with its new and unpredictable patterns of competition affects existing domestic interests and the political balances which are tied to industry. Moreover, the firm's competitiveness—and its contribution to the national economy—depends upon another element not included in customs union theory: the macroeconomic situation of the national economy in relation to those of the other member states.

Consequently, customs union theory must be placed in the context of much more elaborate theories of domestic and regional political economy. This must include the existence of the state and will lead to a distinctly different view of the dynamics of the EC and its industries.

Although the Rome Treaty established a formal equality among the member states and their firms, this did not correspond to the different levels of development of national political economies and the disparities in the size and productivity of their firms and the qualitative differences in their industrial structures. Unfortunately the Community, in order to be a viable association, would have to deal with these differences. However, those members like Germany, which were industrially strong, or at least better off, were concerned that as a result of their commitment to collective policies they would be required to insure that private investments and public funds were transferred to develop other parts of the Community. This would diminish the capital available for domestic investment, and potentially lead to wasteful subsidization of other countries' industries for political rather than economic reasons. Those states which were relatively weak were concerned that such transfers would make them dependent on the strongest members of the Community. Consequently, since the Community could not deal with these disparities except through market integration, the member states felt impelled to implement nationally-oriented industrial policies. For strictly domestic reasons the weaker states were concerned that trade liberalization without counterbalancing EC or national policies would have economically and politically destabilizing effects. The stronger states were concerned that if they too did not engage in some form of policy toward industry they would not be able to maintain their competitive edge in the face of the industrial policies of the other member states.

Even if the member states had not taken as active a role as they have, the administrative and legal integration of national markets would not have reduced the importance of national boundaries for industrial organization and strategy. As a result of its ahistorical and apolitical character customs union theory could not take into account the impact that the national structure and power of public and private banks and their connection with key industries predating the establishment of the EC would have on the development of the customs union. To a large extent, in response to the establishment of the EC, these historically determined constellations of economic power have had a significant influence on the geographic distribution of concentrations and mergers, and have perpetuated many of the disparities between the member states. Since these national industries could not become part of a nonexistent European industrial and power structure, the only way for a country like France to check the expansion of German industrial power was through competing industries of her own. Stated more generally the only way the oligopolistic and monopolistic organization of national markets could be challenged was by the establishment of equally as large industries in other member states or in non-EC countries. This situation has been aggravated by the fusion of national interests with those of particular industries.

Finally, even though industrial reorganization and concentration have occurred almost entirely within states, specialization on the basis of new patterns of comparative advantage have, by and large, not taken place. This is contrary to the development expected from the formation of the customs union and is particularly disappointing because it might have contributed to the process of regional economic integration. As a result of rapid economic growth and access to larger markets, national firms tended to expand production, as in the case of the automobile industry, and to a certain extent to duplicate each other's productive structures.[41] Nowhere was this more evident than in key sectors. Instead of attempting to develop these high-technology industries on a cooperative basis, they were developed on a national basis. The result has been a failure to establish significant national or European capacities which are economical and can challenge American corporations.[42]

Consequently, as a result of these political and economic developments the member states have hedged their commitments to the EC through domestic industrial policies and the intergovernmental formula as a balance to the aspirations of the Commission. This has evolved partly because of the risks to national political and economic stability posed by the unclear implications of intra-EC cooperation and partly because of international factors which have an unequal impact on the member states' political economies not only in regard to their relative industrial competitiveness in respect to non-Community countries, but also in regard to one another. Resistance and competitiveness have been intensified by the unequal pressure of rising petroleum prices on the extent to which member states must now increase their large balance-of-payments deficits. Therefore, intra-European policies must take into account the extent to which the member states are in competition with each other to improve their rates of growth as well as the extent to which there are areas in which cooperation among themselves would be mutually beneficial. However, as the difficulties standing in the way of formulating an EC common energy policy have revealed, the differences in relative vulnerability have led to strong national responses. An example of such a response is a 1974 report issued by the British National Economic Development Office and entitled *The Increased Cost of Energy: Implications for UK Industry.* In conjunction with the Wilson government's plans to nationalize industry and to control the profits from North Sea oil, Labor parties in the EC are apparently no less national in orientation than other parties.[43]

These reasons for the continued existence and role of the nation-state in a regional association are an indirect way of reaching a third perspective to explain the dynamics of the EC and the possibility for Community-level policies toward industry. Although the customs union has fostered some forms of interdependence and the necessity for cooperation it is also a regional association in which the members still attempt to maintain some vestiges of their independence; consequently, while there is cooperation on some levels, the members are also engaged in modified foreign policies toward one another. As a result neither the responsibilities for foreign policy nor defense have been transferred to the Community. Therefore, it is not possible to deal with industry and industrial policy without relating them to foreign policy. This requires a shift in focus from the perspectives of the private goals of firms in a customs union and the efforts of the Community to absorb the member states to a consideration of what goals the states are trying to pursue in and through the EC. To a great extent this will explain the choices governments have made in regard to the industries they wish to develop.

Industrial Structure and International Power

Although customs union theory provided an economic rationale for the formation of a Europeanwide market and a simplistic model for contributing to the transformation of interstate relations, the reasons for establishing a larger geographic basis for trans-European cooperation were entirely derived neither from this limited economic model nor from the immediate political conclusions drawn from the experiences of the Second World War. What was not enunciated clearly at that time was a much more profound trend which implicitly has influenced many of the choices made by the member states concerning the kind of industrial structure they wish to have and which has had a variety of implications for the relationship of the EC and its member states to each other and to the international political economy.

Since the early part of this century as the international implications of American and Japanese competition have gradually become visible European states have increasingly become aware of the economic, political, and military limitations placed upon them by their size. During the interwar period they sought to deal with these limitations on a national basis through protectionist policies or, as in the case of the United Kingdom, through an effort to form an imperial preference system with the Commonwealth countries. In other words, parallel to NATO, the EC in part is a Europeanwide geopolitical and geoeconomic successor to those post-World War I policies through which states sought to maximize their political and economic power on either a strictly national or regional basis and to influence the international distribution of industry.[44] If this motive was not stated clearly in the late 1950s, by 1973 it was described at length in the EC's GATT negotiating mandate which mentioned that the movement toward the formation of a customs union was a result of the political and economic implications of international competition and trade liberalization for the industrial power of small nations.

In the early years of the Common Market the potentially international implications behind national and EC industrial and trade policies and the political motives that shaped these policies remained submerged. The member states were "inward looking" because their attention was focused on the problems of postwar reconstruction and the implementation of the Treaty of Rome. Increasingly however the EC became the vehicle through which the member states projected the remnants of their aspirations to be of some importance in world affairs. This was manifested in their conception of the structure of production which they felt was commensurate with their economic needs and international political goals.

These motives and goals were broached by Jean Jacques Servan-Schreiber in *Le défi américain*, which appeared in 1967. In this book he posed the question of whether the Europeans can really depend on the United States in fields of future importance such as nuclear power, space, aircraft, and computers.[45] This question reflected the fears raised by the "brain drain" and the discovery of the managerial and technology "gaps" as well as the extent to which demands for policies in these areas were based upon a very traditional sense of insuring that the member states of the European Community possess the instruments necessary to insure them their independence from the United States and a place in the world. Since the United States was seen as the major political and economic competitor, Europeans, in order to challenge American industry, would have to emulate the American industrial structure—particularly in regard to the size of corporations and in the new high-technology fields.

In 1969 Christopher Layton, elaborating these themes in greater detail in his *European Advanced Technology*, was also both impressed and disturbed by the accomplishments of American industry.[46] He described the technological imbalance between the United States and the members of the Community, the negative effect of American direct investments in Europe on

European efforts to construct transnational enterprises in key sectors, and the record flow of payments to the United States for industrial licenses. He feared that if Europeans were not prepared to make decisions which would allow them to form a counterpole of growth and development comparable to the United States, they would continue to fall behind in lead industries, become increasingly dependent on American technology, continue to see the locus of control and ownership in important industrial sectors gravitate to the United States, and continue to suffer a negative balance of payments. Layton's model for challenging American industry, like Servan-Schreiber's, was drawn directly from his analysis of the American political economy. Among the points he emphasized as having given American industry its advantages were social mobility, professional training, the size of the internal market and of companies, the role of the government in fostering research and development—particularly in crucial sectors such as chemicals, aerospace, nuclear power, and computers—and the relationship between government-supported research and industrial exploitation of this research by private firms.

Thus in the span of a decade (the 1960s) the role imposed upon national industries had expanded from the more limited economic one of providing the backbone for a European political and economic network by taking advantage of the customs union to one which included challenging American industrial predominance in industries based on advanced technology and providing the foundations for some degree of national and Community independence from the United States. For such EC proponents as Layton this would require a much more interventionist Community, particularly in regard to industry, in order to insure that industry played its role in these geoeconomic and geopolitical designs. This posed a subtle relationship between the pursuit of large Community corporations for economic reasons and the necessity of establishing such firms to achieve the larger international goals of those who thought in terms of a world role for the Community. Would industry fulfill its obligation within the confines of the EC? Would the member state governments accept these geopolitical aspirations and exert the necessary pressure on their bankers, industrialists, and managers?

Although the individual markets and capacities to raise capital are too limited to develop large-scale industries in a strictly national context the general desire to have such "European" industries has not led to cooperative policies to develop them. In addition to the reasons already presented, industrial, science, and technology policy cannot be separated from the fact that the realization of the Community must also be seen as an exercise in three kinds of interrelated foreign policies:[47] those of the member states toward one another, of the EC toward the member states, and of the states and the Community in relationship to the rest of the world.[48]

First, in general, the establishment and evolution of the EC is an exercise in foreign policy—even if in a highly modified form. The degree to which this occurs depends upon whether national governments view participation in the Community as part of their foreign policy or as an extension and continuation of their domestic politics. The degree to which the member states see the Community as a framework through which to pursue traditional foreign policy aspirations will influence the extent to which they attempt to develop important industries on a national basis and to which they are prepared to cooperate with other member states on a Communitywide basis. However, if the EC is viewed as an effort to influence the international distribution of industry and trade between the Community and the rest of the world the member states are also engaged in a regional competition to influence the distribution among themselves. Moreover, national industrial policies are often one of the factors in the miniature balance-of-power politics that exists on many planes among the member states.[49] Thus the larger states have encouraged national industries in the hope that they could achieve economic efficiency by having access to the markets of the other EC members; instead, as in the case of computers, aircraft, and nuclear reactors, this has led to a fragmentation and neutralization of national efforts.

Second, this places a rather difficult burden on the EC. Industrial distribution, whether influenced by private or public policies, must contribute to the construction of Europe as well as support the efforts of the member states to modernize their own industries. However, the delineation of an EC industrial policy is one of the means used by the Commission both to improve the overall economic environment for industry as well as to weaken the powers of the nation-state and to increase the role and responsibilities of the Community. Therefore if from the national level the EC is often seen as a useful vehicle for national purposes, from the Brussels perspective states which qualify their participation in European-oriented industrial projects are viewed as blocking the realization of a larger political and economic entity.

Finally, whether pursued individually or collectively, industrial policies are part of the foreign policies of the member states and the Commission toward third countries. States which command specific industrial capacities of interest to third countries have the choice of either influencing EC policies or pursuing independent policies. This is best illustrated by the conflict between the bilateral arrangements of member states with selected oil producing nations and the unsuccessful efforts of the Commission to prevent competition and outbidding among the Nine by stressing the necessity of negotiating Community agreements for cooperation with energy producing nations.[50] The deal concluded between France and Iran in June 1974 is a manifestation of this conflict, particularly since it includes agreements on industrial sectors such as nuclear reactors and uranium enrichment—sectors where the Commission has attempted to foster cooperative research and development.[51] In addition, these deals include joint ventures, long-term supply contracts, and the promotion of imports from oil producing countries in line with their development plans and of exports of capital goods and services from EC member states. Such agreements weaken Community political solidarity and divert attention from areas where intra-Community cooperation would be desirable. Similar conflicts of jurisdiction and substance arise in the context of East-West detente[52] and in the current negotiations between the Community and the more than forty "associable" developing countries when policies involving industrial development, financial credits, and technical assistance must be formulated.[53]

An extremely interesting example which cuts across these industrial and foreign policy problems is the competition between French and American manufacturers for a multibillion dollar contract to supply new planes to NATO. This has pitted the French Breguet-Dassault Mirage F-1M53 against the American General Dynamics YF-16 and the Northrop YF-17 for a contract to supply 350 planes for the Belgium, Dutch, Danish, and Norwegian airforces. The French insist that European, particularly Community, countries buy a plane manufactured by one of the member states both to support a domestic aircraft capacity and to assert independence from the United States—even though the French plane is not considered as good. The four European governments involved in the purchase have indicated that they would like to tie a potential purchase of the French plane to France rejoining NATO.

Thus industrial policies have both domestic and international dimensions, and efforts to formulate common European approaches are complicated for several reasons. Although there is a collective interest in external trade policy, both trade and industrial policies have foreign political implications. Success in both areas may require prior agreement and coordination among the national governments on the direction of their external policies. Moreover, even though industry is a vital element for intra-EC consolidation and for supporting Community and national foreign policies, its decisions may not support integration. Therefore, some further discussion is necessary about the relationship among industrial policy, trade policy, and foreign policy. Before this can be done, some comments are necessary about the internationalization of capital and production and their effects on the relationship between national governments and industry.

The Internationalization of Production

The establishment of the Community was in part justified by the recognition that many modern industries in order to be efficient need access to larger markets than those provided by small nations. It was hoped that the Community's industries would pursue policies that would contribute to the consolidation of the EC. This depended upon firms preferring the Community to other areas for their activities as well as the EC constituting a geographic area large and diverse enough for economically rational public and private policies.

Unfortunately, the divergence between the Community's responsibility for developing a European economic and political infrastructure and the geographic preferences of industry have occurred on two planes. As previously mentioned, firms have been able to take advantage of the market from a national base without engaging in the kind of cross-frontier restructuring that would support integration. Moreover, for many of these large firms, although the member state may be the center for operations, their perspective on their economic interests is global rather than limited to the EC. This is reflected in the fact that the EC is not always the most efficient or desirable geographic unit for planning and development. Therefore, the political goals to be achieved through the encouragement of intra-Community industrial structures is undermined in those cases where industrialists and businessmen find more desirable partners in non-EC countries or the structure and dynamics of particular sectors such as textiles, chemicals, aluminum, or shipbuilding do not lend themselves readily to economically and politically acceptable solutions on an exclusively intra-Community basis because of international factors which are often beyond the control of EC as well as national officials.[54]

The global perspective, in which the Community is one area among others for economic activity, is part of the more general trend of the "internationalization" of production and capital, and transcends both the national and EC context. To a large extent this internationalization, which weakens national control over the private sector, is a result of both regional and international trade liberalization. The conflict it causes is reflected in national and Commission discussions about the operation and impact of multinational firms in Europe and the inability of the member states and the Community to agree on policies to make them serve EC goals. It is also reflected in the dilemma national governments have faced in their attempts to create large-scale internationally competitive firms on a national basis. As in the case of Pechiney, these firms frequently become "internationalized" with the consequence that the government which encouraged them loses control.

Consequently, even without the political difficulties which have been mentioned such trends in the private sector create innumerable problems for the member states, let alone for the Community, in formulating policies toward particular industries. The possibilities for political pressure being exerted to influence the geographic scope of business activity in any event is limited as long as the Community and the member states are still ideologically committed to the existing distribution of power between the public and private sectors. If political pressure were exerted to influence industries to plan or to merge within the geographic limits of the EC, this might place unnecessary constraints on their competitiveness and efficiency. In addition, if the Community is to maintain its international commitments there are limits to the extent that it can impede international competition in order to maintain threatened industries or to develop "infant" industries. Finally, if the Community were to pursue protectionist or subsidization policies to favor these industries the overall effect might be undesirable; as in the case of a common agricultural policy, separating some part of Community economic activity from the international economy would lead to an uneconomic allocation of industrial resources within the Common Market.

Community efforts to approach the question of sectoral policies involve several issues. As a result of the customs union EC industries collectively are in competition with those of the rest of the world. Therefore, there is a common interest in those aspects of external trade policy that affect the interests of a particular sector. If a sector is affected by changing patterns of international competition the Community can only begin to be a forum for policies if the firms and governments involved feel they have a common interest in seeking a solution in Brussels. However, in weak sectors this may require rationalization which means modernization of firms, mergers, phasing out of inefficient units, and retraining of workers. In other words there is an allocation of burdens. In regard to lead industries there is a competition for growth, employment, and whatever power is to be derived from having such industries on a national basis. Thus the collective interest of business and government in dealing with external competition often dissolves when solutions on a Europeanwide basis require dealing with competition among themselves.

Although the Commission has tried to act as though it were dealing with an established political economy its influence in dealing with these problems on a sectoral basis is limited. It does not have the political authority required for sectoral policies nor does it have the requisite administrative infrastructure and financial resources. In addition, industries affected will alternately seek support in Brussels and in the national capitals, depending on the structure of the industry involved. The EC Commission is not a strong federal government mediating among interest groups, although it would like to be. Furthermore, governments and industries often feel that the Commission proposes sectoral policies to fit a preconceived notion of what will contribute to the building of Europe, rather than dealing with industrial problems on the basis of their economic merits. This programmatic approach to industry was challenged when the British banker Ronald Grierson briefly headed the industrial policy directorate under Altiero Spinelli.

Thus during his brief tenure in office Grierson organized meetings of industrialists, bankers, and trade unionists in Brussels. He hoped that through such meetings they would see the Commission as a useful framework for creating a psychological climate for discussing their common problems as well as a catalyst for assisting various industries in finding viable economic solutions for their problems. He preferred that the industries reach agreements among themselves upon which the Commission could act.

Although these sessions have had some importance for introducing industrialists and trade unionists to the prospects for defining their problems in cooperation with the Commission, their immediate and long-range implications must be counterbalanced by the fact that participants tend to appear "European" in Brussels in contrast to their stance in their national capitals. Such conflicting positions are a reflection that the centers of decision making have multiplied as a result of the establishment of the Community, but the national governments and bureaucracies still are the predominant powers.

Before turning to the question of whether there still is a rationale for Community efforts to deal with industrial problems, the relationship between foreign trade and industrial policy must be explored in greater detail.

Foreign Trade and Industrial Policy

The EC was established under Article 24 of the General Agreement on Tariffs and Trade, which permits the temporary formation of discriminatory customs unions; as a result an important component of national policy toward industry, trade negotiations, was transferred to the Common Market's Council of Ministers and its Commission.[55]

Both regional and international trade liberalization require complex policies to maintain the basis for political cohesion and the balance of economic advantage among the member states and between them and the rest of the world.[56] Thus the increased sensitivity of the member states' industries to damaging and changing patterns of international competition provided another reason in the Colonna Report for the Commission to seek additional authority to deal with industrial questions. This sensitivity had already been obvious at the beginning of the 1960s when the Directorate General for Internal Markets, headed at that time by François Xavier Ortoli, conducted studies to evaluate the effects different Community positions on its tariff would have on EC industries if advanced during negotiations in the Kennedy Round.[57] This entailed dealing with the demands of some industries for protection, consideration of what efforts might be required to adjust, and even eventually to reconvert, in weak sectors and sectors in decline which could not withstand the opening of the Common Market to foreign competition, and determination of which EC industries would be able to draw maximum advantages from access to non-EC markets as a result of tariff reductions. On the one hand, "equality" of competitive capacity was a precondition for an effective reciprocity in trade negotiations, particularly in regard to other countries with powerful industries such as the United States. On the other hand, where such "equality" could not be assured, particularly as a result of competition from developing countries, what transitional policies should the Community formulate?

Although the logic of the customs union suggested the necessity for some dovetailing of internal and external policies this coordination could not and did not occur at Community level. Although the Commission is responsible for trade negotiations it is limited from three directions in pursuing this role to its fullest extent. First, it does not have the power to coordinate external trade relations with internal policies involving industrial development and restructuring and adjustment assistance for workers. The necessity for coordinating these policies has become all the more acute since the EC member nations, like other advanced industrialized countries, are under pressure from the developing nations to permit and to encourage the partial transfer of certain productive activities such as textiles from the EC to the LDC's. Such shifts of production would cause social and economic dislocation in the member states, and consequently these disruptions might best be handled through intra-EC solutions.[58] Second, the full development of the common external tariff requires coordination with foreign policy. However, foreign policy is still the domain of the member states and even though some coordination occurs at Community level it is not through the Commission but through the Council of Ministers and the political coordination committee. Third, commercial and financial resources, technological know-how, and the ability to provide services are mainly in the hands of the Community's private sector and the member states' governments.

Irrespective of this fragmentation of political responsibility and power and the limits to public influence over the private sector, is there still a rationale for an EC policy toward industry? If so, what are its components and how can they be implemented? To what extent can such policies lead to a "European" industrial structure to support political and economic union? The answers to these questions depend upon the influence the Community can exert on industry as a result of its authority for trade negotiations and the implementation of the common commercial policy, its jurisdiction over the customs union, and its potential role as a participant in mergers, concentrations, and sectoral planning.

THE COMMUNITY AND INDUSTRY:
A REAPPRAISAL

Even under the best circumstances it is difficult for governments to influence the private sector for limited purposes. When such efforts are combined with political goals such as the Commission has tried to pursue through the encouragement of a "European" industrial network, the outcome is all the more doubtful. Since the Community will remain a multinational association, policies toward industry, whether national or Community, must be based on the reality that the Common Market is a polycentric bloc which has stabilized as a customs union. This means that nationally based firms, the competitive industrial policies of the member states, and multinational corporations will define the parameters of intra-EC cooperation. Naturally, as the case of lead industries illustrates, continuing national efforts to force the development of such sectors within the confines of domestic market will remain unsuccessful and, in terms of contributing to concentration in aircraft, nuclear reactors, or computers within the Community, counterproductive. In addition, they will perpetuate the unequal distribution of industry in the Common Market which has had a destabilizing effect on intra-EC relations since the Community was established. But this only reveals the depth of tensions inherent in a bloc that cannot be resolved by appeals to the establishment of an unrealizable supranational entity.

If, on the one hand, the member states pursue separate policies toward industries, on the other hand, membership in the EC has led to the necessity to formulate and implement some policies in common that affect the private sector. In addition to their shared interest in the management of the customs union as a result of increased intra-Community trade, the Nine have a general interest imposed upon them by the implications of their common geoeconomic boundary. Since the Community has superseded the states as the political entity responsible for trade negotiations, the Commission in conjunction with the member states can determine the broad relationship of the EC's industries to the international economy. This involves access to the markets of other countries as well as access of the industries of other countries to the Common Market.

In regard to EC access to export markets the Nine's capacity to successfully conclude trade negotiations has been maximized because collectively they are responsible for 50 percent of world imports and exports. In respect to access to the markets of the member states, changes in tariffs and in nontariff barriers can have a detrimental effect on a Communitywide basis as a result of the impact of new patterns of competition. This may compel governments and affected industries to seek some modifications of trade policy in Brussels as has been the case with the shipbuilding, textile, and pulp and paper industries. Simultaneously, in sectors threatened by international competition such as textiles, the Commission has represented the Nine in the negotiation of the Long-Term Arrangement to stabilize international competition in textiles.

However, such trade agreements also require some coordination with industrial and employment policies. Although the Commission has conducted a number of studies on the problems of the textile industry and issued a memorandum proposing a sectoral policy,[59] its ability to deal at Community level with the intra-EC effects of other nations' exports is limited.

Consequently, industries affected by these imports have sought whatever advantages they have been able to derive by placing pressures on their own governments for subsidies and protectionist measures. In general the Commission and the member states have not been able to coordinate Community trade policies with appropriate national industrial and employment policies, nor have the states been able to coordinate their support for declining sectors in order to avoid neutralizing each other's efforts to keep basically weak or noncompetitive firms afloat.

The classic example of the failure to coordinate such policies was the decision to lower tariff barriers to the import of pulp and paper from non-Community countries and the inability to devise measures to concentrate and improve EC-based firms faced with increased competition from lower-cost producers in Scandinavia and North America. Discussions of a sectoral policy for this industry are impeded by its international structure, and those proposals which have been advanced attempt to artificially maintain some comparative advantage for Common Market firms by implementing an ambitious program for improving the utilization of forests including forestation and reforestation policies.[60] Moreover, efforts to work out policies for this sector and at the same time maintain the Community commitment to trade liberalization have posed great difficulties.[61]

Although the member states are still determined to establish advanced industries, it is in these sectors more than any others that their interests conflict over how their firms should respond to the impact of international competition—particularly as it affects the international distribution of key industries. Aside from whether a basis can be found for effective intergovernmental cooperation to foster such industries, these attempts are a manifestation of the contemporary mercantilist response to the determinants of global distribution. They are also a clear indication of the political element involved in attempting to use the Common Market to create new patterns of comparative advantage or to improve declining industries.

NOTES

1. *Industrial Policy in the Community* (Brussels: Commission of the European Communities, 1970), p. 7 (hereafter cited as Colonna Report). The report is the first effort of the Commission to formulate an industrial policy mandate for itself. See also Guido Colonna di Paliano, "Why Europe Needs Continental Scale Firms," *Atlantic Community Quarterly* (Winter 1968-69), pp. 566-569.

2. Christopher Layton, *Cross Frontier Mergers in Europe* (Bath, England: Bath University Press, 1971), p. 10.

3. For a brief history of the origins of the European Community see Uwe Kitzinger, *The Politics and Economics of European Integration* (New

York: Praeger, 1963). On the European Defense Community see Daniel
Lerner and Raymond Aron, *France Defeats the EDC* (New York: Praeger,
1957).

4. *Rapport des Chefs de Délégation aux Ministres des Affaires
Etrangères*, Comité Intergouvernemental creé par la Conférence de Massine,
Brussels, April 21, 1956.

5. For an excellent collection of readings on customs union theory and
market integration see P. Robson, ed., *International Economic Integration*
(Harmondsworth, England: Penguin Books Ltd., 1972). For a thorough
discussion of the various rationales for the Common Market see Sidney Dell,
Trade Blocs and Common Market (New York: Alfred A. Knopf, 1963), chap.
2.

6. For a geographer's positive view on the possibilities for integration
see Geoffrey Parker, *The Logic of Unity: An Economic Geography of the
Common Market* (London: Longmans, Green, 1968). The chapter on how
national boundaries have isolated the development of the member states'
transportation networks from one another would suggest that there are
considerable practical difficulties in the way of establishing a European
political and economic union.

7. *The Market Economy in Western European Integration*, Seventh
Flemish Economic Congress, Louvain, May 8-9, 1965 (Louvain: Editions
Nauwelaerts, 1965). For a survey of what policies market integration requires,
particularly to achieve the goals of economic and political union, see Hans
von der Groeben, *Competition Policy in the Common Market* (Washington,
European Community Information Service, Community Topics, no. 19, June
1965).

8. Competition policy has been one of the major areas in which the
Commission has had authority to act. For discussion of its policies see. D. L.
McLachlan and D. Swann, *Competition Policy in the European Community*
(London: Oxford University Press), 1967. See also J. Zijlstra,
*Wirtschaftspolitik und Wettbewerbsproblematik in der EWG und ihren
Mitgliedstaaten* (Brussels: Commission of the European Communities, 1966),
Kollektion Studien, Reihe Wettbewerb, no. 2; and *First Report on
Competition Policy*, April 1972 and *Second Report on Competition Policy*,
April 1973 (Brussels, Commission of the European Communities).

9. See Walter Hallstein, "European Community as an Economic
Order," *The Market Economy*, op. cit., pp. 19-36, and Hallstein, *Der
unvollendete Bundesstaat* (Düsseldorf: Econ Verlag, 1969).

10. For an analysis of the conflicting intergovernmental and
supranational approaches to EC institutions see Steven J. Warnecke, "The
European Community After British Entry: Federation or Confederation?" in
Steven J. Warnecke, ed., *The European Community in the 1970's* (New York:
Praeger, 1972).

11. Colonna Report, op. cit., and *Stellungnahmen der Institutionen und
Berufsorganizationen der Gemeinschaft zum Memorandum der Kommission*

an den Rat über die Industriepolitik der Gemeinschaft (Brussels: Commission of the European Communities, 1971).

12. Colonna Report, op. cit., pp. 89-95.

13. For a survey of national policies toward industry, many of which preceded the formation of the Community, see Andrew Shonfield, *Modern Capitalism: The Changing Balance of Public and Private Power* (London: Oxford University Press, 1965). The chapters on France, Britain, Italy, and Germany are particularly relevant.

14. In the case of France see Lionel Stoleru, *L'impératif industriel* (Paris: Editions du Seuil, 1969). Also *Le Développement Industriel*, Commissariat Général du Plan d'Équipement et de la Productivité, Paris, April 23, 1958, and "Pompidou's France," *Economist*, December 2, 1972.

15. See Stuart Holland, ed., *The State as Entrepreneur* (London: Weidenfeld and Nicolson, 1972). Also Sergio Barzanti, *The Underdeveloped Areas Within the Common Market* (Princeton, N.J.: Princeton University Press, 1965).

16. Olivier Lorsignol, "Krauts Frogs Wops and Limeys Keep Out," *Vision*, February 1973, pp. 69-71.

17. "IRC's Battle for Change," *Times* (London), May 23, 1968 and "Industrial Reorganization Corporation's Year: Review of Methods and Philosophy," *Financial Times*, June 20, 1969.

18. Lorsignol, op. cit., p. 70.

19. *Wall Street Journal*, October 29, 1974.

20. Robert Gilpin, *France in the Age of the Scientific State* (Princeton, N.J.: Princeton University Press, 1968).

21. Keith Pavitt, "Will Europe Cross the Frontiers of Technology," *European Business*, Autumn 1972, pp. 37-44.

22. Renato Mazzolini, "Behavioral and Strategic Obstacles to European Transnational Concentration," *Columbia Journal of World Business*, Summer 1973, pp. 68-78, and "The Obstacle Course for European Transnational Consolidation," *Columbia Journal of World Business*, Spring 1973, pp. 53-56.

23. Ralph Z. Sorenson II, "US Marketers Can Learn From European Innovators," *Harvard Business Review*, September-October 1972, pp. 89-99. For reference see The Fortune Directory of the 300 Largest Industrial Corporations Outside the United States, *Fortune*, August 1974, pp. 174-187 and European Industries, *Vision*, October 1973, pp. 107-130.

24. "Aviation Supply: The Need for Intra-EEC Cooperation," *European Report*, February 6, 1973.

25. "A Transatlantic Aircraft Venture," *Business Week*, June 9, 1973, p. 36.

26. For an analysis of the relationship between the member states and the EC in formulating policies see Helen Wallace, *National Governments and the European Communities* (London: Chatham House, PEP, European Series, no. 21, April 1973).

27. Colonna Report, op. cit., *passim*.

28. For the most recent developments in competition policy see *European Report*, "European Anti-Trust Policy," pt. 1, November 21 and November 28, 1972.

29. On subsidy policy see *First Report on Competition Policy*, op. cit., pp. 112-143 and *Second Report on Competition Policy*, op. cit., pp. 75-138.

30. *Scientific and Technology Policy Programme*, Commission of the European Communities, Com(73)1250 Final, pts. 1, 2, July 25, 1973, and H. von Moltke, "Le Financement du Progrés Technologique au Regard des Objectifs de la Politique Industrielle de la Communaute," *Revue du Marché Commun*, March 1972, pp. 236-247.

31. Geoffrey Denton, *Planning in the EEC: The Medium-Term Economic Policy Programme of the European Economic Community* (London: Chatham House, PEP, European Series, no. 5, 1967).

32. Robert Toulemon and Jean Flory, *Une politique industrielle pour l'europe* (Paris: Presses Universitaires de France, 1974).

33. Ibid., pp. 122-126, and "Public Works Patriotism," *Vision*, April 1973, p. 47.

34. "The European Investment Bank: The EEC's Financial Arm," *European Report*, June 20, 1973.

35. "Towards the Creation of EEC-Wide Public Purchasing," *European Report*, April 20, 1974.

36. *Towards the Establishment of a European Industrial Base* (Spinelli Memorandum), Bulletin of the European Communities, supp. 7/73, May 7, 1973.

37. "EEC Industrial Policy Put to the Test by the Nine," *European Report*, March 23, 1974.

38. See G. D. N. Worswick, ed., *The Free Trade Proposals* (Oxford: Blackwell, 1960). This is an interesting collection of papers debating the implications of the EC and its customs union for the United Kingdom if it becomes a member of the Community.

39. John Pinder, "Positive and Negative Integration: Some Problems of Economic Union in the E.E.C.," *The World Today*, March 1968, pp. 88-110.

40. Warnecke, op. cit., See also W. Max Corden, "The Adjustment Problem," in Lawrence B. Krause and Walter S. Salant, eds., *European Monetary Unification and its Meaning for the United States* (Washington, D.C.: The Brookings Institution, 1973), pp. 159-202.

41. A preliminary examination of patterns of specialization is included in a study prepared by a consultant to the Commission. See Pierre Maillet, *Quinze Ans de Politique Communautaire 1958-72* (Brussels: Director General for the Budget, Commission of the European Communities, December 1972). In addition, see Bela Belassa, *Trade Liberalization Among Industrial Countries: Objectives and Alternatives* (New York: McGraw-Hill, 1967), pp. 89-91.

42. Pavitt, op. cit.

43. See "The Regeneration of British Industry" (New York), British Information Services, August 16, 1974; for coverage of the report see *The Financial Times*, "Critical Years Ahead for Major Sectors of the Economy," July 2, 1974.

44. Dell, op. cit., pp. 3-26.

45. Jean Jacques Servan-Schreiber, *The American Challenge* (New York: Atheneum, 1967). See also Louis Armand and Michel Drancourt, *The European Challenge* (New York: Atheneum, 1970).

46. Christopher Layton, *European Advanced Technology: A Programme for Integration* (London: George Allen and Unwin, 1969), and *Industry and Europe: An Introduction to the Industrial Potential of Common Market Membership* (Bath, England: Bath University Press, October 1971).

47. Robert McGeehan and Steven J. Warnecke, "Europe's Foreign Policies: Economics, Politics, or Both?", *Orbis* 17, no. 4 (Winter 1974): 1251-1279.

48. Pavitt, op. cit., p. 40. ". . . The formation of effective 'European' companies in 'strategic' technologies, far from resolving problems of national sovereignty, depends itself on the solution of these very same problems."

49. Gilpin, op. cit., pp. 388-389 and pp. 430-431, for examples relevant to French policy.

50. *Relations Between the Community and the Energy-Producing Countries*, Commission of the European Communities, Com(74)90, Brussels, January 23, 1974.

51. On the Franco-Iranian agreement see *Le Monde*, June 28, 1974.

52. "Outlook for EEC Role in Trade and Cooperation Policy with Eastern Europe," *European Report*, December 12, 1972.

53. "EEC/African Association on the Verge of Renewal," *European Report*, pt. 1, April 14, 1973, pt. 2, April 20, 1973.

54. For a discussion of this viewpoint see Jonathan Radice, "Going European Isn't Enough," *Vision*, February 1973, pp. 43-45.

55. For an analysis of the Commission's role in formulating and negotiating EC international trade policy see Frans A. M. Alting von Geusau, *Beyond the European Community* (Leyden: A. W. Sijthoff, 1969), chap. 5.

56. On the conflict between free trade and regional integration see Dell, op. cit., pp. 139-147; also McGeehan and Warnecke, op. cit., pp. 1262-1265.

57. *Premières Etudes sur le "Trade Expansion Act,"* Communauté Economique Européenne, Direction Generales, August 31, 1962.

58. For a discussion of some of these problems as well as the role of the Commission see "Generalized Preferences: Towards a Better Deal for the Third World," *European Report*, October 31, 1973.

59. See study on the textile industry and general proposal for sectoral policy in *L'industrie textile de la CEE: Analyse et Perspectives (1975), Rapport Presenté à la Commission par Professor J. De Bandt* (Brussels: Commission of the European Communities, January, 1969, 5885/III/69/F),

and *Politique Sectorielle pour le Textile*, Sec(71) 2615 Final, July 22, 1971 (Brussels, Commission of the European Communities).

60. "The EEC Pulp and Paper Industry: Need for Action," *European Report*, December 15, 1973.

61. "Commission Official Stresses EEC Policy Role," *European Report*, October 10, 1973.

CHAPTER

7

EUROPE IN
THE AGE OF
PETROLEUM
Dankwart A. Rustow

A "common energy policy" has for many years been high on the list of desiderata of those concerned with the future of Western Europe's industrial economy, and every year a drawerful is added to the already sizable file of reports and memoranda on that subject that emanate from Brussels, Strasbourg, and Luxembourg. But the patient compilation of statistics, usually at second or third hand, the ritual incantation of optimistic formulae, and the setting of goals that no one pursues or guidelines by which no one chooses to be guided—all these scarcely add up to "policy." It took the petroleum crisis of 1973-74 to expose the utter lack of any European energy policy and, through some surprising reversals, to prompt some first remedial steps.

The most far-reaching efforts toward a common energy policy still are those taken early in the process of European integration that resulted in the creation in 1952 of the European Coal and Steel Community (ECSC) and in 1958 of Euratom. When the first generation of European unifiers went to elementary school late in the nineteenth century, the geography textbooks took it for granted that national power had its solid foundations in iron deposits, in coal mines, and in steel mills. And the mines of Lorraine, the Saar, the Ruhr, and Upper Silesia turned out to be among the most tangible stakes of the European wars of 1870, 1914, and 1939. There was nothing more natural, therefore for aging, courageous, and principled men such as Robert Schuman, Konrad Adenauer, and Alcide de Gasperi than to try to convert the spoils of past wars into so many foundations for future peace. Alas, coal had no sooner been unified than it began its rapid and secular decline as the major industrial fuel. Whereas in 1952 it accounted for over 90 percent of total energy consumption within the European Community that proportion now is down to less than 25 percent; and even the fivefold increase in petroleum prices during the 1973-74 crisis is more likely to arrest rather than reverse this decline.

Euratom's role in shaping Europe's nuclear policies has been far more modest than that of the ECSC in controlling the market for coal. And whereas coal still claims a solid fifth of energy consumption, atomic power at present accounts for less than 1 percent.

The interregnum between coal and uranium of course was filled by petroleum; but for petroleum, too, the timing of common European policies proved to be out of step with the onrush of common needs. The high point of European petroleum policy may well be considered to have come as early as April 1920, when the Supreme Allied Council met at San Remo to transfer to France all German interests in future oil production in the ex-Ottoman territories—and when petroleum accounted for an even lesser fraction of energy consumption than does atomic power today. Eight years later, American companies were admitted into the consortium in response to persistent State Department pressure for an "open door." But this pattern of Western imperial control was crumbling just as European dependence on Middle Eastern oil began. (Petroleum, virtually all of it imported from the Middle East, supplied 14 percent of Europe's energy in 1950 and 59 percent in 1973.) The British saw their rich Iranian oil holdings expropriated in 1951, and they withdrew from Suez in 1954. American imperial policy intervened briefly in the early 1950s, with "fifty-fifty" profit-sharing agreements that provided large extra payments to oil governments at the Western taxpayer's expense, and with the CIA-assisted overthrow of Mossadegh in Iran; in return U.S. companies received a 40 percent share in Iranian production when operations were turned back to Western companies in 1954. For half a century multinational oil companies held sway in the Middle East as a direct byproduct of imperialism. By the time the British withdrew their last military contingents from the Persian Gulf in 1971, the emperor's clothes had been found to be transparent and companies were in full retreat in the face of escalating demands by Middle Eastern rulers.[1]

In short, the ECSC and Euratom turned out to be the result of two visions, one obsolescent and the other premature, and both therefore with little relevance to immediate needs. Since Europe's oil was almost wholly imported, Europe's energy policy, in fact was made neither in Brussels nor in the various national capitals, but rather at first by multinational companies and then by OPEC governments.

EUROPE'S SHIFT FROM COAL TO OIL

Europe's shift from coal to oil was part of a brilliant rearguard maneuver by which the eight multinational oil companies managed to hide the emperor's nakedness and to preserve their profitable position in the Middle East for twenty more years (through the 1950s and 1960s). The companies (five of them American, three European) faced the double threat of nationalization, as attempted by Mossadegh, and intrusion of new firms (American independents, ENI, etc.) into the preserve of their tightly interlocking cartel. Their maneuver consisted of (1) keeping the price of oil steady; (2) expanding their markets—tenfold in Europe and ninety-sixfold in Japan; and (3) setting off most of the added payments to Middle Eastern governments against their taxes back home.

The steady price of petroleum throughout the 1950s and 1960s was a major factor in postponing any awareness of the need for a common European energy policy. Generally the price structure of oil illustrates the circumstances in which public policy will or will not intervene in major international market movements. Once petroleum began to be discovered in large quantities in Saudi Arabia, Kuwait, and other countries of the Persian Gulf, the production cost declined steadily; today it is in the neighborhood of 5 to 10 cents per barrel. But production costs in the United States (then as now both the largest consumer and—along with Soviet Russia—the largest producer of petroleum) were in the neighborhood of $1.50 a barrel. Since five of the eight multinational companies controlling Middle East oil production (and the international marketing of production generally) were American, the world price of oil was set in the postwar years at a level where Middle Eastern oil would not make inroads into the markets for American oil. The eight companies, moreover, through a network of joint subsidiaries in the Middle East and elsewhere, formed a closely interlocking cartel, and this enabled them to achieve price stability—the goal that has proved so elusive for most other commodities from coffee and sugar to tin and copper. (Until the nationalization measures of the 1970s the following companies [as of 1974] shared the exclusive or major oil production concessions in the various Persian Gulf countries: Saudi Arabia—California Standard, Exxon, Texaco, and Mobil; Kuwait—British Petroleum (BP) and Gulf; Iraq, Qatar and Abu Dhabi—Compagnie Française des Pétroles (CFP), Shell, Exxon, and Mobil; Oman—CFP and Shell. It should be added that Iran, before Mossadegh's nationalization attempt of 1951, was controlled exclusively by BP; and as a result of the 1954 consortium agreement production was shared among all the eight companies mentioned, with a 5 percent share allotted to American "independents" so as to allay the antitrust compunctions of the U.S. Department of Justice.)

From 1948 to 1970 the price of oil on the world market stayed in the neighborhood of $1.80 a barrel (for Saudi Arabian light crude f.o.b. Ras Tanura—with corresponding differentials for other grades and locations), rarely rising or falling as much as 10 percent above or below that level. Such minor fluctuations in the price as did occur were due largely to fears set off by periodic Arab-Israeli wars and to periodic shutdowns of the Suez Canal through which until 1967 most Middle Eastern oil passed to its major European markets. After the end of the 1948 war the price became $1.88 and $1.75 (April and September 1949); in 1953 it was set at $1.97; from 1957 to 1959 (after the second Arab-Israeli war) it rose to $2.12; and from 1960 to 1970 it was $1.80. Such prices, as mentioned above, kept Middle Eastern oil out of the American market for a number of years. But when by the late 1950s price alone was no longer enough to achieve this protectionist effect, an import quota system (1959-73) was instituted that was volubly justified in the name of U.S. "national security." In effect this amounted to a mandatory "drain-America-first policy," according to H. David Freeman, White House energy adviser under President Johnson.

Needless to say, the enormous differential between production costs in the Middle East and world market prices implied a handsome profit for the multinational companies—in the neighborhood of $1 billion a year for the early 1950s.[2] Since total payments to Middle Eastern countries amounted to only $150 million in 1948 and $240 million in 1950, it was not surprising that nationalist governments, such as that of Mossadegh in Iran, sought a larger share, through nationalization if necessary. The companies managed to ward off the immediate threat through their control of the international transport and processing system of oil tankers and refineries: Mossadegh could not sell what little oil his technicians could produce. Since the companies moverover had secure control in other Middle Eastern countries, increased production in Kuwait and Saudi Arabia soon more than compensated for the production losses in Iran.

For the longer run, U.S. public policy intervened quietly but decisively to prevent further head-on clashes between nationalist governments and Western companies such as had led to the Iranian crisis. The policy adopted—by a resolution of the National Security Council of 1950—was that company payments to the governments of oil producing countries could be claimed as full tax credits against the companies' U.S. tax liability on their foreign earnings, so long as these payments to oil governments were construed as "income tax" rather than "royalty." This ruling enabled Aramco to work out in 1952 the Middle East's first "fifty-fifty" profit sharing agreement with Saudi Arabia. (This followed an earlier precedent from Venezuela and in turn became the precedent for all other Middle Eastern countries, including Iran in 1954. The specific tax laws—British, French, Dutch—applicable to non-American companies differ in their details but very little in their general effect of shifting the burden of additional payments from oil company to home-country treasury.)

The United States thus developed two major public policies regarding international petroleum: that of 1950 in the form of a disguised subsidy to Middle Eastern countries which, it was hoped, would refrain from extreme nationalism and stay out of the Russian orbit; and that of 1959 in the form of a protectionist barrier against imports of cheap Middle Eastern oil. The countries of Western Europe, whether singly or united in the Common Market, had little need to develop parallel policies: they had no domestic oil production to protect and they were in the process of surrendering their once powerful position of imperial hegemony in the Middle East. The major policy of European countries affecting the place of petroleum in their industrial economy thus remained a set of heavy excise taxes on gasoline and other petroleum products.

But protectionist considerations entered the European picture as petroleum, which before the Second World War had been used mainly as a transport fuel for ships, automobiles, and airplanes, began to compete with coal as a fuel for industry, for home heating, and (much more slowly) for the generation of electricity. The coal mines of Britain, Belgium, and West Germany had been worked for centuries, so that the richer seams close to the surface had long since been exhausted. The coal miners, moreover, formed some of the largest trade unions, whose power was often pivotal in the Socialist parties; in short they were a crucial force on the political scene. Every demand by the colliers for a living wage, for decent hours, for safe working conditions, or for medical or accident benefits thus was bound to add appreciably to the already-high price of coal. By the late 1940s and early 1950s Western European coal could not compete in price with coal from Poland's Silesian mines or even with strip-mined coal shipped halfway around the world from West Virginia. By the mid-1950s all sorts of coal—domestic, Polish, and American—were beaten out of many of their European markets by Middle Eastern oil.

The price of petroleum and its products might seem high, considering that multinational companies sold their crude at about ten times its production cost and amortized their investment in Middle Eastern production facilities every year or two; that generous tax credits enabled the companies to retain their full profits while making payments of corresponding size to shah, sheikh, or junta; and that the price of gasoline or fuel oil was doubled or trebled as the result of excise taxes. But in comparison to coal the price of oil was low—and whereas coal tended to keep ahead of general rates of inflation the price of oil kept steady in nominal money and hence declined in real money terms.

The shutdown of exhausted coal mines and generous severance benefits for aging miners or retraining programs for younger ones thus became the major content of the energy policies developed by Western European countries in the 1950s and 1960s. And indeed a major function of the ECSC turned out to be the maintenance of a common market through negotiated adjustments of the subsidies and nonmarket prices resulting from these costly labor policies.

So long as the miners were taken care of, everyone else was happy. The oil companies retained their profits and rapidly expanded their markets; indirectly the political power of the miners provided the oil multinationals with their most effective guarantee against unwanted interference by national governments or by the European Community as a whole. And economic planners, whether in government agencies or the investment departments of private industry, were tempted to think of petroleum almost as of a free good: unlike any other factor of production it seemed to be available in unlimited quantities and at a steady rather than increasing price.

This idyllic situation of the 1950s and 1960s was rudely shattered as the multinational oil companies by about 1970 had exhausted the possibilities of their threefold rearguard maneuver. Customers can switch from coal to oil only once and companies can write off no more than 100 percent of their taxes on foreign production. The oil producing countries, moreover, were no longer attacking singly as in the days of Mossadegh, but in 1960 had banded together in the Organization of Petroleum Exporting Countries (OPEC). If the multinationals were to continue satisfying OPEC's appetites while retrieving their declining profits, petroleum prices were bound to rise. Such has been the nature of the international petroleum revolution of the early 1970s in which multinational companies and Middle Eastern governments have been the major protagonists and consumers in Europe and Japan the major victims.

Beginning in the late 1960s the OPEC governments, with Libya, Iran, Algeria, Iraq, Saudi Arabia, and Kuwait alternating in the lead, showed much ingenuity in devising new demands: increases in the tax rate from 50 percent to 55 and 60 percent; "posted prices" for tax purposes well above the market price; premiums for low sulfur content and short transport routes; nationalization, outright or on the installment plan ("participation"); price corrections for downward, but not upward, movements of the dollar; production cuts for geological, economic, or political reasons; the government share of oil ("royalty" or "participation oil") sold at auction or returned to the company at prearranged "buy-back" prices; and, above all, matching concessions for all those extracted by any other OPEC member. The net result was a ratchet effect by which half a dozen "five year agreements" were signed and renegotiated in half that span of years.

At a crucial point (October 1973 to March 1974) the embargo by some of the Arab producers against the United States, the Netherlands, and others provided an added touch of drama and a somewhat inconclusive test of the oil governments' newly won political power. Israel did stop its counteroffensive at the Suez Canal under U.S. pressure and went to Geneva; but when the embargo was combined with the second round of price rises, imposed by the Shah, Europe and Japan clearly were hurt far worse than the United States. The dollar hence gained rapidly, and Sheikh Yamani, the Saudi oil minister, quickly retreated from his earlier embargo program.

Underneath this maneuvering and the many legalisms four principles have clearly emerged. First, the producing governments alone will decide how much oil flows into the world market. Second, they mean to retain all the profits to be made from oil, except for a residual management fee for the companies. The governments' share accordingly went up from 72 percent in 1970 to 83 percent in 1972, and the current aim is 93 percent. Third, the producing governments mean to charge—or rather force the companies to charge—what the traffic will bear. And the traffic, it turned out, would bear a good deal; the price of Arabian light crude accordingly rose from $1.80 in 1970 to $2.48 in 1972, to about $8 in early 1974, and to over $10 by the end of the year. And finally the companies' position is greatly weakened in that they have lost control over amounts of production, but their technical and marketing services for the time being are still indispensable to the producer countries. Hence these countries still are offering to the former concessionaire companies what amounts to a 7 to 15 percent discount compared with sales to outsiders. Since the companies are able to pass on the price increases they do not suffer financially. Indeed since they raise their product prices as soon as the price of crude goes up, 1973-74 turned out to be a year of exceptional profits, based in part on instant appreciation of inventories.

EUROPE'S 1973-74 PETROLEUM CRISIS

Europe's petroleum crisis of 1973-74 may best be viewed from three angles: the impact of OPEC's cartel policies; relations between the European Common Market and the other major oil importers, notably the United States; and the gradual, fitful emergence out of the crisis of a new European energy policy.

The embargo of the winter of 1973-74 was a mere foretaste of the power of the producers. The core of the petroleum crisis turned out to be a fivefold increase in prices in a period of less than a year—the first two rounds of increases (from about $3 to $8) widely heralded by Sheikh Yamani in October 1973 and then by the Shah in December, the later ones (to $10 or more) disguised behind the scenes in tedious negotiations in Qatar, Kuwait, and Saudi Arabia regarding "participation agreements" and "buy-back prices." The comforting notion that petroleum was a free good that planners could disregard in calculating scarce resources was exploded as a naive fallacy.

To make matters worse, it gradually became clear that oil prices were likely to remain steady for the next decade or so, with possible upward adjustments for world inflation. Indeed they could rise a good deal further if OPEC wished to push its advantage to the limit—where consumption would fall drastically or substitutes become available in quantity. We know too little about the price elasticity of the demand for oil and about the cost of adapting new shale or coal technologies to large-scale production to be sure about either of these limits—except to guess that they are well above the current petroleum price of $10 to $11. But OPEC is unlikely to push that far because this would put the major burden of reducing production on just a few members, notably on the Saudis, who could always threaten to increase production and (like Samson) bring the whole temple down. Any such extreme push, moreover, would severely test OPEC's future ability to retreat in orderly formation. In cartel economics, as in mountaineering, a false step on the way up slows your progress but a false step down may prove fatal. Between the short-run temptations to raise the price and the long-term risks in doing so, the present level seems optimal from a collective and long-range OPEC point of view.

The hope widely cherished in the consumer countries of a glut on the world oil market resulting in a falling out among producers, and hence a collapse of the cartel, turned out to be illusory. To be sure, OPEC production by the summer of 1974 had gone back to September 1973 levels whereas the price had quadrupled—thus raising the question of whether the market would be cleared. Those producing countries that have both additional oil reserves and absorptive capacity for additional foreign exchange income (Iraq, Iran, Indonesia, Nigeria, Ecuador) were expanding their production during the 1973-74 embargo. But a potential glut due to these two factors can for some time be contained by corresponding production cuts by the financial surplus countries. Saudi Arabia, Abu Dhabi, Kuwait, Libya, and Venezuela already have curtailed their production, and by the fall of 1974 OPEC as a whole had coordinated its curtailment plans. In a technical sense, moreover, there can be no "glut" (as distinct from "excess capacity"). In most OPEC countries oil flows; in some it is pumped. Either way no surpluses can arise. Once the storage tanks are full and if no customer appears at the decreed price the further flow is simply cut off by shutting a few valves. OPEC's remarkable success has been based on its shift from the traditional and precarious cartel tactic of allocating production to the new tactic adopted in the mid 1960s of agreeing on common amounts of government revenue per barrel and letting both prices and production find their corresponding levels through the market mechanism. This OPEC formula, moreover, could easily be extended to non-OPEC members. By 1974 the Province of Alberta was levying export taxes to bring the price of Canadian oil in line with the "world market [that is, OPEC] price," and the Soviet Union was selling its oil exports at the same levels. Even U.S. domestic producers were clamoring for the lifting of residual controls so that they too could follow OPEC's price lead. Understandably the Western press quickly fastened on any reports or even rumors of dissension between Qaddafi, the late Faisal, or the Shah, thus overlooking the more important news of their unimpaired cohesion. The OPEC cartel tactic had been too successful to be easily or quickly abandoned.

If this diagnosis is correct—that is, if prices remain at their 1974 levels and consumption stays at around 1973 levels with modest annual increments—the aggregate annual income of OPEC countries is likely to be upward of $100 billion (beginning in 1974). Of this aggregate amount no more than one-third, for a start, is likely to go on current imports including those needed for development programs, with perhaps another $10-to-$20 billion per year going on armaments (the Iranians and Saudis being the most lavish spenders, engaged in a regional arms race as they are). All this implies a cumulative surplus in the oil producing countries of close to half a trillion dollars by the early 1980s. OPEC is embarked on forcing a redistribution of the world's gross product and capital assets perhaps even beyond what its leaders now imagine. Most of this money will come from Europe as the customer for more than half of OPEC's oil. One major financial effect of the petroleum revolution has been to force Europeans and Japanese to try to earn more dollars to meet their galloping energy costs.[3]

The multinational companies have lost their earlier control of production at the wellhead, and lost it more completely than perhaps the public is aware. In the words of the chairman of BP, they have become a vast "tax collection agency for OPEC," although at the downstream end of their operations they remain, as we shall see, far more than that. This has prompted observers such as M. A. Adelman to conclude that governments of importing countries, such as the United States and the nations of Western Europe, could hasten OPEC's collapse by bypassing the companies in their present role as wholesale buyers and distributors of crude, or by reducing their decades-old privilege of writing off the "income taxes" imposed by producers.[4] This conclusion, however, derives from faulty analysis: it is true that OPEC countries could not have pieced together a brand new cartel; but finding one ready-made by the companies, OPEC has proved quite capable of taking it over and no doubt will prove capable of holding on to it. Acting in combination (although without any deliberate plan), companies first and governments later, the oil producers have treated Europe and Japan much as heroin dealers treat their customers: getting them used to the drug by selling it cheap, then extorting a high price when addiction has set in.

There also is the possibility, much discussed lately, that the OPEC cartel will be emulated by Third World producers of bauxite, copper, and other metals.[5] My guess is that such metal cartels will obtain much less financial leverage for three reasons. There is a scrap market for metals, whereas scrap petroleum becomes air pollution; there are many more different metals than there are fuels and metals can often substitute for one another; and in some years manganese nodules (containing many other metals as well) may be scooped off the ocean floor at costs far below and quantities far above those of conventional mining.

Meanwhile the oil companies, with the political impartiality that befits them as *homines oeconomici*, did valuable service during the embargo of the winter of 1973-74 in allocating the worldwide shortage among their customers, and softening its impact on the Netherlands and the United States. But their eviction upstream has meant that they are having to find entirely new ways of surviving in the future. Perhaps Gulf's plans, abandoned under public criticism, to buy Ringling Brothers, Barnum & Bailey stemmed from a correct estimate of the oil multinationals' future need for acrobatics. A more serious symptom of their readjustment has been the major advertising campaign which, at least two years before the embargo, sought to bring the "energy crisis" to the attention of the American public.[6] (When else have corporations spent their advertising budgets on heralding not the availability of their product but its imminent disappearance?) For the companies the crisis—of dispossession in the Middle East—was real enough. Their response was to try to get a better grip on the distribution end in the United States (which remains the largest market for petroleum), where the prevailing free enterprise rhetoric provides the best available guarantee against nationalization, and where vast shale and coal deposits wait to be developed. The companies' favored solution, one may assume, is to have that development undertaken at public expense, after which they will be glad to enter the subsequent, profit-making phase.

During the 1950s and 1960s the companies' ability to supply indefinite amounts of petroleum at low prices had exempted the European Community from any need to update its energy policies. But the same policy vacuum persisted in the 1970s as the companies' position upstream began to decline and prices to rise. A meeting of the Community's Council of Ministers in May 1973, the first in some years wholly devoted to energy, revealed the fundamental divisions that kept any energy policy from emerging. There were those who would have liked to see the EC play some role in coordinating relations with the oil producing countries and with the United States and Japan as the other principal consumers. But this would have involved the EC in the conduct of foreign relations, something to which the French since the days of de Gaulle had been adamantly opposed. There were those who would have involved the EC in regulating the intra-European petroleum market, a *dirigiste* policy such as France and Italy had long pursued at home. But such a course found little favor with the British and the Dutch, with their direct interest in two of the major oil companies (BP and Shell) that were now regulating the European oil market; nor was it agreeable to the Germans with their general aversion to economic regulation. In short those member governments which inclined to activism in Europe were committed to passivism overseas, and vice versa. The result was no policy at all, and the list of areas of disagreement produced at the abovementioned May 1973 meeting was nothing short of exhaustive: relations with exporting and other importing countries; regulation of the internal oil market; the future of nuclear power, coal, natural gas, and other, new sources of energy; conservation of energy; and the environmental implications of all these.[7] The one concrete measure of European policy remained the agreement arrived at late in 1972 to increase the storage of petroleum in member countries to a 90-day supply by January 1975.

But the crisis of October 1973 showed that even in the area of emergency supplies each EC member country was for the time being going it alone. The

Arab embargo against the United States as Israel's major military supplier was also extended to the Netherlands. The official reasons referred to various pro-Israeli attitudes of Dutch government officials but became the less convincing the more often they were restated. The actual effects of the anti-Dutch embargo may provide better clues to the Arabs' motives. The Netherlands, with its ample supplies of natural gas, consumes only about 7 percent of Western Europe's oil imports; yet Rotterdam serves as the major petroleum entrepôt for all of Central Europe and much of Northern Europe. To hit at the Dutch thus was a way of hitting at many Europeans without hitting at any of them very hard.

No Common Market country came forward with any offer to share its supplies with the Netherlands. If there was any such impulse the Arabs effectively thwarted it by demonstratively placing Britain and France on their "friendly list," but threatening that any country found to be sharing its supplies with a country on the embargo list would itself be embargoed. Instead of European solidarity against outside pressure, there was a common declaration by the foreign ministers of the nine Common Market nations on November 9, 1973, in favor of Israeli evacuation of occupied territories, followed a month later by a somewhat vaguely worded invitation by the heads of government to a future European-Arab dialogue. If the aim of the Arab oil ministers in brandishing their oil weapon had been to divide and rule they had succeeded, at least on the level of diplomatic pronouncements, very well indeed.

European energy policy had resulted in inaction, the attempt, at the height of the embargo, to coordinate policies between Europe and the United States started off by producing much recrimination and bitterness.

In the United States the first reaction to the price rises of the winter of 1973/74 was one of sheer disbelief. For example, since quadrupled or quintupled oil prices would conjure up unthinkable problems, the price rises must simply be a nightmare or a temporary aberration. Besides, so much money could not be trusted to inexperienced governments of undeveloped countries. If only the consumer countries bestirred themselves into forming a common front, if only they applied the merest fraction of their vast power or exercised some judicious cunning in playing this producer country against that—then surely prices could be rolled back. All this of course presupposed a solid consumer front in which the United States naturally expected to take the lead.[8]

The desire for a common consumer front seems to have been a major part of the rationale behind the energy conference called by Secretary of State Kissinger in Washington in February 1974. But there was immediately a somewhat rude awakening—from the dream though not from the nightmare. Most of the European countries, as well as Japan, were most reluctant to be part of any consumer front which, they suspected, would be futile, or by antagonizing the OPEC countries, worse than futile. The instinctive reaction of most of the Europeans and of the Japanese was to seek such safety as could be had in just the kind of special bilateral deals that Kissinger loudly and publicly deplored. The conflict came to a head between Kissinger and French Foreign Minister Jobert, who flatly refused to let his country take any part in the Energy Coordinating Group (ECG) resulting from the Washington meeting. Others joined the ECG reluctantly when forced into a choice of following either Washington or Paris.

There was much justice in both the French and the American critique of the other's tactic. Any showdown between oil consumers and producers could only lead to disaster for the consumers. The producing countries, even at rapidly rising rates of income, have well over a year's worth of foreign exchange income stored away—whereas petroleum storage in Europe is barely up to the 90-day level prescribed by Brussels and in the United States only about half of that. The storage of money, moreover, is very lucrative and the storage of petroleum very costly.

On the other hand, there was no question that the spectacle of Western industrial countries such as France, West Germany, and Japan rushing into offers of bilateral economic deals with various Middle Eastern countries could only add to the Middle East's sense of strength and hence to its price intransigence. And in the light of past events two standard items in such prospective deals would be of questionable relevance: offers of financial assistance from countries with mounting exchange deficits to countries with mounting surpluses could at best be of temporary value; and promises of so much oil to be delivered over 3-, 5-, or 10-year periods could carry little confidence in view of the number of agreements with oil companies that OPEC countries had simply disregarded when these no longer suited their convenience.

But beneath the tactical divergences among Kissinger, Jobert, and others there lurked a number of mutual suspicions, and beneath these in turn there hid some rather profound differences of interest. Washington for some years had been sensitive to European restiveness in accepting American leadership and therefore was all too ready to castigate Jobert's stand as yet another instance of infantile Gaullism. Conversely, Europeans could not help consider Washington's manner high handed. The "oil weapon" after all had been aimed at the United States for its support of Israel; yet it was the European countries that bore the brunt of the embargo. Thus in January and February 1974 U.S. total energy supplies, including natural gas and coal as well as domestic and foreign oil, are estimated to have declined by only 2.4 percent, as against 2.8 percent for Japan and as much as 5.6 percent for West Germany (according to detailed estimates by Robert B. Stobaugh of the Harvard Business School). And at the height of the October crisis the United States had not troubled to inform European governments before placing NATO forces on alert against Russia during the so-called Yom Kippur war on October 24-25, 1973; yet Kissinger had later complained, in one of his all-too-transparent off-the-record interviews, of European lack of support and cooperation. But Europeans also tended to view most of the oil multinationals as American and therefore tended to wonder whether the companies' ready agreement to escalating prices did not hide some evil American design to increase prices for European competitors.

Americans in their turn, as the prime target of the 1973-74 embargo, were only too aware of its character as an outside emergency rather than an American contrivance. Because of years of prior concern about the energy crisis and because of lengthening gasoline lines throughout the winter of 1973-74, Americans also tended to forget that they were less hard hit by the embargo and accompanying price rises than were Europeans and especially Japanese. European suspicions, moreover, were bound to be further aroused when Washington one day denounced a European Community plan for a Euro-Arab economic conference as unhelpful to its Middle Eastern peace efforts, and on almost the next day concluded with Saudi Arabia the very kind of bilateral deal against which it had so eloquently warned before.

The basic differences of interest between Europe and the United States in confronting the international petroleum revolution rested mostly on their differential resource endowment and financial stature. The United States, as noted previously, remains the world's largest petroleum producer. If its oil consumption for transport per capita were no larger than Europe's it would not require any imports whatever—and even the shortages of the winter of 1973-74 could easily be overcome by curtailing pleasure driving and by turning lights off and thermostats down. Even at prevailing lavish levels of consumption the United States may well attain self-sufficiency by the end of the 1970s: at $8 or $11 a barrel much secondary recovery will prove economical from existing fields; Alaskan oil by then will be ready; and for the longer run there are ample possibilities of oil from shale and of gasification or liquefaction of coal. The other major consumers have no such alternatives, and, as it is, they depend more heavily on oil for their energy (United States, 46 percent; Europe, 59 percent; and Japan, 76 percent) and on imports for their oil (United States, 36 percent just before the Arab embargo; Europe, 98 percent; and Japan, over 99 percent).

The financial effects were potentially even more divisive. Not only was most of OPEC's income payable in dollars, but the dollar economy, whether in the United States itself or in so-called Eurodollars, offered the only financial market large enough to absorb payments that would run to $20 or $30 billion on every quarterly pay day. Much of the Middle Eastern surplus cash, it soon became clear, was being channelled into arms purchases—the Arabs and Israelis and the Saudis and Iranians each being involved in arms races larger than any except that among the superpowers—and here again the United States stood to benefit as the major supplier.

CONCLUSION

All these differences of interest between the United States and Europe had come to the fore in the clash between Kissinger and Jobert in February 1974 and again briefly in skeptical European reactions to two speeches, one by President Ford and one by Kissinger, in September 1974 that seemed to presage an American shift toward a tough policy with the Middle Eastern oil producers.

Yet there was an undeniable, if more limited, community of interests between Western Europe and the United States (as well as Japan) as the world's major oil importers. While Kissinger's staff had busily been briefing the chief on the economics of petroleum no one had thought of anticipating the possible French reaction. Now after February 1974 the differences were plainly in the open and, on second thought, it was clear that little would be gained from further public recrimination. Although the then newly elected French President Giscard d'Estaing did not care to depart too ostentatiously from previous Gaullist attitudes the change of government in Paris also helped to reduce tensions with Washington. And Washington in its turn, after some initial fumbling, chose to play its leadership role with generosity and self-abnegation.

The notion of a general showdown between consumers and producers was quietly dropped, and the development of technological alternatives to petroleum left for the more distant future. In discussing plans for the pooling of supplies in the face of any new embargo, the United States now made it clear that it was willing to place its domestic production as well as its imports into the common pool. By the summer of 1974, moreover, the development of detailed working plans within the "Energy Coordinating Group" was entrusted to a team headed by Vicomte Etienne Davignon, long known as the most skilful and imaginative diplomatic planner for European political unification. By the fall of 1974 Davignon's temporary ECG was ready with plans for a more permanent International Energy Agency (IEA) to be loosely attached to the Organization for Economic Cooperation and Development.

The initial membership of the IEA consisted of eight of the Common Market countries (all except France), the United States, Canada, and Japan. Norway, eager to retain full control over its new oil riches, remained aloof at the last moment. But other industrial oil importing countries such as Switzerland, Sweden, Australia, and Austria proved eager to join. And France made no objection to the European Community as such joining the IEA in an associated status.

The core of the IEA arrangement is a petroleum sharing plan designed to prevent a recurrence of the disarray in response to the 1973-74 embargo; a complex voting scheme is designed to prevent any one-sided dominance by Europeans or Americans, by oil producers (the United States, Canada, and later Britain) or consumers. Most importantly, the presumption is in favor of common action: a weighted majority is needed to veto implementation of the plan which otherwise takes automatic effect. Conservation and storage are integral parts of the plan and conditions for sharing in its benefits—and this in turn implies a growing function for the IEA, via its member governments, of monitoring and regulating the internal petroleum market of the participant countries. The common financial problems of oil consumer countries are likely to be the next major item on the IEA's agenda.

The eight Common Market members in the IEA constitute less than half of the new organization's membership; even so, their cooperation within the wider IEA framework was a first and highly promising step toward a common European energy policy.

Following World War II the leaders of Robert Schuman's generation sought to lay the foundations for a united Europe in a community of coal and steel. But just as generals are apt to plan victories in bygone wars, so politicians are prone to lay the foundations for the peace of yesteryear. Through a constellation of factors not readily foreseen in the years after World War II, what was to have been the Europe of coal and steel ruled from Luxembourg or Brussels turned into the Europe of petroleum in bondage first to companies in Houston or New York and then to governments in Riyadh, Tehran, and Benghazi.

Early in 1974 a thoughtful observer might well have judged that it will prove fatal to the European dream that its early successes have mostly been in agriculture and its continuing failures mostly in the field of energy. By the end of 1974 there was new hope that the pressure for common solutions in the energy and monetary fields might give a fresh impulse to a wider and closer European unity.

NOTES

1. For a brief account of the shifting patterns of control see Dankwart A. Rustow, "Petroleum Politics 1951-1974: A Five-Act Drama Reconstructed," *Dissent* 21, no. 2 (Spring 1974): 144-153.

2. The most detailed calculations are found in Charles Issawi and Mohammed Yeganeh, *The Economics of Middle Eastern Oil* (New York: Praeger, 1962) p. 188, and in M. A. Adelman, *The World Petroleum Market* (Baltimore: Johns Hopkins University Press, 1972).

3. For summaries of the financial effects see Gerald A. Pollack, "The Economic Consequences of the Energy Crisis," *Foreign Affairs*, April 1974, pp. 452-471; and Dankwart A. Rustow, "Who Won the Yom Kippur and Oil Wars?", *Foreign Policy* 17 (Winter 1974-75): 166-175.

4. M. A. Adelman, "Is the Oil Shortage Real?", *Foreign Policy* 9 (Winter 1972-73).

5. See Zuhayr Mikdashi, Stephen D. Krasner, and C. Fred Bergsten, "One, Two, Many OPEC's . . . ?", *Foreign Policy* 14 (Spring 1974).

6. See series of advertisements by Mobil in New York *Times*, May 11, 1972 to April 19, 1973.

7. See Louis Turner, "Politics of the Energy Crisis," *International Affairs*, July 1974, pp. 404-417.

8. The consumer front was advocated by Walter J. Levy in "An Atlantic-Japanese Energy Policy," *Foreign Policy* 11 (Summer 1973), pp. 159-190; for a more moderate restatement see Levy, "World Oil Cooperation or International Chaos," *Foreign Affairs*, July 1974, pp. 690-713.

CHAPTER

8

THE TEXTILE POLICY
OF THE EUROPEAN
COMMUNITY
Camille Blum

The textile industry in Europe has been in difficulty for quite some time: since the mid-1960s it has layed off an average of 40,000 workers a year—particularly in the woolen and cotton sectors. This reduction in the level of employment has been caused by the drive within the European Community to improve productivity through restructuring firms in response to the increased pressures of both intra-Community and international competition.

Although at a competitive disadvantage, the textile and related clothing industry still play an important role in the Community's economy. They are concentrated in a limited number of regions where in some cases they employ up to 80 percent of the industrial labor force. Moreover, employment of women is extremely high, reaching 50 percent in textiles and over 80 percent in clothing. In addition, these regions are often ones in decline dominated by a single industry. Consequently, the adverse social and economic effects of reducing employment in this primary sector are magnified. The decline in employment is expected to continue at a rate comparable to that since the mid-1960s as efforts to accelerate restructuring and increase competitiveness continue. Thus until the industrial structures of these regions are upgraded and diversified the textile sector will still remain essential to their economic equilibrium.

In part, the competitive difficulties of this industry are a result of the trend of natural fibers being replaced by synthetic fibers manufactured by the Community's expanding chemical sector. In fact, synthetic fibers currently account for some 50 percent of the consumption of the three leading textile fibers—cotton, wool, and synthetics. This proportion according to some estimates is expected to rise to 75 percent by 1980. However, this trend is improving the competitive position of Community textile firms in regard to those of less industrialized countries.

Faced with these problems the industry, national governments, and the Commission of the EC have tried to develop and implement policies to improve the position of this sector.

THE ROLE OF THE SOCIAL PARTNERS

Initiatives Taken By Comitextil

As early as 1966 the EC textile industries, grouped together in Comitextil (Coordination Committee of the EC Textile Industries), had sent the Commission a note describing the problems confronting the textile industry. Comitextil, set up in 1961 in Brussels, the organization's headquarters, has in fact come to act as the "umbrella" organization for a number of branch associations (wool, cotton, silk, synthetic fiber producers, linen, hemp, jute, knitwear, carpets, made-ups, printing, etc.) which had already been organized at Community level since the start of the Common Market. The federative element is to be sought both in the development of the industry and in action by the Community authorities.

Since the 1960s the ever-increasing use of synthetic and artificial fibers heralded the progressive disappearance of the border line dividing traditional branch sectors. Parallel to this process of horizontal integration a phenomenon of vertical integration was beginning to develop.

The textile industries felt the need for an organ to provide liaison, information, study, and coordination, while the Commission sought a single interlocutor representing the entire textile industry. For one thing, the Commission did not dispose of the means—particularly of personnel—to arbitrate between the sometimes diametrically opposed positions of the different sectoral branches. Because of this it wanted the industry itself to be able to arrive first at a common negotiating position; such a position would carry more weight to the extent that it was frequently the result of particularly thorny intraindustry negotiations. Since its inception the Commission has played the card of negotiating with the industrial and trade organizations. Its policy can be defined in a few words: it consists essentially of reserving the prerogative of consultation and permanent relations solely to those bodies which operate at Community level. Thus in principle the Commission does not deal with national federations or confederations nor with organizations operating on a larger scale than the Community.

In the absence of direct citizen participation in the Community processes the Commission thought it could find points of support in this *"eurosphere professionelle,"* sensitive to and aware of the problems of the European authorities and ready, therefore, to support their activities.

The Commission then was not insensitive to the ideas advanced by the textile industry in its 1966 note. The unions, for their part, without being directly associated with the initiative, to a large extent shared the conclusions of management about the causes of the difficulties facing the industry. The unions had had regular contacts with Comitextil since 1964 in an informal forum called the Round Table.

Unions and Management:
A Common Front

Their common analysis led unions and management to conclude that the decline in employment in the EC textile industry was due in large part to disruptions caused by imports from countries at operating prices incompatible with normal competition. In view of this they considered a satisfactory trade policy to be a necessary precondition for the industry's harmonious development.

The causes of this abnormal competition are to be sought preeminently in the policy of subsidies and artificial boosts to business practiced by certain third countries. This kind of competition is a fact as regards individual countries or groups of countries. First, for example, there are the state-trading countries where selling prices are always determined by general political considerations and by economic policy in particular. Abnormally low-priced imports from these countries are steadily increasing; they are in danger of expanding further if these countries succeed in financing their sizable purchases of investment goods by deliveries in kind which are partly made up of a textile quota of growing significance. This "truck" system is moreover in many cases just as ruinous for the whole economy as it is for the sector which more than any other bears the brunt of it.

Second, there are the less developed countries (the LDC's), which can export at prices defying all competition, thanks to different production conditions, subsidies, and other artificial aids like multiple exchange rates; the inadequate competitiveness of these countries is attested to by the prohibitively high tariff barriers they erect. Third, in certain countries like Hong Kong an economic system exists which is reminiscent of the beginnings of capitalism. Hong Kong benefits from a privileged geographical position; her textile industry has specialized particularly in the improving trade, either on her own account or as a subcontractor to foreign importers; and she generally practices a particularly dangerous form of competition thanks to a low-wage policy combined with a high level of productivity.

Fourth, certain European countries like Spain and Portugal, with different economic and social systems, operate an abnormally aggressive form of competition. They do this through more or less disguised export subsidies on particular products or markets. And finally in Japan, thanks to individualistic methods of financing and trading, a small number of big distribution companies make certain of foreign markets at prices well below those ruling on the domestic market. They then compensate themselves behind the shelter of high import duties.

The unions, for their part, put the emphasis in several of their pronouncements on social dumping. According to them the textile industry is not one of those which stimulate the creation of any real industrial potential, and it therefore contributes very little to a country's development. Furthermore, there are few real "transfers," but essentially capital investment comes in from industrialized countries. In the great majority of cases the object is to assume foreign capital a very handsome return based on the exploitation of a very poorly paid labor force that enjoys no social guarantees. Profits are repatriated and only wages remain in the country. This is a form of aid which is astonishingly like a certain form of neocolonialism. Nevertheless the industry was the only one to present a sectoral policy plan. In reality its proposals were very limited in the field of industrial policy (properly called) and could only be regarded as measures to complement the moves to be taken on commercial policy; essentially they envisaged getting the support of Community authorities for economic and scientific research projects, or securing the opening of the Community's Social Fund to include textile workers. As far as industrial structure was concerned only the aspect of "trimming back" was considered. These propositions were inherent in the logic of the analysis of the situation; that is, the industry's difficulties are essentially attributable to competition from certain third countries.

ACTION BY THE EC COMMISSION

The Conception of Industrial Policy

The Commission was aware of the difficulty it would encounter in establishing a Community industrial policy. In fact, the Treaty of Rome (1957) gives it very little power in this field. To attain this objective the Commission could choose between two approaches: it could define a number of general principles valid for the industry in general, with, if necessary, different provisions applying to the various sectors (the global approach); or it could define a number of sectoral policies which taken together would amount to an industrial policy (the sectoral approach).

The Commission hesitated for a long time between these two approaches. If the first approach seems officially to have won the day in reality it appears that only sectoral policies defined around (but apparently not as a function of)

industrial policy have led to any concrete results. We are not going to look
into the underlying philosophy behind the Community's policy, but rather to
examine the process which led to the formulation by the Commission of the
principles governing its textile policy.

Consultation Between the Social Partners

During the two years (1966-68) that followed the presentation by
Comitextil of proposals for a textile policy, the Commission organized a
series of consultative meetings, some bilateral (Commission and employers or
Commission and unions) and some tripartite (Commission and both social
partners). Dialogue between the social partners and the Commission was
particularly difficult. The former believed as long as abnormal competition
persisted the textile industry would be unable to develop, no matter what its
structure or how competitive it might be. The Community authorities, on the
contrary, thought it was right, given the hypothesis of a gradual opening up of
frontiers, to determine what industrial policy should be adopted to enable the
industry to face external competition. The Commission services had
undertaken a series of monographs concerned with the different branches of
the textile industry. It quickly became apparent that a description of the
sector's situation was not enough; what was needed was an examination of its
prospects in the medium and long term. These were, in particular, the
conclusions of the Medium-Term Economic Policy Committee which had
been apprised of the question.

The de Bandt Report

The EC Commission then decided in October 1968 to commission J. de
Bandt, assistant director of the Centre d'Etude des Techniques Economiques
Modernes (Ecole Pratiques des Hautes Etudes, Paris) to prepare a study of
the Community textile industry and its development prospects up to 1975.[1]
His task was to add depth to the monograph studies done by the Commission,
to make trend forecasts based on the general performance of the economy,
and finally to consider as one of the directions of future policy the possibility
of a wider opening of the market to the products of the LDC's. The
conclusions of the de Bandt report were very badly received by the social
partners. They may be summarized as follows. There is excessive production
capacity in the textile industry and the elimination of worn-out plants is too
slow. This excess capacity is a burden on the profitability of the textile
industry particularly since marginal enterprises are exercising abnormal

competitive pressures. In addition, production units are thoroughly fragmented ranging from a host of artisan-type units to small companies which predominate in the sector. Both production conditions and company efficiency levels vary widely. This extreme variation is another indication of the importance of marginal firms in the textile sector. Furthermore, cyclical fluctuations are undermining the already underutilized capital.

The continuation of these trends would suggest an increase in production of 30 percent and a reduction in the labor force of 15 percent—or 250,000 people—by 1975 in comparison with 1966 levels. However, taking into account the greater intensity of competitive pressures that forecast should be revised. As a result of the necessity to increase productivity or see the trade position worsen the cutback in the labor force would have to be of the order of some 15 to 20 percent or 310,000 to 350,000 people. It seems impossible to quantify the impact of trade liberalization apart from making quite arbitrary and extreme hypotheses. Beyond the demands of harmonization of trade policies there are hardly any objective criteria by reference to which one could define the term "abnormal prices." Lacking a definition of an optimal level of protection, protective agreements and measures can only be understood as transitional measures carried out in the context of a restructuring plan. In the final analysis a better organization of production would enhance both labor productivity and the efficiency of the capital currently employed.

In general, de Bandt indicated that it is both right and wrong to say that the Community textile industry cannot be integrated, for precisely the same reasons that it is not in a position to be assured an adequate level of profitability given existing conditions. These are reasons bound up with its structure and operation. Nevertheless, it appears that it could adapt if it carried out essential restructuring, a process acknowledged to be painful both for management and labor. In this regard, trade liberalization aimed at improving the international division of labor was considered relevant to the Community textile industry, because it would compel the industry to face external competition, particularly from the LDC's, from whom, de Bandt indicated, trade sensitivity is the greatest.

The de Bandt report advocated a restructuring of the industry based on two policy guidelines: elimination of plant and production units with the aim of mopping up existing excess capacity and removing marginal companies from the market; and organization of structures of production along lines of vertical and horizontal concentration. The report triggered off a great deal of controversy in textile circles. If opinions on the causes of the sickness continued to diverge, they were united in thinking that a systematic opening of the market would lead to social troubles that would hardly be acceptable. One of the merits of the de Bandt report, laying stress as it did on the need for more pronounced vertical integration, was to bring out the fact that no textile policy could leave out of account the situation affecting the principal customer, the clothing industry. The Commission therefore decided to approach a private consulting agency for a study on that industry; the result was the Capelin report.[2]

The Capelin Report

The conclusions of the Capelin report were much more subtle in tone than those of the de Bandt report. It should also be pointed out that the consulting agency was given a less open-ended brief. De Bandt, as noted above, had been asked to evaluate the consequences of a systematic opening up of markets, on the assumption that such a political posture would be beneficial both to the industry and the whole economy as well as unavoidable in terms of world politics and the international division of labor. These principles were not imposed as a starting point for the new study. What is more, the Capelin report actually cast doubt on these conceptions:

> "Thus, we believe the question may be summed up in terms of the following choice: a costly social policy involving support of the industry, or its abandonment to the profit of the leading industries, the L.D.C.'s and the European consumer. Indeed such a supportive policy is social in character not only in the narrow sense of the word but also in aiming at the general collective welfare. It is a policy which can prove itself to be economically profitable in the medium term, since those sectors of the clothing industry capable of absorbing capital and know-how can become internationally highly competitive (as some already are).
>
> In the last analysis, the choice is above all a political, even an ethical one, between two policies on which it is difficult to decide from the economic and even the social point of view."[3]

The report advocated the following policies.

1. Allow the sector to be restructured. In particular, a speedy liberalization of trade at Community level would stimulate rates of growth of net imports in such a way that the vaccine would kill the invalid rather than cure him. Nevertheless, in the medium and long term this industry would have to adapt itself to conditions of international trade freed of restrictions. An appropriate policy would be to limit temporarily (for four or five years) global imports by volume by an annual growth rate of 12 percent to 15 percent taking as a base the figures for 1969 or 1970, then progressively to liberalize trade with the LDC's while clearly informing trade associations and unions of the policy being pursued.

2. Agree on Community regulations of foreign trade in clothing and in particular harmonize nontariff restrictive trade practices. Regarding different

countries of origin the report recommended the following distinctions: a firm attitude toward the state-trading countries where objective conditions for dumping are fulfilled; a firm attitude toward Hong Kong, which cannot any longer qualify as an underdeveloped country and whose price advantage is partly a result of the supply of raw materials (and sometimes semimanufactured articles) by the People's Republic of China which is a state-trading country; a firm attitude toward Macao and Timor, for the same reasons, but which apply here with even more force; a liberal attitude to all the other LDC's.

3. Demand and strictly control labels of origin; prevent and sanction the practice of relabeling; and demand authentic certificates of origin and sanction contraventions by a reduction or even a revocation of licenses granted or to be granted.

4. Favor the decentralization of the industry, reserving to it a privileged place in national as well as Community development regional policies.

5. Facilitate productive investment with the help of available fiscal and monetary instruments.

6. Suppress in the medium term export subsidies, the logical consequence of progressive liberalization carried out in the medium term.

7. Improve the total flow of information, elaborating and disseminating valid statistics which serve as a basis for entrepreneurial decisions. This is seen as very important and must be considered in collaboration with the trade federations, whose statistical equipment is still often derisory.

THE FORMULATION AND APPLICATION
OF THE EC TEXTILE POLICY

The Commission spent the entire year that followed the submission of this study (in July 1970) in a series of consultations devoted to formulating a sectoral policy for the textile industry. On July 21, 1971, it issued a proposal which has remained the charter for the Community's entire approach toward textiles. In preparing these proposals the Commission recognized that there were certain limits set for public bodies at both the national and Community level, since initiatives for change would remain in the hands of entrepreneurs. Public authorities could create conditions which would favor necessary developments, but they could not force the private sector to respond. In addition, care would have to be taken to avoid structural adaptations that would cause serious social disturbances.

Thus in light of the range of difficulties faced by the textile sector the Commission agreed that any improvement for the industry would require a greater degree of competitiveness at company level. This would involve accelerating the pace of restructuring already underway, and, in particular, insuring that it led to a higher degree of concentration and reduction in excess capacity. Such policies would have proved increasingly necessary in any case as new techniques were applied to fibers, manufacturing materials, and finished products. In addition, they would provide Community firms with an offsetting advantage to compensate them for the labor-cost disadvantages normally felt in those sectors that must compete with firms in certain less developed countries. Consequently, the Commission proposed policies in several areas: the implementation of a commercial policy capable of making the progressive opening of the Community market compatible with the demands of adaptation unique to the textile sector; the adoption of measures likely to speed up restructuring; and the continued implementation of measures designed to give the Community market the same characteristics as a national market, including fiscal harmonization and elimination of obstacles to the free circulation of goods, an improved capital and bond market, the provision of adequate sources of finance for industry, and the general pursuit of the policies outlined in the EC memorandum on industrial policy (described in Chapter 6).

In the following sections the implementation of these goals will be discussed.

Commercial Policy in the Textile and Clothing Sectors

The main component of the commercial policy the Commission has followed is the progressive opening of the Common Market to imports from third countries, particularly from LDC's. This direction was confirmed when the EC included textiles in its offer of a Generalized System of Preferences (GSP) to the developing countries. However, the very fact that most other industrialized nations excluded textiles from their preferences indicates the difficulties experienced by the industry in adapting with ease and rapidity to competitive conditions ruling on the world market for products from this sector.

An orderly and smooth structural adaptation of the textile industry under conditions of an "open markets" policy presupposes several factors working in unison, in particular the social partners being adequately informed on the timetable of the proposed commercial policy. In regard to the implementation of the GSP the Community has established a system of quotas and buffers for sensitive products. Over the next five years any further tariff concessions will generally have to take place within the framework of this system. After the completion of the present offer to the countries benefitting from the Council of Ministers decision of March 30, 1971 (that is, the countries belonging to the group of 77 which are also nonsignatories to the

Long-Term Arrangement of 1962 delimiting world trade in textiles), the size of the Community's offer ought not to be a matter for further negotiation, either because of the enlargement of the system to include other countries— should such a case arise—or because of any possible increase in the ceilings at a rate in excess of 5 percent per annum of the global offer.

As to quantitative restrictions, the progressive elimination of still-existing limitations should take place with due regard to the attitude of other trading partners. The schedule of liberalization, with yarns already largely liberalized, ought to affect fabrics before affecting more made-up articles. Such a policy would be consistent with the progressive industrialization of the LDC's. Finally, the Commission should seek the establishment of a structure of competition compatible at world level with GATT rules, and capable both of avoiding the permanent dangers that lurk in the currents of world textile trade and of gradually achieving the conditions for a new international division of labor. If it turned out to be impossible to define a code of good conduct with principal trading partners, there would be a danger that it might be necessary in one way or another to withdraw once again into restrictive policies.

On December 20, 1973, the representatives of 50 governments, meeting under the auspices of GATT at Geneva, renegotiated the 1962 Long-Term Arrangement, which covers international trade in cotton, woolen, and man-made fibers.

On July 31, 1974, a total of 45 countries, accounting for 85 percent of world trade, acceded to the arrangement. Article 1 defines the object of the agreement in these terms:

"The fundamental aims regarding textile products will be to achieve the expansion of trade, the lowering of restrictions to trade, and the progressive liberalization of world trade. At the same time the orderly and fair development of trade in these products will be assured, avoiding the effects of disorganization on markets and on types of production in both importing and exporting countries."

It recognizes further the necessity of avoiding damage to the minimum "viable" production of textiles in any particular country, while at the same time emphasizing the willingness to favor economic and social development in the LDC's. To this end it presents policies designed to encourage companies which are less competitive on the international level either to engage in more viable fields of production or to transfer to other sectors of the economy. In reality, it organizes a new approach to international trade, since it envisages, over the first year of the application of the agreement (which came into force on January 4, 1974), the presentation by all the contracting parties of a trade policy for textiles which over a three-year period would progressively eliminate existing restrictions.

Import restrictions will only be allowed when they can be justified in terms of the new arrangement, that is, in line with a certain number of objective criteria. It is still too early to have an overall view of the policy which the Community will follow in applying this arrangement. Up to now the EC Council of Ministers has only announced a mandate for negotiations with India and Pakistan. It appears that the Community intends to adopt a selective approach, by products and by countries. These restrictions would only apply on products which are clearly causing disruption on the EC market and to countries which are a really disruptive influence.

With respect to tariff preferences the Community has kept textiles as part of its general offer; it has also kept the annual growth factor to 5 percent in line with the declaration of July 21, 1971.

Industrial Policy Properly Called

As a result of trade liberalization the accent was placed on the need for a program to improve companies' competitiveness. Increased investment, above all, was to be used to improve productivity as well as adapt output in quantitative terms to consumer demand. Since the Commission did not control funds for this purpose, it outlined complementary European-level policies in regard to scientific and economic research.

Scientific Research

Both research and the exploitation of technological progress are essential to the achievement of the aims outlined in the Commission proposal (July 21, 1971) for the textile sector. Indeed, in the production of synthetic fibers as well as the manufacturing and making-up processes research has played a vital role in lowering production costs and adapting the quality of supply to foreseeable developments on the demand side.

Synthetics producers generally operate an autonomous research program which allows them to experiment and discover new fibers. Research aimed at achieving technical progress in textile machinery, which is ultimately linked to productivity in the manufacturing industry, is carried on efficiently under the general auspices of the mechanical engineering industry, frequently in liaison with the machinery users.

Textile research as it is properly called takes place at all stages—the treatment of fibers, conversion (into cloth / fabric), and the final completion of the made-up article. Certain companies and groups of companies independently carry out the particular branch of research which interests them. However, the low level of profitability on which most companies operate does not generally permit them to lay out the kind of financing necessary for a sustained research effort. At the interindustry level the beginnings of research coordination have been set in motion for all the textile subsectors grouped within Comitextil. Nevertheless, this trend is still far from representing a satisfactory solution to the problems the industry is confronting. In addition, research institutes are partly financed by the public sector in certain member states.

Therefore, the Commission indicated in its proposal that it was interested in any program that might be envisaged by the textile industry, and that it would be able to ascertain in the light of the general EC policy governing advanced technology whether the Community could consider channelling support into these projects. If that were the case, the Commission would then propose such action to the Council of Ministers.

Moreover, the Commission's action could take the form of an effort to coordinate individual and collective research. On the other hand, there is scope for pursuing Community-based research programs that have been going on since 1964 under the auspices of Eurisotope for the application of nuclear techniques in the textile industry.

Consequently, the Commission proposed to the Council of Ministers at the end of September 1974 a program of technological research in the textile sector. This was based on the Council's resolution of January 14, 1974, concerning the coordination of national policies and the definition of action of Community interest in the field of science and technology. A sum of 250,000 units of account has been set aside as the EC financial participation in carrying out this research program. It consists of three elements: thermal treatment for synthetic fibers—this will be a matter of obtaining an optimalization of the processes of manufacture with a view to improving output and quality, particularly in small and medium-sized textile companies that generally do not dispose of the necessary research capability; treatment of textiles by organic solvents, the aim of which is to reduce water pollution and energy consumption, either by changing manufacturing processes or by adopting processes that make use of organic solvents; and fire-proofing of textile fibers, the aim of which is to protect consumers by improving the fire-proofing of clothing and furnishings. Preliminary research carried out by Comitextil has proved the utility of this program, and the textile industry proposes to participate in it with a financial stake double that of the Community. The import of this program goes well beyond the sums that can be brought to bear by the EC, because it is a manifestation of concern about a declining sector as well as an incentive to develop research programs coordinated at Community and industry level. Certainly this habit of working in common already existed in the past, but the EC's financial participation provides a secondary motive for deepening cooperation.

Economic Research

The periodic but significant fluctuations in the trade cycle affecting the textile industry have constituted a serious handicap to any progress toward essential restructuring and modernization. Moreover, they have a detrimental effect on companies' liquidity, and their amplitude has presented difficulties in making short-term forecasts for this sector. What is needed is a Center for Cyclical Observation (Centre d'Observation Conjoncturelle), operating at Community level with sufficient means to assemble all the requisite data for making these forecasts, data which would help to deal with the aforementioned problems. Thus the Commission in 1972 entrusted the Center for Economic and Management Research at Lille with the responsibility of carrying out a study consisting of the following:

    1. analysis of the phenomena which are at the root of the cyclical fluctuations affecting the textile sector

    2. determination of the kinds of information that should be collected and published periodically to support short-term forecasts

    3. preparation of an inventory of the data available at national level and determination of the ways in which it might be exploited at Community level

    4. formulation of proposals on the work that could be done by an observation center on cyclical fluctuations at Community level and make suggestions on the organization of such a center.

The study came out strongly in support of such a center and proposed several functions for it.

First, the center would have the task of encouraging and sustaining efforts made to improve statistical tools and to develop research and studies in the field of textile economics. Second, in order to avoid duplication of what is already being done, the center would have to organize a close degree of cooperation between the relevant national organizations and promote the harmonization and exchange of information. Whenever possible it would also be the center's task to make a synthesis of these findings. Finally, having centralized information, the center would have to see that it was widely published and found its way to the appropriate end-users. At the same time the study indicated that such a center would only be possible if it were supported by appropriate financial resources. Though not necessarily exclusively, the principal contribution would have to depend on Community levies. Since the submission of this study in June 1973 nothing new has occurred, apart from the decision taken by the EC statistical office to give priority to the textile and clothing sectors in harmonizing industrial statistics. This harmonization was in the opinion of both the Commission and of the industry a prerequisite to any action in the textile sector.

Public Sector Intervention

The Commission has indicated that national aid programs ought to contribute particularly to a speeding up of the restructuring process and its orientation toward the Community goals already cited. In this regard it distinguished among three kinds of governmental intervention: aid channelled to the textile industry as a whole, aiming either at stimulating research or at improving short-term forecasting; aid of a structural nature—elimination of excess capacity, retraining outside the sector, and company concentration; and aid to investment in textiles—modernization and retraining within the sector. Although the Commission has entirely reserved its right of appraisal, it should be remembered that in this sphere the role entrusted to it by the Treaty of Rome is essentially one of coordinating national policies. Its actions consequently are directed toward the avoidance of distortions in competition which can result from autonomous aid and subsidy policies. In line with this it also directs member states' actions toward Community objectives. However, the Commission does not dispose of its own resources that it would be able to bring to bear on aids to industry. Moreover, until now no agreement has been reached at the level of the Council of Ministers concerning the creation of a regional fund.

With these various parameters in mind—and most notably the minimum degree of interference with free competition—the Commission considers that intervention in the form of industrywide or structural aid would be beneficial, while intervention to aid investment ought to be in response to a much more strict set of criteria such as justification in the light of acute social problems. Furthermore, investment aid ought not to lead to increases in capacity, and it should take into account the situation at Community level of the sector concerned.

The Examination of National Policies

In 1971 and 1972 the Commission undertook an examination of aid measures for the textile sector, either existing or planned, in member states in order to make them consistent with the criteria envisaged in the declaration of July 21, 1971. All of 1973 was essentially taken up with an examination of the systems in application in the new member countries. On the whole, and with the exception of some modifications of detail, national measures were judged compatible with Community policy.

However, faced with the difficulty of identifying and comparing concrete applications of the various systems of national aid in force in the member states, the Commission at the beginning of 1974 was led to deepen and complete its former initiatives. To this end it informed the member states that it had decided to develop its line of action on the following levels.

1. The formulation of a sectoral policy for the textile industry involving special conditions for granting direct aid with application in the framework of agreements between industry and state; and if necessary, the application of a system of indirect aid (general assistance, regional assistance) which must be

communicated to the Commission in advance and placed in the context of
sectoral policy.

2. The development of a procedure for bilateral—even multilateral—
consultation will be organized by the Commission to look into all justified
complaints made by national governments about assistance granted to certain
textile concerns that might seriously affect trade and competition (whether
the assistance in question results from applying systems specific to the textile
sector or systems having a more general application).

3. The preparation of a list of aids from which the textile industry stands
to benefit will be compiled each year, and an annual statistical survey will list
all aids and assistance from which investments may be augmented.

Italian Textile Law

The only piece of legislation which has really necessitated official action
is the Italian law no. 1101 of January 2, 1972, regarding the restructuring,
reorganization, and conversion of the Italian textile industry. Indeed the
Commission has often been called upon to take a public view of this outline
system of assistance as the Italian government has proceeded to define its
criteria and modes of application.

By May 27, 1970, the Commission had already taken a partial stance
on what at that stage in Italy was still no more than proposed legislation. Indeed, in 1969 it had set in train the procedure under Article 93, Paragraph 2 of
the EC Treaty. The proposed Italian legislation envisaged various kinds of
aid: credit facilities and tax advantages designed to assist in the financing of
restructuring operations, modernization, and reequipment of textile concerns; credit facilities favoring the creation or extension, in so-called textile
areas, of nontextile industrial activities; and a decennial exemption on all
direct taxes on revenue for investment placed in so-called textile regions.

The partial decision of the Commission focused on the suppression of aid
for work in progress that the decennial exemption on tax on revenue
amounted to. It was also concerned with the necessity of taking into account,
in the light of aid being granted to textile investment, the problems of
overcapacity not only from the national but also from the Community point
of view. The Italian government took cognizance of this decision in
elaborating the final text, known under the name of "Law no. 1101."

This legislation is a framework or outline law in which the Italian
authorities specified aid criteria (notably geographical and sectoral) and the
manner of application of aid by successive stages according to procedures
envisaged in the legislation itself. That is why the Commission moved at the
end of 1972 to take up a new provisional position on the law and certain of its

articles, although this position still did not exhaust the subject. The substance of this latest position, communicated by the Commission to the Italian government and other member states in a letter of December 15, 1972, is as follows:

"The difficulty of determining which branches and regions are to be the beneficiaries of investment aid as well as the possible overlap of this aid with assistance from other sources [is] well on the way to being resolved. The Commission has taken note of the prohibition of any overlap in assistance stemming from the textile laws with assistance forthcoming under other laws. It has, however, stressed that given the possibility for companies to choose between these two forms of advantage, the application of other systems of aid to textile companies must also be looked at in the light of the general guidelines to be laid down for the application of the textile law. The Commission has further reminded the Italian authorities of the necessity for them to inform the Commission beforehand of the policies that the ad hoc interministerial committee set up under the law intends to implement, firstly as regards a concrete definition of the criteria which will determine textile activities, operational plans and the location of benefiting investment; secondly regarding the apportionment of the credits available (200 billion discounted bills) between schemes for reconversion and restructuring. Only on the basis of this information will the Commission be able fully to appreciate the impact of the law on the sector. The Commission has further indicated to the Italian government that it was not raising any objection to the eight textile regions which have been designated by ministerial decrees of July 31 and August 21, 1972; in these areas the textile industry predominates and there are serious employment problems."

During the parliamentary procedure for adopting the law a new move governing aid to textile and clothing companies had been introduced, without prior notification to the Commission. This was a temporary (three-year) and partial (reduction of the rate from 15 percent to 10 percent) tax on the social charges payable on family allowances. According to the Italian authorities this measure would reduce the appropriate charges on companies concerned by about 31 billion lira, or some 0.8 percent of their turnover. It would therefore have significant effects on intra-Community trade and competition, in a sector where competition and trading are intense. On July 25, 1973, the Commission moved to adopt a new interlocutory decision under Article 93, Paragraph 2 of the EC Treaty, with regard to the intended moves.

The factors that led the Commission to take this position may be summarized as follows: this was a case of a type of aid being channelled to the production process toward which the Commission generally takes a negative attitude, since it is not the kind to give effective encouragement to companies receiving it to carry through essential reorganization programs. In the particular case of the Italian textile industry this aid is not suitable for the objective of resolving difficulties of certain branches or concerns, because it is distributed to all textile companies without distinction. In addition this aid is such as to have a direct effect on intra-Community trade and competition since it is immediately reflected in cost price and in companies' competitiveness—this in a sector already marked by significant trade and very lively competition.

The Application of the Social Fund
to the Textile Sector

Since more rapid restructuring and increased productivity will accelerate the decline in employment in the textile sector regional and social policies are required to assist workers who lose their positions. The reconstituted European Social Fund will be able to play a determinant role in facilitating the transfer of redundant workers within and outside the sector.

In 1971 the Social Fund, which had been established by the Treaty of Rome, underwent a fundamental reform; the basic elements are described in decision 71/66 of the Council of Ministers. The purpose of this change is to make the fund the instrument of a more active employment policy and to relate it more firmly to the aims of Community policies. Thus its primary objective now is to promote not only an improvement in the situation of workers in the Community, but especially the development of policies designed to better prepare them for changes in employment opportunities. These policies most frequently involve some training readaptation.

The new system is characterized at once by selectivity in its intervention role (as opposed to the automaticity of the former system) and by a stronger emphasis on the hortatory function of its interventions. The Fund may intervene either sectorally (under Article 4) or on an individual basis (under Article 5).

Regarding sectoral intervention, up to now two sectors have received support—agriculture and textiles (albeit the converting part of the textile industry, excluding the production of synthetic fibers and clothing.) The textile sector has further benefitted from a certain number of interventions carried out under Article 5 as "regional" interventions. However, on the whole the sums allocated to textile workers are comparatively low. This situation may be explained by the fact that companies, at least small and medium-sized ones, are not always aware of the possibilities offered by the Social Fund, with almost all the funds available having been absorbed by big groups. It is certain also that the social partners, in particular the unions, have taken a very reserved attitude toward opening the fund to the textile sector. They fear that the fund constitutes an alibi for the Community, authorizing it to follow a policy of unconditional opening up of the market without any real alternative choice being possible insofar as the paucity of the sums earmarked in the budget precludes an active employment policy.

If, however, the activities of the fund are to be coordinated with a sectoral policy for the textile industry its decision will have to be based on very rigorous selective criteria, and the fund will have to be provided with sufficient financing to accomplish this and other tasks that it is given. The fund could give priority to actions in areas fulfilling the following conditions.

1. Retraining within the textile industry which would permit the development of those specialized subsectors in which under open market conditions Community products would find it easier to face external competition. A study is now being conducted to determine which subsectors might answer this description. The results will be submitted to the industry for its reaction and suggestions.

2. The reduction of the textile industry labor force if it were coordinated in a program supported both by textile firms who need to rid themselves of excess labor and other sectors capable of absorbing this manpower.

3. Restructuring inside the textile industry where the effort of retraining labor would go hand in hand with a program of reequipment and technological conversion. This would enable the optimum utilization of the manpower thus retrained.

Priority, however, would be given to those actions consistent with one of these three criteria which are most relevant to the needs of regional policy.

CONCLUSIONS

The formulation and implementation of a sectoral policy for the textile industry shows the limits within which the EC Commission must act with regard to industrial policy.

The Commission currently enjoys a certain amount of competence in the field of commercial policy, but in contrast its powers with respect to industrial policy are still very restricted. It is against this background that it negotiated in the name of the member states the international arrangement on wool, cotton, and synthetic fibers. However, at the time it was signed the question was raised whether the arrangement ought not to have been signed conjointly by the Commission and the member states. This dilemma arose since the arrangement—especially in its preamble—made reference to structural adaptations it envisaged in the industrialized countries. In any event the Commission was authorized to sign the arrangement singly, since the agreement is regarded essentially as an act of commercial policy. This anecdotal fact shows that member states remain distinctly jealous of their prerogatives and autonomy in the field of industrial policy. In commercial policy, too, sectoral policy would seem to have been applied essentially in this spirit. Nevertheless in decisions of a general character, whether affecting the Social Fund, regional policy, environmental policy, and even industrial policy, the Commission has always taken the "textile fact" into account and planned special measures for the sector whenever that was desirable. It is in this sense that one may speak of a textile sectoral policy.

NOTES

1. J. de Bandt, *L'industrie textile de la C.E.E.: Analyse et perspectives 1975*, Brussels, EC Commission, January 1969.

2. *Les industries de la Confection dans la C.E.E.: Analyse et perspectives 1975*, Capelin Associates Limited in collaboration with the University of Geneva, July 1970.

3. Ibid.

9

FRENCH ELECTRONICS POLICY: THE COSTS OF TECHNOLOGICAL INDEPENDENCE
John Zysman

The dissolution of the Délégation à l'Informatique almost a decade after it began marks the end of the *Plan Calcul*, the program intended to foster a viable French presence in the computer industry. Giscard d'Estaing's new government, faced with the ever-mounting subsidies required to float the plan and the unwillingness of at least one of the industrial partners to increase its capital investment, is moving to change the commitments of the state. Three options appear open. The government can take control of the strife-torn CII (Compagnie Internationale de l'Informatique) and manage it directly, perhaps under the authority of the French Atomic Energy Commission (CEA). The entire game could be reconstituted on a European scale within the framework of Unidata, the technological and marketing alliance in computers struck among Philips of Holland, Siemens of Germany, and CII. Finally the French holdings could simply be sold to Honeywell or another American firm, as has been discussed for some time. Taking control of CII now does not exclude a European or Franco-American solution later, it should be noted. Ever since it became evident that CII could not be profitable except in the dim future, if ever, the French have claimed their support of a computer plan would give them a bargaining position in assembling either a European company or, with American participation, a viable multinational competitor to IBM. Thus for the French government to take control of CII now might well imply that a suitable bargain had not been struck, not necessarily that it had decided to permanently keep control. Certainly the most symmetrical finale would be the sale of CII to Honeywell, for in this case the electronics story would close where it opened, with the sale of the French computer holdings to an American company, and, as in the first case, at the behest of

Giscard d'Estaing, then Minister of Finance and now President. Whatever the outcome, the exit of the *Plan Calcul* lowers the curtains on an epoch in French policy for electronics, and perhaps on an epoch in French planning and industrial policy as well. The decision points to the evaporating power of the planning commission and is perhaps one more hint at the industrial policies that will follow. The policy that is beginning to show from the slow accumulation of choices, rather than any general statement of principle, seems to rest on four elements: (1) a general pull back from direct government industrial initiatives, thus (2) ceding the lead to private companies and most importantly the holding companies and banks, while (3) leaving the government to intervene on a selective basis when required, using the vast array of financial instruments in the hands of the finance ministry, and (4) insulating the social and political community from the turmoil of the market by such massive welfare programs as one-year unemployment insurance for those left out of work in the stops and starts, twists and turns of the marketplace. The open question of course is what purposes this will serve, whether the technical wizard of the Ministry of Finance can, as President of the republic, find a policy that will at a minimum avoid social and political turmoil.

Ending the *Plan Calcul* at any rate forces the French to reevaluate past policy for its electronics industry and its stance in the search for joint European ventures. The case of the *Plan Calcul* is instructive both about efforts at European technological cooperation and national initiatives to foster advanced industries. The focus here will be on the French initiative, but several remarks about European efforts are in order.[1]

There has not been a European electronics policy but rather a strategy in each of the several nations to promote a national computer champion, and occasional efforts to link those approaches together. In keeping with experiences in other advanced industries, there have been efforts at collaboration but no unification of national efforts in electronics. As Warnecke notes in this volume, the development of the European Community has seen a "strengthening of the national authorities over the private sector at the expense of multinational cooperation." It would appear in fact that more than the desire of each government to conserve its influence over the character of industrial development by maintaining some control over its national actors was at stake. France and Germany had very different approaches to economic policy and, in particular, to the responsibility of the state to shape the direction of growth and to protect the society against fluctuations in the marketplace. In and of itself, the different notions of the authority and influence the state should exercise over corporate strategies and the mechanisms by which such intervention should be made would tend to exclude unified industrial management. Moreover, this problem is all the more acute in advanced industries and electronics in particular where the strategies and technological choices of the companies involved reflect sharply different priorities, although the policies of all the countries reflected a concern with American technological domination. The French government, the central actor in the history of that nation's computer industry, was most concerned with national technological independence, and used subsidies and guaranteed markets to induce a single local producer to develop particular products. The German and Dutch companies were in pursuit of corporate profit and followed the lead of the commercial and industrial marketplace. The differing goals urged different technological choices and were reflected in the companies' current product lines. In computers, as in the other advanced industries, when cooperation is in fact tried, the management structures of the joint enterprises reflect the politics of collaboration rather than the need for competitiveness in the marketplace. This simply adds to whatever other handicaps the Europeans may have.

Since there is no unified European policy any analysis must focus on the individual national policies. The French experience of state intervention in the electronics industry suggests the limits on a government's ability to shape the growth of a domestic industry that forms an integral part of an international marketplace. The French government pursued a political goal of technological independence by directly supporting and protecting certain electronics firms. Its policies, however, appear to have had the unintended economic consequences of damaging the conduct and performance of the very firms that must serve as the instruments of policy. A French state accustomed to imposing its will on the marketplace has been unable either to alter the structure of the international industry or to isolate French firms from its pressure. In this setting forcing firms to conform to the political goals of the state rather than the necessities of the market can slowly weaken them, damaging not only the firm but impeding the original state policies. The government's ability to pursue its technological goals dwindles as the position of national firms in the international industry erodes. In this case the difficulty has been that allowing or encouraging the firms to conform to the constraints of the market would require that the government at least redefine its policy goals. We must, therefore, begin by considering these policy goals and the character of the bureaucracy that made them.

TECHNOLOGICAL GAPS AND INDUSTRIAL POLICY —THE ORIGINS OF FRENCH POLICY

French policy for the electronics industry was set forth in the "era of the technology gap" and inspired by the fear that national independence would be lost and France shoved into the second or perhaps third rank of nations by the rush of technological advance that came from America. The particular wave of electronics technology developed in the 1950s and 1960s posed apparent security questions but the malaise was more widespread. An undoubted concern existed that the magnitude of American aid, the structure of American industry, and the organization and management of American firms would end with a permanent French political and economic dependence on foreign technology and a domination of certain industries by foreign capital. It appeared, therefore, that the state should intervene to support the development of vital technologies and to modernize the industry to insure that French firms could defend the national position.

There are those though who argue that the fundamental goal of the government was always the modernization of the industry and that the "technology gap" rhetoric and its security implications were consciously manipulated to promote this end. In this interpretation the Control Data computer temporarily denied by American policy was not in fact essential to atomic development in France, but rather the incident gave force and legitimacy to government demands for change. Since the government's conception of a modern industry called for a few large producers capable of competing in all products, both interpretations led to the same end—the government should assist the reorganization of the industry and support efforts at research and development (R and D). Similarly, whether the fears of a technology gap prompted the policies or legitimated them, an atmosphere of national glory through noble technology emerged in which the engineers had little difficulty engaging government support for technically—not commercially—inspired projects such as SECAM, the French color television system. The "technology gap" debate faded away, perhaps, as Jean-Jacques Salomon argues, because the problem was finally clearly seen and everything remained to be done, only to be renewed when in the face of sudden trade deficits the Americans began asking whether they had "lost their technological lead."[2] In its new version the "technology gap" has exchanged political perspectives and concerns for the economic problems of trade.[3]

Multiple meanings for the term "technology gap" have long clouded our understanding and confused the formulation of policy. The economic reality which inspired the label and the policies that might have been appropriate were markedly different from the political imagery in the term. Most importantly the needs of security, economic policy, and political symbolism conflicted at some points and required separate approaches at others. Grouping them together as "technology issues" obscured the difficult choices that were in fact necessary. Given the biases of the decision makers and the political mood of the time, the problem perhaps could not have been defined differently. However, articulating the multiple meanings of the "technology gap" will both suggest the origins of certain policy dilemmas and perhaps suggest some of the ways out of them.

In the most literal sense there probably never was a "technology gap" between Europe and America, certainly not of the kind that might characterize the technological relations of Third World and industrial nations. With very few exceptions, military products such as certain atomic techniques or integrated circuits in their earliest phase, there were no products the French did not have and could not use. That is, the French had available the full range of advanced technologies, and the scientific and industrial infrastructure to use them existed. Differences in productivity levels certainly existed, but differences in the quality of the capital stock reflected a myriad of social and economic factors such as the reluctance of noncompetitive and often family-owned and small firms to adopt new methods and relative factor prices. Under any circumstances the productivity problem, although of concern to the French, is one of effective uses of standard technology in basic industries and not a matter of advanced technologies in science-based sectors of the economy. Productivity questions were never really part of the debate.

Nor could it be said that the products were not made in France by French nationals. In electronic components, for example, production of each new generation began in France as the market grew large enough to justify manufacture, not import. Similarly IBM and Honeywell Bull manufacture computers in French plants manned by French engineers and even managed by Frenchmen. Furthermore, Machine Bull when it was still in French hands produced two innovative computers, the Gamma 3 and the Gamma 60, which were undoubted technological leaders. Therefore, it was not even true that France lacked the capability to produce these advanced goods.

Although the "technology gap" implied a literal difference in technological capacity, it referred in fact to something much more limited and specific. French firms—that is, firms composed of French capital—could not assure the production of certain products nor maintain technological advance in certain fields. Thus at its core the "technology gap" was a question of the market position of different national firms. Although technological prowess may have affected those market positions the difficulty more often than not was the inability of French firms to translate technological possibilities into competitive products and defensible market positions. Certainly this was the case in the failure of Machine Bull and Cosem. It was as much a failure of the firm that produced a technology gap as the other way around. In this context strategies aimed at particular technologies or specific gaps never came to grips with the real problem, and may simply have perpetuated it.

What should be done about the fact that French firms do not produce particular goods depends, of course, on what difference it makes. Apart from a simple defense of the interests of national capital, there are reasons why the French government felt uneasy with foreign firms, particularly foreign electronics firms. Foreign firms may be less responsive to French government policy and less bound by the rules of the business game in France. For example, they may be less willing to assure stable employment and exports, two central elements of French economic policy. In fact, employment in electronics, particularly in foreign firms, is very small while exports require a competitive position in some goods not necessarily the most advanced. Neither would seem to justify the major programs that were initiated. Second, early access to certain technologies such as components may affect the competitive position of product firms in a variety of sectors, and, therefore, a national producer and innovator might be considered essential. Since American manufacturers, the argument runs, tend to produce only standard catalogue items in France, developing new generation products in the United States, there is a need for a national producer to maintain the national R and D capacity. There are, though, many more effective and less expensive solutions than the present floating of a national producer, some of which the French are beginning to toy with. For example, some form of implantation in the United States, or a tie between a French group and one of the American components manufacturers such as was envisioned in the proposed tie between Motorola and certain European competitors, might resolve the problem. Finally, it is argued that a dependence on foreign technologies is simply a threat to national independence—in some distant and not clearly defined way, and here we come to the heart of the issue. As Raymond Vernon notes:

> When advanced nations find themselves reliant upon outside sources for the technology essential to their national objectives, a deep sense of insecurity is generated. Whatever the economic analysis may suggest, therefore, nations are likely to feel more at ease if the sources of technology seem to lie within their control than if they are largely external.[4]

One working group of the French Planning Commission argued that failure to maintain a semiconductor capacity would mean that France would start down the road to underdevelopment. Although real economic and security issues were involved, simple insecurity underlay much of the technology gap debate. Commercial production of particular technologies was not required to resolve the substantive problems and, in fact, was a symbolic gesture and not a real solution of insecurity.

Even if the French government were denied the use of a technology controlled by a company with a foreign base exactly at the vulnerable moment when a new generation of products became available, the older products would probably suffice—although they would be less efficient—for a number of years. The time to react and develop a French product would still exist. One policy might, therefore, be to maintain the capacity to develop that product if it became necessary. Thus it may not be essential for companies controled by French capital and sensitive to French policy to produce the most advanced products, but for them to maintain the capacity of producing them if necessary. Since the prototype and the industrialization of products represent the bulk of its overall cost of development, the applied and basic research necessary to maintain a defensive position is relatively low. If the firm, moreover, is producing related or more traditional products in the same sector much of the research costs would be absorbed by other products, reducing the necessary subsidy even further. Actual product competition with the international leaders, on the other hand, would probably demand subsidies that were factors of ten of the minimum defensive subsidies. Finally, if the level of subsidy were the only issue the discussion would be academic since the state would most likely pay a higher subsidy to reduce the uncertainty inevitable in a defensive position and to purchase the symbols, even if it clearly perceived the cost and choice. However, the insistence that particular high-technology goods be produced by French capital, not simply that a defensive reaction capacity be maintained, has generated serious dilemmas in French policy. Producing these goods today may in fact make it increasingly difficult to maintain a defensive position tomorrow. The problem is a political one, technological independence, but the underlying cause is economic. Addressing the political symptoms may simply aggravate the economic problems.

BUREAUCRATIC POLITICS OF BUSINESS AND THE STATE—THE BASIS OF CHOICE

Before considering the difficulties the French strategy encountered, it is worth considering why that choice was made.[5] Whatever the wisdom of the decision, it certainly appears that government bureaucrats choose to do what they know best—wield the power of the state and manipulate the web of school and social ties between the top echelon of businessmen and government officials—to create operating companies, channel capital flows, and establish guaranteed markets. In this instance the civil servants recruited allies in the business community much more than responding to pressures from them, and the *fonctionnaires* may well be said to have devised and imposed the strategy of the *Plan Calcul*. Two commercial strategies were proposed but neither found strong allies in the government and, by the end, all the policy options were defined as means of achieving technological independence for France. The options themselves reflected the responsibilities of the agencies involved, while the common experience of all the state officials tended to exclude a competitive and dynamic business strategy as an option. (De Gaulle was certainly involved in the final choices, but who actually made the decision and the precise criteria and reasoning remain obscure to me.)

Three different groups of actors were involved in molding the *Plan Calcul* and the structure of the electronics industry: the ministries and agencies within the state responsible for formulating government policy, the holding companies and *banques des affaires* representing the major companies, and the operating subsidiaries charged with making and selling products. The nature of the links between these groups, particularly between business and the state on the one hand, and between the holding companies and the operating subsidiaries on the other, is important to almost any economic or business events in France and must be briefly noted. The administrative power of the French government rests in the hands of career civil servants recruited almost exclusively from two schools with quite limited enrollment, Polytechnique and the Ecole Nationale d'Administration (ENA). Access to the most prestigious and influential posts in the government is controlled by the Grands Corps, at once exclusive clubs and unions, which organize the careers of their members within the public and often in the private sectors as well. For the most significant posts, membership in a particular corps is an unofficial requirement, and of course membership in these corps is open only to the top students in *Polytechnique* and ENA, with different corps recruiting from different schools. After a career in the civil service these men can move directly to the top posts in the business world. One study showed that of the largest French companies nearly half had a *polytechnicien* as chairman of the board or president, and most of the rest had one vice-president from the school. In the reverse of the American experience the flow is from government to business. Consequently, virtually no ranking administrator will have had independent experience in the business community, while virtually every important company will include in its leadership those who have held important posts in the government, if only to assure its position in negotiations with the state. The perspectives of state administration therefore permeate a business community long cartelized and sheltered from competition. Second, French business long lived in a hothouse environment; protected from outside competition the internal market was divided by negotiation not competition.

Cajoled by the state and pressured by outside competitors French industry has undergone substantial reorganization, but the anticompetitive tradition remains despite the changes. In many industries the dominant firms are fixed holding companies, often unwieldy networks of operating subsidiaries that retain considerable autonomy. In the electronics industry the smaller, often family-owned, firms were absorbed by the holding companies which in turn arranged matters of market shares and products between themselves and sometimes the state. An important mechanism for reaching agreement between the groups has been the joint subsidiary, held in common by competing groups. Furthermore, limited access to the capital markets and negotiated access to many markets makes it very difficult for a new company to penetrate the citadels of financial and industrial power, however innovative its business strategy. In this environment skills at politics and negotiation are at least as important as an ability to implement a competitive business strategy, and a man's career inside a company is not directly related to the profitability of the "*groupe*" or subsidiary. In fact there are often sharp hierarchical splits within the company and those at the top of the important companies have normally arrived there through family or school ties. Such a setting fosters business strategies of negotiation and accommodation in which the operating subsidiaries are pawns in a struggle between "*groupes*," rather than tightly executed competitive strategies.

The state took the initiative in formulating and implementing the *Plan Calcul*, but even as it did so the industry was changed by the collapse of important French firms and the American penetration of the market. The holding companies and the *banques des affaires* had the initiative in restructuring the French-held portion of the industry, but the state played an important role throughout. Importantly, though, the strategy of the *Plan Calcul* set the priorities of the government in the entire industry. There were two decisions to be taken. First, what would the goals of the state be, and after technological independence became the objective, what would that independence mean in operational terms. Second, who in the state and the private sector would organize the activities of the industry and thus be the instrument of policy and the recipient of state assistance.

After several years the choices were finally formulated by the head of the Planning Commission. Those who set the options and took the choice had working experience inside the government ministries managing state research or production facilities, managing companies almost exclusively dependent on state purchasing for success, or in the politics of merger and joint venture. Virtually no one had experience managing a market-oriented company, let alone one in the competitive and difficult field of computers and components. One set of proposals came from the Permanent Planning Group for Electronics (COPEP) set up at the Planning Commission even before the Machine Bull affair. A second early lead came jointly from the civilian and military research agencies, DRME and DGRST. Throughout, the planning group was more concerned with the impact of the computer industry in the economy as a whole, while the research agencies were more concerned with scientific and military applications. Each emphasis became a formal policy option. Neither group really focused on what was required to foster a competitive and profitable computer company. The question of business strategy was only addressed after the basic purposes the agency urged on the government were defined. The computer subsidiary of Schneider and an independent consulting firm urged a strategy of aggressively exploiting competence in particular sectors, but this seems never to have found widespread support in the business community or in the government, although it remained a formally stated option. Certain of the holding companies and the banks urged an entirely different solution; some kind of agreement with Bull-G.E. to assure a profitable but not autonomous French independence was decided as one of the objectives of the plan, but this approach was rejected.

Each of the final options was linked to a different notion of independence. If strategic independence meant the ability to develop the atomic weapons required by the Gaullist *force de frappe*, then large-scale computers primarily for scientific use, such as those of Control Data, were required. If independence meant the ability to use and produce computers when needed, then support could be given to companies to exploit the market niches in which they had the greatest competence. If independence meant the ability to develop an industrial capacity in the range of computers of greatest importance to industry and business, then medium-sized computers similar to those already produced by IBM were required. Although this last option was thought of as an economic strategy, it is dubious that subsidizing the use of French-produced business computers in French firms, products they could have anyhow and which were not strategically important, would be of more economic value than competitive companies turning a profit in a less difficult sector of the market. This last strategy, though, was chosen, and it meant that the new company would find itself in direct competition with IBM. At the same time the government could help it with a guaranteed market among state agencies. Equally significant, the large-scale effort involved permitted a merging of the computer subsidiaries of nearly all the large groups, thereby assuring everyone a piece of the action. This produced enormous organizational problems that handicapped CII, but it solved the political problem of who would benefit. Although hopes of early profitability were expressed at the beginning, these hopes faded quickly and the real message the choice conveyed to the firms was that they should turn their face toward the state, not the market. Given the organization of French business and the French state, the decision is not surprising, but the consequences of that choice must concern us now.

French Policy and the Evolution
of the Electronics Industry

French policy as it emerged was aimed at sustaining a French presence in certain technological sectors of the electronics industry, such as computers, semiconductors, and radars. However, by the time the state intervened American firms had already taken up powerful positions in computers and semiconductors, and the structure of the international industry which favored the Americans in certain products from the beginning, therefore, led to a government policy to protect French firms from the consequences of the market, not to help them adapt to it. French policy was intended to compensate for what were seen as three weaknesses in the competitive position of French firms: the firms themselves were too small; the French market was too restrictive; and American firms were subsidized by military and space programs. Intervention thus took three important forms: the fusion of small firms and the creation of a national champion; the support of French exports in semicompetitive markets; and the creation of internally protected markets for the national champion and other privileged firms, and the outright subsidy of these firms. The Délégation à l'Informatique was organized as the instrument of this policy, and M. Balley of the French Atomic Energy Commission and former manager of one of its plants, was appointed as the *délégué*.

A National Champion

The Thomson group emerged from a decade of maneuvering and fusions as the French electronics champion. As a national champion Thomson has the right to claim the aid of the state to maintain the position of the firm and thus of the French; as its president has expressed it, "I ought, moreover, to underline that this effort is indispensable for maintaining French electronics in the first road which it occupies on world markets and cannot be continued without adequate financing of research and development equal to what the major foreign companies receive in their own countries."[6] Thomson's demands have been met, and it has been the single greatest benefactor from the programs of the state, but not the only one.

A Protected Market

Active government support for exports to the Eastern bloc and Third World countries, where competition has been more political than commercial and technical, has been the second part of the electronics policy. The justification of what sometimes sounds like a deemphasis of efforts directed at early competitive markets has been that the French presence should be extended throughout the world. Occasionally such a policy is even overtly defended as when the weekly paper of the French electronics industry commented on export figures that showed that over two-thirds went to the Third World:

> In the reverse situation of other industries, the French electronics sector judges that it is better to pursue a global strategy than to limit itself to the Common Market. Thus, it believes that assuring a strong position in these markets against international competitors, including America, is a priority.[7]

The result in practical terms is the extension of a protective umbrella over at least a portion of the market, reducing the pressure on French firms to match the international development pace or to develop their own competitively based export policy. Some industry observers contend that these state-supported exports are essential to a continued French electronics capability in many areas. Not only does it provide important income to firms such as Thomson that exports 25 percent of its production, but also provides sufficient production to reduce average costs, and thus the price of these products to the government, to acceptable levels. Furthermore, these exports tend to cover the import of advanced products from the United States. A strategy emphasizing export to the industrial world would have forced firms in the state to develop an economically based commercial strategy to effectively enter the market. Eastern bloc and Third World exports, at the same time that they reduce competitive pressure, permit the continuation of a bias toward technological self-sufficiency.

Such export markets, of course, simply supplement the market that the state can provide through administrative purchases primarily by the military and the government-controlled telecommunications system (PTT). Such government markets, of course, are not created to support the electronics industry, but they can be manipulated to serve industrial objectives. Both the PTT and the military have offices of industrial policy which serve to coordinate their policies with the more general industrial policy of the government.

Programs of Subsidy

The third technique has been direct subsidy of particular firms. Aid has passed through a variety of programs, some like the *Plan Calcul* aimed directly at the electronics industry, and some, such as the DGRST's *action concertée*, aimed at industry in general. The two primary goals have been to subsidize the development of particular technologies and to create a French national champion as an instrument of that technology policy.

The result of these policies has been a bipolar industry that at once expresses the competitive pressures of the international electronics firms, and the protective heritage of France clearly expressed in current policy. Very schematically the larger firms that now dominate the industry were created by two distinct processes that represent quite different business instincts and purposes. On the one hand, there were the subsidiaries of foreign companies that have established themselves in France with the intention of capturing part of the French market as part of the parent company's strategy of internal expansion. Among the American firms there are those like IBM that had been established in France for many years before the postwar electronics revolution, and others like Texas Instruments and Honeywell who have only entered in recent years. The second group are French firms that grew to current size by mergers and acquisitions rather than internal growth. Though no reliable data exists, industry sources unanimously report a steady movement of mergers and fusions among French firms. In the 1950s the industry was composed of a few medium-sized and many small firms. The number of firms has remained the same but the domestic market has continually expanded. The smallest firms have exited and their place has been taken by American firms producing in France and specialized small equipment manufacturers. In fact, these two processes of American penetration and French regrouping have been intimately connected because the French state, faced with the American domination of what it perceived to be a critical industry, acted to encourage fusion and merger among French firms.

The policies of the state have left two strategies open to French electronics firms: either they can compete without state resistance on a price and quality basis with electronics firms of other national origins in the industrial and commercial markets, or alternatively they can seek the direct and indirect protection of the state and follow a political as well as an economic strategy. The dominant French firms, the centerpins of the state's policy, are clearly the sheltered firms.

The Costs of a Technological Strategy

If the electronics industry were static with stable product lines and production costs, then a policy of protection and subsidy that insured fabrication of particular technologies might work. In the highly competitive and rapidly evolving electronics industry, however, these policies can lead to costly flaws in the strategies and organization of the sheltered firms. This discussion will concentrate on the strategy dilemma the French have faced in pursuing predominantly technological goals, but it must be remarked as well that policies of protection have interfered with badly needed organizational changes in the firms themselves. Policy ignored or underestimated the importance of appropriate organization to business success in competitive markets, particularly in innovative industries like electronics.

Debates over the technological options open to Europe have often confused the perspectives of the firms and those of the nation-state. For the firm the problem is to make a product it can sell at a profit, and other than for reasons of corporate strategy it doesn't matter what that product will be. The problem for the nation-state, particularly as the French have defined the matter, may be to insure that there are firms making particular products that it needs for one or another national goal. Difficulties begin when the products the government desires are not those which will permit the firms their profits. Thus for the firm the market structure represents a set of constraints to which it must adapt when selecting, making, and marketing products, while for the government that market structure may be a set of obstacles blocking particular policy objectives. The French electronics firms might be able to prosper both in size and technological capacity, but whether firms making particular clusters of products, such as a broadline French semiconductor or computer producer, can survive and prosper is a very different question. The market constraints on firm strategies represent limits on state policy, unless the state can change the structure of the industry or provide a sufficient direct or indirect subsidy to balance the costs of ignoring the constraints. By encouraging and often forcing the firms to ignore these constraints in order to pursue a national supplier of particular technologies, the state endangers the firms and undermines many of its own policies.

The thrust of French policy has been to insulate French firms from the market's constraints so that they could be responsive to the demands of the state that have called for a presence in every important sector of technology. American military and space spending, the small size of French firms, and a limited French home market have indeed put French firms at a competitive disadvantage in those product sectors of greatest interest to the state; but that does not mean that the French cannot be competitive in other sectors, nor that they could not maintain a position in many of the important sectors. Thus, for example, no French firms are competitive in large central processing units for computers, but several firms are able to compete in the markets for smaller machines and peripherals. The French state has simultaneously ignored and raged against market constraints because its political goal of technological independence required French firms to compete in the very sectors of the market where they were most handicapped.

Since France is only a medium-sized country with limited resources whose market represents but a fraction of the world electronics industry, the French state could never hope to change this economic reality. Although programs of direct transfer and administrative purchasing have created a small shelter, the firms huddled there still remain deeply vulnerable to the evolution of a competitive world outside. As the industry develops there is no assurance that marginal positions for favored firms can be maintained except at ever-increasing levels of subsidy and continued dependence on the state. At the same time effort expended in noncompetitive sectors can only distract attention and divert resources from the firm's essential task of choosing competitive products and taking up defensible positions on the world market.

Since the state's purpose in intervening in the industry was political the success of its programs cannot be judged by the profitability of the firms. Nonetheless, the market position and competitiveness of the firm affect the cost of achieving any particular goal. The dilemma then is that a politically inspired technological strategy that flies in the face of economic constraints that the state cannot change contains the danger of undermining the long-run well-being of the firms who must be the agents of that policy by imposing unprofitable strategies on them. The effort to close a technology gap by assuring a French producer of specific "modern" goods may only have perpetuated a traditional industry looking to the state and the French market rather than toward its competitive situation in a world industry.

The technological strategy thus both puts firms at a competitive disadvantage for the products they are obliged to produce and distracts them from more profitable products and product strategies. This is, moreover, an equally serious problem for the state. Confronted with the rapid product evolution of the industry each firm must develop and market new generations of products. A subsidized and privileged, but economically marginal, national producer cannot assure the state a secure national source in the future. As a follower, and probably a distant follower, the firm will almost certainly have low profit margins and few if any advantages to offer clients in competitive markets. In many cases, in fact, the image of being a subsidized and noncompetitive firm gives a second-class aura to the products, making it even harder to sell them in an unprotected market. In France the small size of the administrative market for many goods has prompted a search for other administrative markets in Eastern bloc or Third World countries, but these markets, even if they can be found, will always be vulnerable to the political relations between these countries and America. The growth of American trade with Eastern bloc countries for example will permit Control Data and IBM to sell computers in previous French preserves and will weaken the French position. Whatever protected markets can be created, the basic problems remain since the major markets are competitive ones. With low profit margins, a weak competitive position, and limited production, the firm depending on protection will almost certainly have difficulty mustering a competitive development effort on its own. It may be unable to respond to a sharp product jump, thus finding itself in an ever-weaker position without ever assuring a national source of the technology in the future. Then the symbol of a current producer will have been purchased, but not the political security of a permanent supplier. The primary problem remains the weak competitive position of the firms.

Another glance at the *Plan Calcul* will suggest both the problems of a technological strategy and the alternatives to it. Not only did the plan create a firm, but it specified its first product—a large computer based on a central processing unit of French design. Therefore, from the moment of its birth CII was in competition with the bread-and-butter products of its established American competitors, hardly an enviable position for a fledgling firm. It is estimated that in this sector of the computer business a firm must control a minimum of 5 percent of the world market if it is not simply to be squeezed by its larger competitors. Even now CII does not control a much higher percentage of the French market—a market in its entirety little larger than 5 percent of the world market. The plan's subsidies of $40-to-$50 million dollars a year, which have benefitted CII almost exclusively, were originally intended to put the firm on a competitive footing. Now there is little hope that the subsidies can soon be ended. In fact current plans call for substantially increased subsidies. It is an altogether different question of course whether Machine Bull, at the time of the sale to G.E., could have established a secure position in the world computer business. Bull had an undoubted technological virtuosity and an invaluable sales network, but a thorough reorganization of the management systems and financial controls would have been required. Whether the effort was not undertaken because, as Scott and McArthur argue, no one at Bull understood what in fact was required or whether the reasons were more political, as is suggested by some government officials, is unimportant. A strategy that might just have worked with Bull was impossible with CII. At best CII is in a marginal and vulnerable position, but SESCOSEM—the semiconductor filiale of Thomson-Houston—has been the real victim of a technology policy.

Since the central processing unit of a computer is little more than a collection of semiconductor components, a French computer manufacturer requires a French semiconductor manufacturer to guarantee national production. However, since SESCOSEM was not a strong firm,* CII machines are designed around components of the American firm Texas Instruments, a world leader. SESCOSEM though is obliged to develop and produce the catalogue of Texas Instruments products to insure a French second source although it is only a fraction of the size of Texas Instruments. In an industry where late entry is fatal SESCOSEM is relegated by decree to this role and must develop products for which it is not even the primary source. At the same time that the need for an independent French semiconductor producer is repeated the cost of subsidies continues to mount and an endless downward spiral ensues. Thus because SESCOSEM is weak, it cannot be guaranteed a market, but because it must guarantee production, it is impossible to develop a sound economic position. Reversing the situation now would be difficult at best, and SESCOSEM, never particularly robust, would still have deep problems. The technological objectives of the state have set the economic trap. Importantly, the current desperate position could perhaps have been avoided had more competitive policies with a greater market emphasis been adopted a decade ago.

A similar process has been observed, it should be noted, among other producers who use the state's umbrella of preferential purchasing to produce thoroughly uncompetitive goods—often products in which they have a hopeless position. A technology strategy in electronics can thus create French producers but cannot assure their future. Furthermore, in forcing them to imitate the giant world leaders without their resources or market position, they cannot become aggressive and effective challengers either.

What happened a decade ago, however, cannot be undone today and the

---

*It has since been absorbed into Thomson-Houston.

issue is not simply what might have been but what is possible now. If the state cannot change the market constraints the alternative is for French firms to select market segments in which they can compete and develop their strengths as they grow, one of the original strategy choices. Two apparent market constraints on French ambitions and tactics should be noted, neither of which, it must be emphasized, is incompatible with long-term technological independence. First, given the more limited resources of the French state and firms, it would appear that initially it would have been desirable to select for major investment those areas where the undeniable French technological capacity could have been turned into defensible market positions. Thus a careful market strategy is essential for any technological hopes. Second, since the cutting edge of electronics technology was coming from America for clear reasons of market structure and government spending, it was necessary for all others to become effective followers in certain sectors, that is, to minimize the time it took for new technologies to be absorbed and ideally modified, applied to new uses, and exported. Product innovation and even innovation in component applications remains possible, but it is essential to acquire the most advanced technologies by license if necessary and then build on the back of the work the Americans have done. The French appear to have fought either for utter independence of licensing arrangements, as was the policy of CSF, or accepted relative technological dependence, as has often been the habit of other firms. Both strategies force the French firms to follow directly in American tracks.

A healthy electronics industry, the essential piece of any policy of industrial or technological independence, requires above all that the technological needs of French security or prestige be sharply distinguished from the product requirements of competitive and profitable companies. The companies must not be made to bear the financial or managerial costs of state-determined technological objectives; unless the state can provide a sufficient market for the firms to make a profit and keep up with the evolving technologies in the industry, the firms will have to survive by competing in the market even if they receive massive subsidy. In this case the firms bear costs whenever they develop or manufacture products that do not lead to a defensible market position.

The message of government policy must be that the state will help the firm to become competitive and profitable, not that endless subsidy will be provided for the firms which pursue technological goals of state interest. The initiative for strategy definition and product choice in a competitively and technologically volatile industry such as electronics must be with the firms. Despite the massive expenditures on military needs and space, government agencies in the United States never selected the appropriate horse to back in the semiconductor industry. Only when the firms define and execute or learn to define and execute a product and marketing strategy that can be profitable and be defended against competition can state policy achieve its goals.

European Collaboration—Escape Valve or Quagmire?

In the computer field European collaboration has often been proposed as a route out of this dilemma. The joining—the word "merger" would imply greater unity than in fact exists—of the computer efforts of CII, Siemens, and Philips in the joint venture called Unidata was intended to extend the product line, enlarge the marketing network and customer base, and concert their computer-related research. The serious danger is that the difficulty of managing the alliance will simply outweigh the advantages of increased size. The current crises, even if CII stays in the partnership, can only underline the difficulty of establishing and managing a unified strategy, particularly when CII is so sensitive to governmental policy changes and the conflicting wishes of the several holding companies that share in its stock. CII was formed by the merger of several small companies, and the management problems that resulted ought to have served as a warning of the difficulties of mergers.

Importantly, cosmetic adjustments in institutional arrangements must not be allowed to substitute for more basic change in the French approach to policy. Since Unidata is an alliance, not a merger, the terms of the arrangement must be examined carefully, because without unification of profits and costs the French may be left supporting the same policy on a grander scale. The companies will share their sales networks and specialize their R and D and production. CII will focus on the larger business computers (although Siemens may manufacture one larger but specialized machine) leaving it in head-on competition with IBM and Honeywell, digging CII even deeper into the big machine trap by closing off the small machine escape.

Furthermore, one must have serious reservations about the future sales of CII products outside France, because within France CII has not been overly successful selling to anyone except the state. Moreover, its line of machines in particular requires an effective service network to provide software as well as hardware and guarantee the continuity of the information processing service it is in fact selling. Neither Philips nor Siemens has experience with such products and their sales network are unlikely to be adequate to this critical task. Moreover, if profits for all products are not generally shared—that is, if profits are assigned to the product's producer and developer rather than entering a general pool from which all draw—the bargain may be a bad one. CII may provide her sisters with a French sales network while using the reciprocal sales networks to market a product that has been less than brilliantly successful in France. In addition, such a sharp split between marketing and production and development responsibilities leads to serious interorganizational conflicts in electronics firms. It would seem that unless a unified strategy and organization is established then an expanded marketing network or greater R and D resources will be wasted.

CONCLUSION

Despite European collaboration in advanced technologies the individual nations remain the focus of activities. The French experience suggests the limits on a government's ability to shape the growth of a domestic industry that forms an integral part of an international marketplace. The French state has attempted to maintain at least one national supplier of each politically important electronic technology. The dilemma has been that the protection and support required to produce specific products of interests to the state may in fact have weakened the firms that must be the long-term instruments of state policy. Without strong firms the development of new technologies cannot be assured in the future. Strong and healthy firms with competitive market strategies and efficient organizations must be the centerpiece of any successful government electronics policy, and financial mergers or joint ventures which increase the volume of capital will not prove a substitute for often painful change in the firms' strategies and organizations. Before the reality of technological independence can be realized the symbol of particular goods produced by subsidized but feeble national companies may have to be abandoned. Certainly in the computer industry where France's partners will not be other governments but individual profit-making companies, it would appear that any real unification of efforts will require not only that the French renounce a veto over corporate policy but also that they encourage their own companies to define and pursue competitive policies. The new government has dissolved the Délégation à l'Informatique, the agent of the last decade's policies, but it will be some time before it is clear whether the basic thrust of policy has been altered.

NOTES

1. This study draws heavily from "Between the Market and the State: Dilemmas of French Policy for the Electronics Industry," *Research Policy*. Both this chapter and the above article are part of a larger study of change in French industry to be published by the University of California Press.

2. Jean-Jacques Salomon, "Europe and the Technology Gap," *International Studies Quarterly*, October-November 1970, pp. 5-31.

3. See Richard Nelson, "World Leadership, the Technological Gap and National Policy," in *Minerva*, July 1971.

4. Quoted in Salomon, op. cit., p. 19.

5. This material draws from my own research on the French electronics industry and from Pierre Gardoneix, "The Case of the Plan Calcul" (Ph.D. diss. Harvard Business School).

6. *Electronique Actualités* (Paris), July 1971.

7. Ibid., March 24, 1972.

INDEX

active labor market policy, 96
Adenauer, Konrad, 16
aircraft industry, 180
Andean Pact, 70, 157
Atlantic Community, 156

Belgium (*see* Economic Expansion Law)
Biedenkopf Report, 105
Boddewyn, Jean, 6
Burke, Edmond, 133

Capelin Report, 214-15
cartels, 3
civil servants, France; careers, 35ff; education 35ff; influence of, 233-34; pantouflage, 37, 39, 120, 234
coal industry, 196; British policy, 106; French policy, 106; relation to oil price, 193-94 (*see also*, energy policy, European Coal and Steel Community)
Cohen, Stephen, 29
collective bargaining, 108
Colonna Report, concentrations, 160-61; conclusions of, 168-78; and U.S. firms, 168
Comitextil, 209ff
Commission of the EC, powers of, 156-57, 159; Social Action Program, 110 (*see also*, European Community)
Compagnie Internationale de l'Informatique (CII), 241
competition policy, 159
computers, 164; European policy, 228-29, French options, 227-28; French Planning Commission, 232-33, French state, 235; Thomson-Houston, 242, (*see also*, French planning)
concentrations and mergers, 7, 26ff, 160-62 (*see also*, Colonna Report, computers, European Industrial Base)
Confederation of British Industries (CBI), and CNPF, 134; and government, 126; leadership and French planning, 139; and market forces, 138; organization, 135; and planning, 140
Conseil National du Patronat Français (CNPF), and CBI, 134; and government,

126; and market forces, 138; opinion poll, 137; organization, 135; and planning, 140
Customs Union, and national inequalities, 174ff; and political integration, 8; and specialization, 175; theory of, 171ff

de Bandt Report, 212-14
Delegation à l'Informatique, 227
Department of Trade and Industry (DTI), 120ff
Devlin Report, 131-32
Drancourt, Michel, 38

Economic and Social Committee (ESC), 108ff
Economic Development Committees (EDC), 140-41
Economic Expansion Law, 48ff; application of, 63ff; and EC objections, 56ff, 65ff; and Federation of Belgium Enterprises, 61; Flemish-Walloon controversy, 47, 55ff; and French planning, 59; and national unity, 10; and regional policy, 6; and Socialists, 10, 55ff, 60ff; and U.S. Embassy, 62 (*see also*, industrial policies, national governments, industrial policy, national response)
economy and government intervention, 58ff, 67ff; limits to, 71; and new forms of, 71-72
Ehrmann, Henry, 32
employer associations, fragmentation of, 123, 131; in France, 127ff; internal consensus, 131, 133, Olson on, 133-34.
employment, economic mobility, 83; geographic mobility, 83; job security, 8; rate of unemployment, 82; structural unemployment, 86; structure of, 82; vocational mobility, 83
employment policy, 81-82, 84ff; adjustment assistance, 99; and demand expansion, 85ff, 90ff; and EC, 90; and management, 100; and structural policy, 89; and trade liberalization 85ff (*see also*, active labor market policy; trade unions)
Energy Modernization Commission, 140
energy policy, Arab-Israeli War, 194-95; common consumer front, 202; and EC,

247

National Economic Development Council
(NEDC, United Kingdom), 3
National Investment Society (SNI, Belgium),
52

OECD, 4
Olson, Mancur, 133-34
OPEC, 9, 17, 197

petroleum industry, 4
Plan Calcul, 228, 233-34, 235
Prioret, Roger, 32
Puchala, Donald, 69
pulp and paper sector, 187

regionalism, 9
regional policy, 55ff
Royer Law, 11, 32, 127
Rustow, Dankwart A., 9

Servan-Schreiber, Jean Jacques, 61, 177
Sik, Ota, 5
small business, in France, 11, 127, in United
Kingdom, 128
social dumping, 211
Socialism, 12, 16
sovereignty, 3
Spaak Report, 158
Spinelli, Altiero, 170
state aides and subsidies, 221-22, 238
Stoleru, Lionel, 6, 13
Suleiman, Ezra, 7
Swedish labor policy, 96

Tavitian, Roland, 14
technology gap, 230-32
textile industry, 13; Capelin Report, 214-15;
competition, 208, 210-11; de Bandt Report,
212-14; economic research, 219-20; in

France, 145; and government intervention,
215ff, 220; in Italy, 222-24; scientific
research, 218-19; European Social Fund,
224; subsidies, 221; synthetic fibers, 208; in
United Kingdom, 145
trade associations, 129ff
trade liberalization, regional, 7; international,
156; and industrial policy, 2; and
employment, 84ff
trade unions, 14ff; concept of role, 95; concept
of strike, 106; and employment policies, 94;
and EC, 107ff; inclusion in national level
policy institutions, 95; in Italy, 104; joint
employment committees, 102; and
multinational corporations, 111ff; and
"social plans", 10; special collective
agreements, 102-03; in Sweden, 104;
voluntary concentration, 99 (*see also*,
active labor market policy, employment
policy)
Trade Union Congress (TUC), 108

UNIDATA, 164
United Kingdom, economic tradition, 120ff;
policies toward industries, 125ff
United States, European image of, 54, 178;
planning in, 19
Upper Clyde Ship Builders, 107
Uranium enrichment, 8

Venturini, V. G., 26

Warnecke, Steven, 8, 228
Weber, Max, 24
West German codetermination law, 16
worker participation, 15, 101

Yugoslavia, 15

ABOUT THE AUTHORS

STEVEN J. WARNECKE is Associate Professor of Political Science at the Graduate School and Richmond College of the City University of New York, and contributor to and editor of *The European Community in the 1970s* (1972) and is currently working on the external relations of the European Community.

EZRA N. SULEIMAN is Associate Professor of Political Science at the University of California, Los Angeles. He is the author of *Politics, Power and Bureaucracy in France* (1974) and is currently completing a study on elites in French society.

J. J. BODDEWYN is Professor of International Business at the City University of New York and coordinator of the international business program. He is co-author with Jack Behrman and Ashok Kapoor of *International Business-Government Communications* (1975) and *Organizing for External Affairs in Europe* (1975).

CAMILLE BLUM is Director of the Economic Affairs at COMITEXTIL, Comité de Coordination des Industries Textiles which groups the employers organizations of the textile industries in the nine countries of the European Community.

HANS GUNTER is senior staff associate at the International Institute for Labor Studies in Geneva. He is a contributor to and editor of *International Labor and the International Enterprise* and *Transnational Industrial Relations* (1972).

JACK HAYWARD is Professor of Politics at the University of Hull and the author of *The One and Indivisible French Republic* (1974) and co-editor of *Planning, Politics and Public Policy, The Experience of Britain, France and Italy* (1975).

DANKWART A. RUSTOW is Distinguished Professor of Political Science at the City University of New York. Among his publications are: *Middle Eastern Political Systems* (1971), *Philosophers and Kings: Studies in Leadership* (Editor, 1970) and *A World of Nations* (1967). He is a member of the Council on Foreign Relations and former Vice President of the American

Political Science Association and the Middle East Studies Association of North America.

ROLAND TAVITIAN is head of the European Social Fund Directorate for Studies of the Directorate General for Social Affairs at the Commission of the European Communities.

JOHN ZYSMAN is Assistant Professor of Political Science at the University of California, Berkeley and author of *French Industry Between the Market and the State* (1975).

THE EUROPEAN COMMUNITY IN THE 1970s
edited by Steven
Joshua Warnecke

LABOR MOVEMENTS IN THE COMMON
MARKET COUNTRIES: The Growth of a
European Pressure Group
Marguerite Bouvard

TRADE RELATIONS OF THE EEC:
An Empirical Investigation
Mordechai E. Kreinin